Using a straightforward rational-choice approach, Professor Ramseyer explores the impact that law had on various markets in Japanese history and the effect that those markets had on economic growth. In doing so, he applies an economic logic to markets in a different world in a different historical period with a different political regime and a different legal system. He looks hardest at those markets that have most often struck traditional observers as "exploitative" (e.g., the markets for indentured servants and for sexual services). Within those markets, he focuses on the way participants handled informational asymmetries in the contracting process.

Ramseyer finds that Japanese courts generally defined important property rights clearly, and that Japanese markets generally protected an individual's control over his or her own labor. As a result, that the Japanese economy grew at relatively efficient levels follows directly from standard economic theory. He also concludes that the legal system usually promoted mutually advantageous deals, and that market participants (whether poor or rich, female or male) generally mitigated informational asymmetries shrewdly by contract. He finds no systematic evidence of either sex- or age-based exploitation.

# ODD MARKETS IN JAPANESE HISTORY

Editors
James E. Alt, Harvard University
Douglass C. North, Washington University of St. Louis

Other books in the series
Alberto Alesina and Howard Rosenthal, *Partisan Politics, Divided Government and the Economy*
Lee J. Alston, Thráinn Eggertsson, and Douglass C. North, eds., *Empirical Studies in Institutional Change*
James E. Alt and Kenneth Shepsle, eds., *Perspectives on Positive Political Economy*
Jeffrey S. Banks and Eric A. Hanushek, *Modern Political Economy: Old Topics, New Directions*
_Yoram Barzel, *Economic Analysis of Property Rights*
Robert Bates, *Beyond the Miracle of the Market: The Political Economy of Agrarian Development in Kenya*
Peter Cowhey and Mathew D. McCubbins, eds., *Structure and Policy in Japan and the United States*
Gary W. Cox, *The Efficient Secret: The Cabinet and the Development of Political Parties in Victorian England*
Jean Ensminger, *Making a Market: The Institutional Transformation of an African Society*
Kathryn Firmin-Sellers, *The Transformation of Property Rights in the Gold Coast*
Murray Horn, *The Political Economy of Public Administration: Institutional Choice in the Public Sector*
Jack Knight, *Institutions and Social Conflict*
Michael Laver and Kenneth Shepsle, *Making and Breaking Governments*
Michael Laver and Kenneth Shepsle, eds., *Cabinet Ministers and Parliamentary Government*
Brian Levy and Pablo T. Spiller, *Regulations, Institutions, and Commitment*
Leif Lewin, *Ideology and Strategy: A Century of Swedish Politics (English edition)*
Gary Libecap, *Contracting for Property Rights*
Mathew D. McCubbins and Terry Sullivan, eds., *Congress: Structure and Policy*

Continued on p. 190

# ODD MARKETS IN JAPANESE HISTORY

## Law and economic growth

J. MARK RAMSEYER
*The University of Chicago*

CAMBRIDGE
UNIVERSITY PRESS

PUBLISHED BY THE PRESS SYNDICATE OF THE UNIVERSITY OF CAMBRIDGE
The Pitt Building, Trumpington Street, Cambridge CB2 1RP, United Kingdom

CAMBRIDGE UNIVERSITY PRESS
The Edinburgh Building, Cambridge CB2 2RU, United Kingdom
40 West 20th Street, New York, NY 10011-4211, USA
10 Stamford Road, Oakleigh, Melbourne 3166, Australia

© Cambridge University Press 1996

First published 1996

Printed in the United States of America

Typeset in Sabon

*Library of Congress Cataloging-in-Publication Data*
Ramseyer, J. Mark, 1954–
Odd markets in Japanese history : law and economic growth / J.
Mark Ramseyer.
p.   cm. – (Political economy of institutions and decisions)
Includes bibliographical references.
ISBN 0-521-56386-0 (hc)
1. Law – Japan – History.   2. Law – Economic aspects – Japan.
3. Commercial law – Japan – History.   4. Trade regulation – Japan –
History.   5. Japan – Economic conditions – to 1868.   6. Japan –
Economic conditions – 1868–1945.   I. Title.   II. Series.
KNX120.R36   1996
330.952 – dc20                                    96-3302
                                                       CIP

*A catalog record for this book is available from
the British Library*

ISBN 0 521 56386 0 hardback

For my critics:

*Howard Blair*
*Arthur Rosett*
*Theron Schlabach*
*Frank Upham*

# Contents

# Contents

# Contents

# Contents

# Tables

# Series editors' preface

The Cambridge series on the Political Economy of Institutions and Decisions is built around attempts to answer two central questions: How do institutions evolve in response to individual incentives, strategies, and choices, and how do institutions affect the performance of political and economic systems? The scope of the series is comparative and historical rather than international or specifically American, and the focus is positive rather than normative.

Property rights shape the incentive structure of a society and so determine its economic performance. In his thoughtful and provocative analysis of Japan before 1940, Mark Ramseyer argues that governments created and courts enforced legal rules that made people economically autonomous agents in many ways, providing the motive force behind economic growth. His evidence rejects oft-stated claims that Japanese courts enforced autocratic family law, for instance. But his arguments from the field of law and economics go further than this, analyzing the historical evolution of Japanese property rights in such diverse areas as land and water, children, families, factory labor, and sexual services. Many of these markets feature severe information asymmetries and thus sometimes depend more on cartelization and bargaining than on simple decentralized exchange among individuals. This magnifies the role of rules and laws in such markets in promoting economic growth. Ramseyer shows how the Imperial courts confirmed explicitly what customary practices of Tokugawa markets in land, water, and labor had conveyed implicitly, namely, secure specific rights to individuals to use factors of production under their control as they saw fit.

How can politicians be induced to provide good laws in odd markets? Contemporary concern for the construction of market institutions in many transitional societies makes Ramseyer's attack on this question timely. His use of unusual, even fascinating, cases gives the book relevance well beyond those interested in Japan.

# Acknowledgments

I have puzzled over these issues too long. Intermittently but regularly, I have toyed with these issues nearly since graduate school in Japanese studies (mostly history) nearly two decades ago. This book is the result. Stated simply, it is a book about markets in history: about the property rights that structure those markets, about the contracts that people negotiate over those rights, and about the economic growth that can ensue.

Over the many years I have worked on this project, dozens of people thoughtfully read chapter drafts and contributed to the workshops at which I presented the drafts. Believe me, without their comments this book would have been much worse. More recently, Margaret McKean tirelessly and generously read through the entire book and offered invaluable suggestions. To all of these friends, I offer heartfelt thanks.

Two housekeeping notes: I have written modern Japanese names in the American format, with the given name first and family name last. In the interests of simplification but at the admitted risk of irritating reviewers, I have omitted macrons over Japanese names and words.

To complete this book, I received generous financial assistance from the University of Chicago Committee on Japanese Studies, the John M. Olin Foundation, the Lynde and Harry Bradley Foundation, and the Sarah Scaife Foundation.

Earlier versions of parts of this book appeared as: "Water Law in Imperial Japan: Public Goods, Private Claims, and Legal Convergence," 18 *Journal of Legal Studies* 51 (1989) (© the University of Chicago Press); "Indentured Prostitution in Imperial Japan: Credible Commitments in the Commercial Sex Industry," 7 *Journal of Law, Economics & Organization* 89 (1991) (© the *Journal of Law, Econmics & Organization*); "Credibly Committing to Efficiency Wages: Cotton Spinning Cartels in Imperial Japan" (1993) *The University of Chicago Law School Roundtable* 153 (© the University of Chicago Law School); "The Market for Children: Evidence from Early Modern Japan," 11 *Journal of Law,*

## Acknowledgments

*Economics & Organization* 127 (1995) (© the *Journal of Law, Economics & Organization*).

I dedicate this book to four people who taught me to write, rewrite, and then start all over again. They taught me my trade. I doubt they will agree with much of this book. So long as they are not bored with all of it, I will be delighted.

*The University of Chicago*
*Summer 1995*

# Introduction

"Weird markets." A friend suggested the phrase in 1991 over burnt coffee in one of those nouvelle-Italian restaurants that plagued the East Coast that year. "That's all you do, you know. Write about weird markets." She had a point, I guess. And even if she had not thought the phrase a compliment, it did have a nice ring. It may have been a bit too cute to work as book title (I tried it, but prudent friends said no), but it does capture an important facet of this project.

If this is a book about weird markets, it is also a "law & economics" book about Japan. Solidly within the genre of positive (nonnormative) "law & economics," it explains the relation between legal change and economic growth through a model of individuals who rationally maximize their utility (generally, wealth). Where most studies in law & economics either develop formally theoretical (mathematical) models or test theories with empirical data from the United States, however, this book uses data from Japanese history. It is data from a different world: For much of the period at stake, the Japanese government was an oligarchy rather than a democracy; the judges operated a civil rather than common law regime; the economy grew modestly but erratically; and social customs changed rapidly and radically. As a result, this book applies an economic logic, but to markets in a vastly different environment – to markets in a different historical period with a different political regime, a different legal system, and a different cultural context. And sometimes, as my friend indelicately put it, to pretty weird markets at that.

## I HISTORICAL CONTEXT

In the Japanese legal world, the last decades of the nineteenth century were decades of change. From 1600 to 1868, the Tokugawa government (the shogunate) had controlled Japan. In law, it had consciously adopted a federal approach: it issued laws and adjudicated cases on those matters

1

most important to it, and delegated the rest to local domainal govern-ments. From time to time, it issued decrees on subjects from real estate transactions to the sale of humans. From time to time, the domainal governments followed it with their own decrees. In the courts, both the Tokugawa and the domainal governments adjudicated criminal cases and heard complaints on a motley variety of civil disputes.

All this changed in the nineteenth century. By 1868, renegade samurai from several powerful domains had grouped themselves into an uneasy coalition, "restored" the Meiji emperor to power, and toppled the Tokuga-wa regime. They spent the next several decades in a variety of tasks: most prominently, quarreling with each other, consolidating their collective oligarchic control, and fighting to keep the West from colonizing Japan.

The exsamurai who ran this new government placed legal reform high on their collective list of priorities. The Western governments had de-manded treaties that effectively placed their citizens in Japan beyond the control of Japanese courts. To renegotiate these terms, government lead-ers had somehow to convince Western governments that their courts were both predictable and fair.

Toward that end, the new oligarchs initiated massive legal changes. They hired judges, built courts, passed statutes, opened modern univer-sities with legal departments. By the end of the century, they could boast several thousand sophisticated and articulate judges and prosecutors and a panoply of complex codes. Through the codes they defined property rights to scarce resources, and through the courts they enforced them. By the end of the century, they could also boast a growing economy with high levels of private investment and smoothly functioning factor, prod-uct, and capital markets.

## 2 PROPERTY RIGHTS AND JAPANESE STUDIES

Through the work of economic historians like Douglass North and econo-mists like Harold Demsetz, we now understand well the basic relation between claims to property and economic growth (discussed more fully in Chapter 1). Growth occurs only when individuals have incentives to under-take activities that are socially beneficial. Necessarily, that generally happens only when they face private incentives that track the social benefits they generate. And the simplest way to align private incentives with social benefits is usually through a property rights regime: a legal system that gives individuals the right to use property themselves, to exclude others from it, and to transfer it. Like most of the greatest insights in social science, in retrospect the point is nearly obvious: growth requires incen-tives, and incentives generally require rights to use, to exclude, and to transfer.

Those property rights are central to this book. That makes it something of a curiosity in Japanese studies, for observers of Japan have largely ignored the relation between property rights and growth. Although non-Japan specialists have clarified the theoretical relation between property rights and growth, few have studied the empirics of property rights in Japan. In this book, I address that empirical lacuna – how the law influenced the development of property rights, and how private parties bought, sold, and rented those property rights.

In many markets (e.g., most commodities markets), sellers and buyers have much the same information about the goods and services transferred. When they do, they will find writing a contract to be relatively straightforward. In other markets (markets that often seem more "odd"), however, one of the parties may have better information than the other. An employer may know things about the workplace (like safety hazards) that the employees do not; the employees may know things about themselves (like their propensity to shirk, steal, or run away) that the employer does not. When parties to a deal face these informational asymmetries, they necessarily find writing a satisfactory contract harder. How they drafted contracts in the presence of those asymmetries is a second focus of this book.

Generally (and with exceptions to be sure), for at least the last century the Japanese government enforced most private claims to scarce resources. For at least the last century, it enforced basic property rights. In doing so, it facilitated growth-enhancing investment and markets. The story of Japanese economic growth is thus no surprise. It is instead a story of the commonplace: growth occurred when the government protected private claims to scarce resources, and thereby encouraged market allocations and private investment.

That this could be controversial at all testifies to how myopic our work on Japan has been. It is controversial only because so many of us interested in the Japanese economy have for so long done so little but interview government bureaucrats and read government white papers. It is controversial only because we have both assumed that Japanese bureaucrats created growth by farsighted leadership, and concluded that they thereby proved standard market economics wrong. It is controversial only because we have believed that "industrialism in Japan," as the ever-quotable Chalmers Johnson (1990: 72) put it, "owes nothing to the 'invisible hand' of Adam Smith."

## 3 THIS PROJECT

### 3.1 *Coverage*

At stake in this book are the connections among factor markets, legal rules, and informational asymmetries. In turn, these connections generate two questions that focus much of the analysis below: (1) How do legal rules, by defining the property rights people can hold, shape factor markets? (2) How do parties who transact in these markets manipulate contractual forms to overcome the informational asymmetries that so often plague them?

To address these questions, I explore several markets for land and labor (see Section 3.3 for selection criteria). In Chapter 2, I examine the property rights to land, water, and irrigation-based improvements to land. In Chapter 3, I examine the way the law effectively (but sensibly) limited those rights – limited the way that one could harm others through the use of one's property. In Chapters 4 through 7, I examine a series of labor markets: the markets for children (Chapter 4), for intrafamilial services (Chapter 5), for sex (Chapter 6), and for factory workers (Chapter 7). Less cryptically, perhaps, I explore several sets of market-related institutions: those that facilitated the creation of investments in land (Chapters 2 and 3), those that gave workers control over their own lives (Chapters 4 and 5), and those that enabled employees (whether prostitutes or cotton spinners) and employers (whether brothels or factories) to contract in their mutual best interests (Chapters 6 and 7).

### 3.2   Caveats

At the outset, three caveats may be in order. First, I span several discrete historial periods. Although I deal primarily with the late nineteenth and early twentieth centuries (what I call the imperial period), Chapter 2 (on water and land) covers most of written history. Chapter 4 (on labor) deals with the seventeenth through early nineteenth centuries. The other chapters then return the reader to the early twentieth century. Historically better-dressed readers may blanche at this chronology, but they should at least rest assured that it is not haphazard. Instead, I take these chronological liberties self-consciously. They will, I hope, help clarify the relationships among factor markets, legal rules, informational asymmetries, and economic growth.

Second, I make no normative claims. In this book, I trace the impact that legal rules had on economic change. In general, more goods and services are better than less – but we all know the necessary normative caveats. Here, I deal only with the empirical issues, and leave to others the quarrels over whether the net effect was "good."

Last, given the conjunction of legal and economic issues, the book necessarily draws on two qualitatively different types of data. Some data are economic. Chapter 4 aggregates surviving Tokugawa contracts, for example, and Chapters 6 and 7 compile economic data from the early

4

decades of the century. Readers should judge these data by the usual canons of economic history.

Other data are legal and involve radically different interpretive issues. Chapters 2, 3, 5, and 6, for instance, rely heavily on reported court cases. Readers who try to handle reported decisions in the same way they handle standard economic data (e.g., to aggregate and count them) will often miss the point. Reported decisions are not a random sample of all litigated cases, and litigated cases are not a random sample of all disputes (Priest & Klein, 1984).

Readers should instead consider reported decisions a clue to how courts planned to handle similar disputes in the future. Necessarily, they should also consider the decisions a clue to how rational disputants actually *settled* later disputes. Although technically not a common law system, imperial Japanese courts usually followed precedent, particularly when the precedent was by a higher court. As a result, the parties to disputes with significant assets at stake could use that precedent to decide how to settle. They could resolve their disputes out of court, in other words, "in the shadow" of what reported cases disclosed about the expected litigated outcome. By doing so, they could reach roughly the same result as they would in litigation, but pocket much of the money they would otherwise pay their lawyers (Ramseyer & Nakazato, 1989; Mnookin & Kornhauser, 1979). In short, court cases did not *sample* the way parties resolved disputes – for they were not a random sample. Rather, they *shaped* the way parties resolved later disputes.

### 3.3  Selection criteria

To explore the connections among courts, statutes, markets, informational assymetries, and economic growth, I chose several case studies. In selecting them, I followed three principles. First, I chose factor markets, primarily markets for land and labor – though several of the studies involve other markets as well. Economic growth depends crucially on these markets. Obviously, other markets matter too. Farmers will not invest in paddies at efficient levels unless they can sell their rice on competitive markets. Adam Smith's famous pin makers will not invest at such levels in pin production unless they can buy steel and sell pins on competitive markets. More generally, economic actors will not invest at efficient levels unless *all* factor, resource, product, and service markets operate efficiently. I focus on land and labor markets, however, because (the largely intractible second-best problems aside; Lipsey & Lancaster, 1956–7) these two factors are basic to most productive projects. It is not that other markets do not matter. It is that land and labor markets matter almost universally.

Second, for several (not all) of the chapters, I chose "weird" or "odd" markets. These markets are not weird in involving phenomena beyond rational maximizing models. Quite the contrary: those models fit the markets well. Rather, they are weird in involving phenomena that most observers of Japan have – wrongly – placed beyond the scope of those models.[1] Given that all but the most intransigent irrationalists admit standard economic models apply to some Japanese markets (e.g., modern financial markets), I would not have pushed the economic model very far with those more standard markets. Instead, I purposely chose markets where many observers have claimed rational maximizing models could not apply. They thought the models could not apply, I argue below, only because they did not think very much about rationality, very hard about competition, or very systematically about markets.

Last, I chose areas where I found our collective understanding of Japanese history most radically wrong. If this seems perverse, my reason is simple. Surely most readers have read at least one of those standard reviews of a rational-choice book. They are formulaic projects, and either start or end with something like this:

> Unfortunately, so enamored with his obscurantist theory is this author that he tells us nothing of substance that we did not already know. Instead, he retells in cryptic equations and polysyllabic jargon a story that the rest of us read in far clearer prose as sophomores in college. It is a sad commentary on the state of the modern university that this sort of rehashing, etc.

The review is seldom fair. But as in love and war, in book reviews too some scholars seem to think fairness beside the point. A man cannot be too careful in the choice of his enemies, Oscar Wilde once noted, but (as critics of the rational-choice approach love to observe) in some matters a man seems to have little choice. Because so many reviewers hope to find so little of substance in rational-choice monographs, most ignore any but the most obviously contrary claims. With that hostile reviewer in mind, I have deliberately chosen areas of Japanese history where some of the orthodox understandings are flatly wrong.

## 4   LAW & ECONOMICS AND HISTORY

Readers more familiar with Japan than with economics will find this project peculiar. I don't get it, a friendly historian (politely) told me. If I were trying to explain anything important, "rational maximizing mod-

---

[1] As noted earlier, several of the markets (those in Chapters 4, 6, and 7) involve informational asymmetries.

els" would be the last thing I'd use. Ramseyer obviously has no sense of history, an anonymous referree on another manuscript once (less politely) noted. Granted, there is something intuitively implausible about the law & economics project, something almost downright wrong. We have tried too hard to find more contextualized approaches to human behavior, formulated too many theories addressing the basic ideational and communitarian sides of life. In positing that everyone greedily maximizes his or her selfish best interests, law & economics – particularly the rational maximizing model used here – sounds altogether neolithic.

Yet even Wagner's *Ring* may be better than it sounds. Too often in Japanese history, we have assumed that explanatory breadth is everything, and theoretical coherence and parsimony nothing. Too often, we have let the rewards go to the scholar with the "richest" and most "contextualized" discussion, or the most nuanced account of ideological change. By contrast, this book is not about explaining everything everyone did. It is not even about explaining every (or any) shift in intellectual "discourse." Instead, it is about using economic theory to explain several prominent aspects of Japanese history. At root – and the point goes to the crux of the economics enterprise – it is about applying simple theories to complex phenomena.

Some readers will complain that the book shows no historical imagination, no empathy, no concern for how people thought "back then." They may be right that it shows none (at least none they would accept), but any such lack is intentional. It is also less perverse than it may seem. As an analogy, consider our discussions of culture in contemporary Japan. After decades of dissertations on the subject, few self-respecting scholars any more start their analysis of Japanese behavior with an analysis of Japanese culture. They do not avoid the subject because they find no cultural differences between Japan and North America. Obviously, they do. Neither do they avoid it because they find the differences unimportant. Obviously, many find them vital.

Instead, modern scholars avoid the culturalist approach because starting with culture too often stops the analysis. Once we look for cultural differences, we can too readily take surface variations as fundamental, and explain artifacts of institutional differences as cultural. As those of us in Japanese studies know but seldom admit, it is precisely because of this easy reference to culture that we are now saddled with so much of what is so bad in Western accounts of Japan – that Japanese never sue because they value harmony, for example, or that there are no takeovers because Japanese see the corporation as a family, and that bureaucrats are powerful because Japanese defer to authority. One can use culture to explain almost anything about Japan, and at one time or another we in the West have done just that.

Where we start our analysis of Japan importantly determines where we conclude. Just as we know Japanese culture differs from American culture, we also know that in crucial ways Japanese and Americans follow the same internal logic. But whether to start with that cultural difference or that essential commonality is not a proposition that sums to six one way, half dozen the other. Starting with cultural differences lets one start with the answer (culture) to one's questions (why the observed difference). Starting with the essential commonality instead forces one to check whether the difference is more than superficial, and whether institutional reasons might not account for any difference.

In the end, it is a matter of self-imposed discipline. Bodhidharma did not stare at the wall in Loyang until his legs fell off because he saw something there. He stared at it because it helped him concentrate. Like Bodhidharma, like Gary Becker and George Stigler. Becker & Stigler (1977) did not urge economists to banish discussions of consumer "tastes" because they thought all tastes identical. They urged economists to avoid them because they too often turned the analysis tautological.

And like tastes, like history. Just as we know Tokugawa peasants saw life differently from the way that Nomura securities analysts see it, we also know that in crucial ways they followed a similar internal logic. We could start with the historical difference, or we could start with the essential commonality. Unfortunately, those who propose to start by unpacking the difference too often stop the analytic project cold. Ultimately, it is just too easy to "explain" historical phenomena by positing differences in the way people saw the world – by whatever variant of neo-Confucianism was in the air, or whatever the level of antimarket prejudice, imperial reverence, or patriarchal deference. Too often, ideology, tastes, and culture are things we fail to measure independently of the phenomena we hope to explain. Too often, the result is simple circularity.

In the book that follows, I explain the relation between market behavior and legal structure, but do so with a simple model of individuals who rationally maximize their personal utility (generally wealth). If by the rules of some disciplines it shows no "sense of history," so be it.

# 1

## Law and economic growth

### INTRODUCTION

"I see the world in very fluid, contradictory, emerging, interconnected terms," Jerry Brown once observed, "and with that kind of circuitry I just don't feel the need to say what is going to happen or will not happen."

Life is subtle. Life is complicated. Life is hard. But Jerry Brown notwithstanding some things are less subtle, less complicated, less hard than they first seem – and the relationship between legal rules and economic performance is one. Legal rules structure institutions, and institutions determine economic growth. Rules that clarify and enforce rights to scarce resources tend to promote efficient growth, and those that muddy those rights tend to retard it.

In imperial Japan (1868 to 1945, though I largely end my discussion with 1930), these connections between law and growth raise at least two questions: what role did law play in Japanese economic growth; and what caused the Japanese government to adopt the law that it did? In this chapter I begin with the argument about the first of these questions and follow it with a more tentative hypothesis about the second. In later chapters I focus on the legal rules themselves and on the ways people manipulated those rules by private agreement.

Accordingly I begin this chapter by outlining the theoretical relationship between legal regimes and economic performance (Section 1). I describe the Japanese regime in place during the first half of this century, and explain how it tended to promote efficient growth[1] (Section 2). I then

---

[1] I use the phrase to refer to Kaldor-Hicks efficient growth: growth in which resources are allocated in ways that maximize aggregate social utility. It should be obvious from the discussion, however, that I use the phrase loosely and do not purport to measure this in any precise fashion. I am arguing instead that the Japanese economy (particularly in the imperial period) was relatively free of the large-scale rent-seeking, rent-avoidance, and common-pool problems that have crippled so many societies.

speculate about why the government adopted so efficient a legal regime[2] (Section 3).

## I THE PROPERTY RIGHTS PARADIGM

Economic growth depends on incentives, and incentives on property rights. Growth will not occur unless people have an incentive to engage in economically productive activities, and they will seldom have those incentives unless they have stable rights to that which they use and produce. Jerry Brown notwithstanding, the point is simple.

Douglass North and Robert Paul Thomas put it nicely in their famous whirlwind history of the West (1973: 1): "Efficient economic organization is the key to growth," and "the development of an efficient economic organization in Western Europe accounts for the rise of the West." In turn, efficient organization requires both appropriate "institutional arrangements and property rights" (id.), and means for people to transfer those rights (North, 1991: 481).

Institutional arrangements and property rights matter because they can align the private incentives an individual faces with the social consequences he or she causes. Properly designed, as North and Thomas (id., at 2) put it, private property rights bring "the social and private rates of return into closer parity." Properly designed, they "create an incentive to channel individual economic effort into activities that bring the private rate of return close to the social rate of return" (id.). Properly designed, they induce people to do good by enabling those who do good to live well.

Over the last two decades, scholars using this "property rights paradigm" have extensively studied the ties among law, institutions, and growth. As one example of the genre, take a recent study by Robert Barro (1994). Using a historical panel of about 100 countries, Barro regressed economic growth on a variety of factors. Concluded Barro (1994: 25), "With respect to the determination of growth, the cross-country analysis brings out the favorable effects from the maintenance of the rule of law, free markets, small government consumption, and high human capital." The key is the right to property rather than democracy, for democracy less causes growth than results from it. "[P]olitical freedom emerges as a sort of luxury good," wrote Barro. "Rich places consume more democracy because this good is desireable for its own sake" (1994: 25; see Scully, 1992).

As another variant of the genre, take George Shultz's recent keynote address to the American Economic Association (1995: 2):

[2]I use the phrase to refer to a legal regime that tends to promote growth at Kaldor-Hicks efficient levels.

We can now see a wide variety of countries that have experienced strong and often sustained economic development. . . . If we ask whether there is a common denominator among these economic success stories, the answer clearly is yes. The common demononinator is that they have found their way to economic policies that use the marketplace, that use incentives, that emphasize enterprise, that have some recognition in one way or another of private property, that are open to the global economy, and that have managed to exercise reasonable budgetary and especially monetary discipline.

Simpler than Jerry Brown's world, perhaps, but also more promising, more logical, and more testable.

Partly because of its stark, almost monocausal simplicity and partly because of its political overtones, to many scholars the property rights paradigm is the academic equivalent to the *Ring* cycle – an acquired taste they never acquired and pray they never will. What of literacy, they ask? What of numeracy, of habits of industry, of normative cosmologies, of propensities to save? What of lumpy markets, others ask? What of strategic behavior, of cooperation in iterated games, of asymmetric information?

These qualifications and complications can fascinate, but they can also obscure. In the comparative economic inquiry, they obscure with a vengeance. For in comparisons of national economic performance, these qualifications and complications pale in importance beside the basic role that simple property rights play. Indeed, to the extent a society maintains appropriate property rights, many of the qualifications and complications disappear.

For example, will people save? The right answer is that it largely depends on the returns they expect, and those returns depend on the property rights in place. Will educators build schools, and if they build them will students come? The answer is that whether educators will build and whether students will come largely depend on the returns to education. Will workers work hard or carefully? Once again, the answer depends on the incentives the institutional regime provides. Do market aberrations like informational asymmetries complicate the analysis? Most assuredly they do (I devote most of Chapters 6 and 7 to the issue). They complicate it, though, in ways that market participants largely anticipate and (given enforceable property rights) mitigate through rational contracting practices.

## 2   LAW AND EFFICIENT GROWTH IN JAPAN

With exceptions to be sure, imperial Japanese law generally provided the right incentives for stimulating efficient growth. It gave people clear rights to scarce resources. It let them enforce those rights through the courts. It stopped them from harming others unless they produced a net social benefit. And it let them freely transfer their rights. To explore these themes, turn to the argument in the chapters below:

*Chapter 2.* Consider first the rights to land and water. In the seventh century, the Japanese government (in fact, it ruled only a small part of what we now call Japan) had imposed on the country a Chinese-based system much like the Levitical "Year of the Jubilee": every six years it returned title to whoever owned the land under the initial allocation. Had it enforced this system long, few people would have invested extensively either in land or in the irrigation facilities necessary to make the land productive. Fortunately for Japan, the system was not enforced long. Within a few centuries, the government lost power to local militias. These militias effectively did enforce private rights to the land under their control, and enforced as well the private claims to the water people used to irrigate that land.

By the time courts faced land and irrigation disputes in the late nineteenth century, they could draw on an elaborate body of customary law. Largely, that law protected private rights to land and water. For land itself, they could turn to the Prussian-based Civil Code. For water, they faced a harder problem, since water-rich Prussia did not face the problems that arose in the effectively water-scarce Japan. As a result, Japanese courts could not use the Code to solve irrigation disputes. They could, however, use custom. By rephrasing it in modern legal terms, they continued into the twentieth century the traditional property rights to water that had so effectively fueled agricultural growth in the recent past.

*Chapter 3.* Critically, imperial Japanese law did not promote economic investment at all costs. Instead, it promoted only relatively efficient investment. If one landowner harmed his or her neighbors (i.e., if one imposed negative externalities on his or her neighbors), it forced the owner to compensate the neighbors whenever their losses exceeded his or her gain. As a result, it did not generally encourage entrepreneurs to produce at inefficient levels. It encouraged them to produce primarily only when the net social gains were positive.

Obviously, the imperial courts sometimes hesitated and sometimes erred. Most prominently, in pollution cases they regularly alternated between a strict liability regime (where the tortfeasor compensates victims for all losses) and a negligence regime (where the tortfeasor compensates victims only if the tortfeasor's conduct is inefficient). That indecision should not, however, obscure the fact that strict liability and negligence both create incentives to produce only at relatively efficient levels. Indecisive as the courts may sometimes have been on some matters, they persistently tried to force entrepreneurs who produced at inefficient levels to compensate their victims.

*Chapter 4.* Imperial Japanese law did not just protect rights to land and water; it also protected rights to labor. Importantly, it protected a worker's right to his or her *own* labor. Scholars make much of the patriarchal and familistic ideology of nineteenth- and early twentiety-century Japan. Turning reflexively from ideology to behavior, many then describe a world where the oldest male of each generation treated other family members nearly as serfs.

In leaning so heavily on ideology, these scholars miss both behavior and the law. The labor market did not let family heads dominate other members, and by the early twentieth century neither did the law. To explore the impact of the market, turn first to the seventeenth century. By most accounts, fathers in 1600 held enforceable claims to their children's work. Perhaps they did. But by the middle of the next century, they had lost them. By then, most people – whether male or female, adult or teen – effectively controlled the property rights to themselves.

Rather than legal change, it was the development of a large and anonymous nonseasonal urban labor market that guaranteed this autonomy. Once that market developed, workers who absconded could support themselves independently. Because of this new-found ability to abscond, employers, parents, and the children themselves all began to negotiate contracts that reflected the inability of parents to control their work-age children. In effect, the potential to abscond and survive (even thrive) gave work-age children the right to choose their own work and keep what they earned. Ultimately, the labor market itself mitigated family hierarchy.

*Chapter 5.* This effective autonomy which the Tokugawa (1600–1868) labor market conferred, the imperial courts confirmed. To date, most Japan scholars describe a legal regime (1) that gave the head of the family strong control over other adult members (whether male or female), and (2) that favored husbands over wives. In doing so, they misstate the law.

Imperial courts did not enforce a rigidly hierarchical legal structure. The family head could not force other members to live where he pleased, could not veto the other members' marriages, and could not freely expel members who flouted him. Husbands could not freely send home wives (even before they registered the marriage), and could not engage in adultery without risking divorce. The law did not require primogeniture, and did not automatically give husbands child custody. Lest any family heads have residual power, virtually all adult members except the next head abandoned their natal family by age thirty anyway.

To gauge the relative economic efficiency of family law regimes, pause

13

here to ask what economic effect an autocratic legal regime (i.e., one that gave the family head extensive power over collateral members) would have. All else equal, free labor is more efficient than bound. After all, people are more likely to work hard when they can keep what they produce. Because all else may not be equal, however, ask in what circumstances an autocratic regime would be least inefficient.

First, autocratic law will be less inefficient when the labor market is poorly developed. The less efficient the labor market, the greater the returns to employing family members at home. Second, autocratic family law will be less inefficient where household production enjoys large economies of scale. The greater the scale economies, the greater the gains from a large workforce in the household, and the greater the need to control it. Last, autocratic law will be less inefficient when a family head can readily monitor other family members. Bound labor is inefficient because of its incentive problems. The more a family head can mitigate those problems through close monitoring, the less the inefficiency to autocratic family law.

Such are the circumstances where autocratic family law would be least inefficient, but by the late nineteenth century those circumstances pointed away from autocratic law in Japan. By the turn of the century, most Japanese workers and firms did not sort themselves in inefficient labor markets. And most Japanese families did not engage in household production with large-scale economies. As a result, a legal regime that gave a family head extensive power over collateral adult members would probably have lowered total social production. Crucially, Japan did not maintain such a legal regime.

*Chapter 6.* To explore what deals workers and firms cut in these labor markets – particularly in the most problematic labor markets – I study the contracts between prostitutes and brothels. Theirs was a market plagued by large informational asymmetries. The brothel had extensive information about how much income a woman could reasonably expect to earn; the potential prostitute had less. The brothel could diversify its risks by keeping a portfolio of labor contracts; the prostitute could not. The brothel, when recruiting a woman, had an incentive to exaggerate her future earnings; the potential prostitute knew this, yet could not (because of the reputational loss she incurred in selling sexual services) cheaply test its claims.

To mitigate these informational problems, brothels and prospective prostitutes negotiated long-term indentured servitude contracts. To commit to compensating the woman for her reputational loss (as well as for the disamenities of her work), the brothel advanced her an extremely large sum of money. In exchange for the money, she agreed to work

14

several years (generally, a maximum of six). If she worked that term, the brothel had no further claim against her. If she quit prematurely, it could demand back much of the advance.

If a prostitute merely agreed to work several years, however, she had no incentive to work conscientiously. After all, her job was an unpleasant one, even if (as happens in most labor markets) those for whom it was least unpleasant disproportionately chose the work. To induce her to please customers, the brothel agreed to apply a portion of the revenues she generated against her initial loan. If she worked hard and generated large revenues, she could quit early. Crucially, many did quit early.

Prostitution was harsh work, but it was not slavery and it was not debt peonage. Instead, for most of the women who took it, it was a lucrative job in which they worked only a few years. Most prostitutes earned high wages, and many fulfilled their contractual terms early. To commit credibly to paying those high wages, brothels advanced them large portions of their expected earnings at the outset. Through the contracts, brothels and prostitutes effectively mitigated the informational asymmetries in their market. Through the contracts, they mutually, rationally – even, one is tempted to say, intelligently – promoted their respective best interests.

*Chapter 7.* This rationality characterizes the more conventional labor markets in imperial Japan as well, and I explore this point in the market for cotton-spinning factory workers. This cotton-spinning industry raises another issue too: the extent to which cartels dominated product markets in imperial Japan. Lacking as the legal regime did an antitrust statute, observers have sometimes claimed that it facilitated cartels, and that pervasive cartels cheated consumers and created large dead weight losses. The most prominent of those cartels – the "most durable and powerful," in Miles Fletcher's words (1989: 15) – was the cotton cartel.

Readers should be skeptical. We have known at least since George Stigler's 1964 study that pricefixing cartels tend to be unstable. We know from several modern industry-specific studies that many apparent cartels create no deadweight losses (Bittlingmayer, 1982; Pirrong, 1992; Dick, 1992). And we know from Fred McChesney's (1995: 336) recent work that antitrust law imposes large inefficiencies: that it is "clearly costly – in enforcement budgets, wrongly decided cases, and private suits filed only to extort settlement offers."

Skepticism pays handsomely here, for the Japanese cotton-spinning cartel did not raise prices. It did not, and was not designed to, earn its member firms monopoly rents. Instead, it helped them overcome a pair of subtle but important informational problems: (1) because of the team character to the manufacturing process, the firms could not cheaply verify each employee's marginal contribution; and (2) during downturns, they could not easily determine why the demand for their product fell. The cartel mitigated both of these seemingly disparate problems.

The logic follows: The cotton-spinning firms paid their workers two to three times the market-clearing wage. By doing so, they created a large penalty for any workers they fired. Through that penalty, they induced their workers to work hard. In many other industries, employers motivate workers through piece-rate pay scales. The cotton-spinning firms used this high-wage (known as an "efficiency-wage") strategy instead because the team character of the productive process precluded such piece-rate contracts.

The cotton-spinning firms formed the cartel to prevent their plant managers from cheating on the high-wage strategy. Given the noisy information in the industry, a firm's owners could not readily learn why the firm faced declining demand. The decline could result from industry-wide problems, or it could result from poor management. Rather than risk inquiries into their conduct, plant managers had an incentive to keep firms operating at full capacity in the black. On a short-term basis they could so so by cutting wages. In the process, though, they jeopardized the firm's high-wage strategy. To protect that high-wage strategy, therefore, the firms formed a cartel that automatically imposed production cuts during times of industry-wide slack. Ultimately, the cotton-spinning cartel – the most famous of all pre-War cartels – was not a pricefixing cartel at all.

### 3 WHY RELATIVELY EFFICIENT LAW?

#### 3.1 *General theories*

*Efficiency.* That Japanese law tended to promote efficient growth raises the second question posed at the outset: why? Why did the government adopt so efficient a legal regime? One might try to ascribe an inevitability to it. Richard Posner, for example, once proposed a theory of common law efficiency. As he (1972) initially articulated it, turn-of-the-century American judges developed a tort law that usually induced parties to avoid accidents at an optimal level. As he later formulated it more generally, American judges developed legal doctrines that "form a system for inducing people to behave efficiently, not only in explicit markets but across the whole range of social interactions" (1986: 229–30).

The idea generated an enormous literature. Some like George Priest (1977: 65) agreed, and claimed that in common law systems there is a "tendency of the set of all legal rules to become dominated by rules achieving efficient as opposed to inefficient allocative effects." Others found close analogies. Yehoshua Liebermann (1986) and Geoffrey Miller (1993) both found in the Jewish legal tradition a set of rules structured by an economic logic. David D. Friedman (1979: 400) did the same for the tenth to thirteenth-century Icelandic law.

Unfortunately, Posner never offered a mechanism for the phenomenon he identified. He never said why judges would necessarily pick wealth-maximizing rules. From time to time, others did offer mechanisms (e.g., Rubin, 1977), but none worked well. Because Posner's judges were autonomous moral and political agents who decided cases independently, Posner himself seemed to rely (even if he never so said) on simple psychology: judges made efficient law because they wanted to.[3] Unfortunately for comparative purposes, it is hard enough to believe American judges would generally promote wealth-maximizing principles over others (e.g., redistributive goals). It is harder still to think judges everywhere else would necessarily do the same.

*Convergence.* More recently, Saul Levmore proposed a general legal convergence thesis. According to Levmore (1987: 44; 1986), legal rules tend to converge when the issues at stake concern "self-interested behavior that threatens the general welfare." They diverge when the rules either "do not much matter" or "raise issues about which reasonable people . . . could disagree." In effect, he claimed, societies develop relatively efficient (and similar) legal rules over issues that matter dearly, but may maintain wildly divergent rules over everything else.

Unfortunately again, the hypothesis harbors its own problems. Japan and most Western countries are rich, and Japan and most Western countries have similar and (mostly) efficient legal rules.[4] That they have those similar rules, however, is exactly what one would expect, given the wealth; that they are wealthy is exactly what one would expect, given the rules.

By contrast, most of the world is not rich. Most societies have not experienced rapid economic growth, and that fact itself suggests that many societies may have very different inefficient legal regimes. That "growth has been more exceptional than stagnation or decline," notes North (1981: 6), itself "suggests that 'efficient property rights' are unusual in history." Given the effect efficient legal rules have on economic growth, it would be strange indeed, in a world as plagued by economic stagnation as ours, to find efficient rules pervasive.

---

[3]Posner himself explores the question more fully in Posner (1993).
[4]Note that Levmore (1986) has indeed applied his theory to non-Western, nonadvanced societies.

### 3.2   *Federalism in Tokugawa Japan*

So why *did* the Japanese government adopt a set of legal rules that tended toward efficiency? If legal efficiency is not necessary, and if legal designs do not converge, why did the Japanese government adopt the law that it did? Consider first what we do know. To maintain a relatively efficient legal regime, a government must be strong enough to specify and enforce property rights; it must be too weak to regulate excessively. It must be strong enough to facilitate the market; it must be too weak to debilitate it.

The Tokugawa government was all this, and the reason lies in its federal structure. In a federal world (defined in Weingast, 1995), the national government has structurally limited but geographically broad regulatory power; the local governments have structurally plenary but geographically constrained power. In this federal world, the local governments regulate markets, but regulate subject to the constraint that disaffected citizens can emigrate. Should they regulate too heavily or protect property rights too loosely, entrepreneurs will take their business elsewhere (e.g., Tiebout, 1956; Easterbrook, 1983). The national government largely escapes that constraint (emigrating to a different nation is harder), but exercises only structurally limited power.

Federalism describes the pre-1930s United States. It also describes the Netherlands in the sixteenth and seventeenth centuries and even England from the seventeenth through the nineteenth centuries (Root, 1994; Weingast, 1995: 3). In each of these countries, the government with the structural power to regulate competed in a market for optimal legal regimes, while the government beyond that market constraint operated within strict institutional bounds.

Federalism also describes Tokugawa Japan. The national government only indirectly controlled most domains. Instead, independent families controlled and regulated most areas. And federalism explains why much of the regulation was as benign as it was. Had the national government enjoyed real regulatory power, it could have caused a regulatory catastrophy – for the ideologically and politically based regulatory plans it announced were disastrous: to end social mobility, to stop real estate transfers, and even to ban interdomainal migration. Fortunately for the country, it lacked the power to enforce any of them.

### 3.3   *Legal efficiency in imperial Japan*

For at least three perhaps paradoxical reasons, the leaders of imperial Japan continued relatively benign economic regulation: (1) they inherited a legacy of limited government, (2) they faced aggression from a forthrightly imperialist West, and (3) they suffered chronic competition among themselves. Consider each in turn.

*The Tokugawa legacy.* The Meiji (1868–1912) oligarchs began their rule with a limited government, and no mandate for reform. They had inherited the Tokugawa tradition of weak, often ineffective governance. They enjoyed no broad support, and no mandate for radical change. During the earliest decades of the regime, they had to work cautiously to alter anything much at all.

*The imperialist threat.* The Meiji oligarchs also faced serious threats from an unabashedly imperialist West. Collectively, the Western navies made clear that what had happened to China could happen to Japan – indeed, that unless the oligarchs cooperated with the West, it would. Having no real choice, the oligarchs agreed to a series of treaties. These treaties, however, placed foreigners beyond the jurisdiction of the Japanese courts.

Determined to regain judicial sovereignty over foreigners in Japan, the oligarchs began the process of convincing Western governments to relinquish consular jurisdiction. As the price for doing so, the Western governments demanded a familiar legal system. Largely to regain its judicial sovereignty, therefore, the oligarchs modeled their new legal system closely on continental European (usually German) models (Haley, 1991: 68). By the close of the nineteenth century, they had constructed a three-tiered court system with professional judges and an elaborate panoply of legal codes (see Ramseyer & Rosenbluth, 1995: ch. 6). It was a system that effectively defined and protected private rights to scarce resources. But it was a system they adopted primarily for other reasons: as the price of ridding the country of consular jurisdiction.

*Structure-induced equilibria.* Once it had adopted a Western property rights regime, the Japanese government kept it largely intact until the 1930s. Part of the reason it did so is easy, for stability is a phenomenon we understand well. Even in contemporary democracies where coalitions should endlessly cycle (Arrow, 1951), institutions are relatively permanent. They are permanent because in modern legislatures legal structure and procedure generally create "structure-induced equilibria" (Shepsle & Weingast, 1981). Indeed, institutions are often stable even when inefficient. Even then, the coalitional conflicts and transactions costs of change can prevent a government from improving the legal regime (e.g., Kantor, 1991, 1995; Libecap, 1989).

Much the same phenomenon explains the legal stability in imperial Japan. The Meiji oligarchs had created a wide variety of equilibria-inducing structures (described at length in Ramseyer & Rosenbluth, 1995: chs. 2, 3): from a carefully crafted Germanic constitution, to detailed procedural rules for issuing and amending regulations, to a complicated gatekeeping function for the emperor, to rules about who had access to (and who thus controlled) that emperor. By creating these structures, the oligarchs effectively tied their own hands.

These structures created stability only because the government was a fractious oligarchy (and by the 1920s, almost a democracy).[5] Had it instead been a unitary actor, the structures would not have created stability. But the Meiji oligarchy was not a unitary actor. In effect, it was a cartel, and suffered from the same suicidal impulses that plague most cartels. In economic markets, rivals may organize a cartel, but they seldom abide by its terms long. Unfortunately for them (fortunately for the rest of us), they usually gain by cheating on the cartel. Although they can raise their aggregate revenues by setting monopoly prices, they raise their individual revenues by underselling their rivals instead (Stilger, 1964).

Like cartels, like oligopolies. Although the oligarchs in Japan might have raised their aggregate political welfare by cooperating with each other, they raised their individual welfare by cheating on each other. As oligarchs, they earned political rents which they necessarily divided among themselves. Yet that division constituted a game in which they regularly found it advantageous to prove that they could threaten the others. To threaten the others, they regularly solicited support from groups outside the oligarchy. Precisely because of this competitive process, they found it hard to make fundamental legal changes by collectively manipulating the structures they had created; precisely because of this competitive process, the institutional apparatus produced a structure-induced equibrium.

*The rent-seeking market.* This competitive character to the oligarchy also improved the character of the laws and regulations that the government did pass. Because the oligarchs competed with each other chronically, the rent-seeking and rent-extractive game in imperial Japan acquired a competitive market cast. That competitive cast, in turn, probably mitigated the dead weight loss to the regulatory schemes adopted.

To understand why competition within the oligarchy would reduce the dead weight loss to regulation, consider Hinton Root's (1994) recent comparison between old regime France and Britain. In prerevolutionary France, argued Root, the concentration of the national power in the

[5]The discussion that follows borrows from Ramseyer & Rosenbluth (1995: 7).

crown led to "cronyism": the discreet allocation of benefits to favorites. Because the crown regulated in secret, those harmed by the regulation could not negotiate better arrangements, and grossly inefficient regulation ensued.

By contrast, in Britain the diffusion of power among multiple elites led to a competitive rent-seeking game that involved a broad segment of the population. In effect, the rivalry among political elites created a forum for competitive bribery. Wrote Root (1994: 47), "Corruption in Britain was the equivalent of an auction market for rents and political favors. That rents could be auctioned to the highest bidder increased the liquidity of the social system by creating a market for privilege. In France, rent-extracting possibilities or favors could only be placed privately, preventing a public market or deals among rent seekers from developing." Where (as in old regime France) regulatory power is concentrated, cronyism results and the government allocates property rights "according to nonmarket criteria. . . . As a result, the chance of resources being misallocated is greater" (id., at 47). Where (as in Britain and imperial Japan) regulatory power is diffused, that distribution "is open to market forces and indirectly allows for the allocation of resources according to a criterion of efficiency that cronyism lacks" (id., at 46).

*Summary.* Return to the basic question: Why did the imperial Japanese government adopt and retain a legal system that recognized clear and enforceable claims to scarce resources? A tentative – and necessarily speculative – answer might proceed in three steps. First, the Meiji oligarchs inherited from the Tokugawa regime a government of limited powers. The Tokugawa regime was a relatively weak federal system, and coming to power as they did through a palace coup, the oligarchs initially lacked the power to change matters radically.

Second, the oligarchs had the paradoxically good fortune to face Western imperialism. Having little choice in the matter, they adopted the treaties the Western powers imposed. Just as the most-favored-nation status in these treaties benefited Japan by opening it to international trade, so too did the consular jurisdiction clauses benefit it by inducing the oligarchs to adopt a relatively efficient legal system.

Last, the diffusion of power among the oligarchs both prevented them from changing the legal regime radically, and mitigated the negative effects of market-displacing regulation. They were an oligarchy, not a dictatorship, and their group status made all the difference: the competition among them created a structure-induced stability, and transformed Japan from a potentially cronyist French-style regime to a competitive (and more efficient) rent-seeking regime in the British tradition.

21

## 4   CONCLUSION

The imperial Japanese government enforced a property rights regime that tended to promote efficient economic growth. It defined rights to scarce resources. It enforced those rights. It tried to stop people from using the resources in ways that inefficiently harmed others. It let people agree to transfer the rights. And it enforced most transfer agreements they made. Such is the basic thesis of this book.

That very legal efficiency, however, raises a second question: Why? A much more tentative answer follows from the diffusion of power. Because the Tokugawa government was federal, the local governments regulated the economy. Because dissatisfied citizens could move, these local governments regulated subject to market constraints. Although the Meiji oligarchs eliminated that federal structure, they now had to assuage the West. To do so, they adopted Western codes that – incidentally – protected property rights.

Once the oligarchs had adopted the Western codes, the diffusion of power among them made radical change hard. Because the competition among them was chronic, major change required privately costly cooperation. Because the competition was public, regulation operated by a market logic. That market logic, in turn, eliminated the most egregiously inefficient forms of regulation. Law facilitated relatively efficient economic growth, in short, and the diffusion of government power facilitated relatively efficient law.

# 2

## Property: Water and land

### INTRODUCTION

As the film *Yojimbo* opens, director Akira Kurosawa shows matinee idol Toshiro Mifune ambling past a ramshackle hut. A young man, apparently the son and heir apparent, dashes out of the cottage. Mifune watches bemused as the son yells at his father. Go on and eat your rice gruel, he shouts. My life may be shorter than yours, but it won't be half as dull. The father is unimpressed. Get back to farming, he replies. The life of a swordsman is not fit for you.

Nor, Kurosawa seems to tell us, is the life of a swordsman fit for many of us – or of much use to any of us. For at least one of the themes in *Yojimbo* is the Hobbesian inefficiency of it all. The mythic world of *Yojimbo* is a world where no public authority enforces private claims to any scarce resource, and no private parties cooperate without that authority. Instead, those with money dissipate their fortunes by hiring Mifune and his fellow mercenaries to protect their wealth and rob their neighbors.

Were the farmers and merchants in *Yojimbo* willing and able to cooperate, they could agree to respect each other's claims and fire these private armies. But agreements to cooperate often presuppose a public mechanism to enforce them. Notwithstanding game-theoretic models of the evolution of cooperation or of self-enforcing contracts,[1] the merchants in *Yojimbo* defect whenever it pays – and it pays often. No matter how badly they would like to respect each others' property claims, each individually finds it more profitable to hire thugs.

Enforceable claims to scarce resources are critical to economic growth (see Chapter 1). Growth depends on private investment, and investment on the size and security of the expected private returns. In turn, those

[1] See Sugden (1981); Axelrod (1981); Maynard Smith & Parker (1976); Klein & Leffler (1981); Telser (1980).

returns depend on the enforceability of private claims to scarce resources. Each entrepreneur could enforce those claims on his or her own, to be sure. Nevertheless, law enforcement tends to generate economies of scale, and private armies tend to have a rent-dissipating character.

Accordingly, efficient growth generally depends on the public enforcement (e.g., through courts) of private claims to scarce resources (i.e., of property rights). In this chapter, I trace the history of the public enforcement of private claims to land and water in Japan. I begin by outlining the history of private claims to water flow and farmland (Section 1). Only during the last few centuries, I argue, have people been able to enforce such claims. As a result, only during the last few centuries have they been able to invest in agricultural technology with much assurance of appropriating the returns to their investments. Because most important traditional investments in land depended on water, water law shaped the market for land as well. I thus turn to the details of the customary Japanese water law as it developed in recent centuries (Sections 2, 3). This customary law effectively protected private claims to water flow. By privatizing water, it facilitated water-dependent investments. And in so doing, it tended to promote efficient economic growth.

## I   PUBLIC ORDER AND PRIVATE CLAIMS

Rice is critical to Japanese agriculture, and water is critical to rice. During many months each year, Japanese rice must stand in flooded fields; during others, it must stand dry. Few issues matter as dearly in such a society as irrigation. In fact, the cosmic fall from grace in Japanese mythology occurs when the sun-goddess's brother breaks down the ridges between the paddies and blocks the irrigation ditches. A violation of the communal irrigation rules was thus not just a crime or a tort, it was a sin (Philippi, 1968: 79). Of the prehistoric eight cardinal sins, four were crimes against irrigation rules: breaking down ridges between the paddies, covering up ditches, releasing the water in the sluices, and double-cropping rice (id., at 403–4)

To ensure the availability of this water, Japanese farmers today perform an elaborate, almost endless series of tasks: they grade paddies, store water in pools, divert rivers, dam streams, build reservoirs, fix sluices, dig ditches, dike terraces. They need enough water to flood their fields in the precise amount, at the precise time. Just as exactly, they need those fields drained. To ensure that they can do so, they refashion the landscape in their own image.

Japan was not always this orderly collection of paddies, sluices, ditches, and dikes. For Japan was not always a society in which farmers could safely enforce their claims to the harvest. Instead, with respect to large segments of the population, vast areas of arable land, and long periods of history, people who invested in major agricultural improvements had no assurance that they would earn a return.

Initially, the risks to investments in agricultural projects resulted from the basic insecurity and ambiguity of water rights and land tenure. Bodies of water, during the earliest periods of Japanese history, were resources to which no one had enforceable claims (Yasuda, 1933: 2–7). Land, if held privately, was nonetheless held only tenuously. Under the Chinese system adopted in the seventh and eighth centuries, the state reexamined land holdings every six years.[2] As in the Levitical "Year of the Jubilee" (Lev. 25: 8–19), it then redistributed the land according to prescribed formulae. Unfortunately, the extant records do not reveal for how long and over how much of the country the state carried out this redistribution scheme. By the tenth century, it had abandoned it entirely (Ishii, 1983: 115–16).

Even after the tenth century, however, land tenure remained unclear and insecure. As in prerevolutionary France (Rosenthal, 1992), land ownership remained a tangled mass of overlapping central and local claims. As it did in France, that chaos itself discouraged claimants from making substantial agricultural improvements.

This relatively insecure land tenure coincided both with an abundance of land and with low levels of agricultural capital investments. Most intricate networks of ditches, sluices, and paddies in place today are relatively recent inventions. Notwithstanding the importance of irrigation to Japanese cosmology, for centuries only peasants in a few communities in central Japan maintained complex irrigation facilities. Peasants elsewhere used land as though it were an unlimited resource. They cleared an area, burned off the vegetation, and raised crops for several seasons. When they exhausted the soil (as they all too quickly did) they moved on (Farris, 1985: 116; Tomosugi, 1984).

Without enforceable private rights to the continued use of land and water, few Japanese tried to adopt more elaborate agricultural techniques. After all, the more productive technologies did not come cheap. Instead, they entailed large investments in both land improvement and river control. Whether peasants, soldiers, or merchants, few people were willing to invest in such techniques without both the assurance of secure returns and the ability to spread the cost of the technology among the parties who would benefit from it. As Douglass North and Robert Paul

[2]See Ishii (1983: 113–17). Note, however, that various exceptions existed. See Sato (1974).

25

## Odd markets in Japanese history

Thomas (1973: ch. 7) demonstrated in Europe, such situations can create stability – but it is a particularly vicious stability: the population stays within the level that this basic agricultural technology can support only because famines and diseases keep it that low.

During the fourteenth and fifteenth centuries, security and clarity in ownership patterns finally emerged. Yet it was not market bargaining that streamlined these patterns – it was opportunism coupled with military power. The central aristocrats had assigned armed guards to their provincial farmlands. These militia had their own interests, and increasingly used their control over the land to further those interests. As the aristocrats lost control of their claims to these guards, ownership effectively passed to them as well.[3]

For agricultural investment, this change in land tenure apparently had several crucial consequences. First, because the local claimants kept larger shares of the yield than before, they had a greater incentive to increase the land's productivity. Because they were on site, they also had better information about how to do so than the central aristocrats. Second, since there were now fewer claimants to the harvest, those remaining were less likely to find that negotiation and contract costs prevented them from splitting the expense of the agricultural improvements among themselves.

Third, because the increased local power made political and military control more stable, land tenure itself became more secure. True, during the late fifteenth and early sixteenth centuries, warfare destroyed this security in many areas. Yet the increased local control actually enhanced the security of land tenure in most.[4] The security of tenure, in turn, reduced the risks to investing in agricultural improvements.

The population now increased steadily. By the seventeenth century it had reached record levels. Agricultural land and water flow, correspondingly more scarce, became effectively and elaborately privatized (subject to private claims enforced through public means). Officially, the Tokugawa regime banned the alienation of farm land. Yet landowners devised an elaborate array of means (generally mortgages) to buy and sell their lands (see Chapter 4). The once uncertain and idiosyncratic claims to land became interests close to fee simple, and eventually the village, domain, and central governments all protected private interests in water flow.[5]

[3]On changes in the concept of land ownership during these periods, see generally Berry (1982: ch. 2); Mass (1974).
[4]See Hall (1981); Murata (1979: 3, 5); Nagahara & Yamamura (1977: 107–12).
[5]The Tokugawa regime attempted a variety of other regulatory devices over agriculture, including limitations on the types of crops peasants could grow and on the minimum sizes of holdings that could be devised to children (Ishii, 1983: 448–9). On the privatization of water flow, see id., at 313–14. Note that the Tokugawa government preferred not to hear water rights cases if it could avoid them. See id., at 521–2.

26

## Property: Water and land

With the scarcity and privatization of farmland and water flow came increased investments in agricultural technology. By the time the American gunboats arrived in 1853, investments in land and irrigation had reached unprecedented levels. From the fifteenth century to the seventeenth, the amount of cultivated land in Japan had doubled; during the two-and-a-half centuries that followed, it doubled yet again (Tamaki, 1984: 8, table 1–1; Hanley & Yamamura, 1977: 74). Irrigation capacity grew at similar rates (Hatate, 1984: 57–60; Yamamura, 1981: 334, table 11.2): some of the facilities were large – great ditches carrying water for dozens of miles. Others were small – thousands of wells, waterwheels, and ponds. By the mid-nineteenth century, one-half to three-fourths of all basic irrigation facilities used today were in place.[6] New fields had been opened, dry fields converted into paddies, and existing paddies double-cropped. In effect, two phenomena had occurred: Japan had privatized farmland and water flow, and it had adopted capital-intensive agricultural and irrigation techniques.


## 2  WATER LAW IN IMPERIAL JAPAN

It was within this world of enforceable private claims to land and water that the Japanese government of the late nineteenth century adopted a modified version of the Prussian Civil Code.[7] Together with other measures to make land more readily transferrable,[8] the new Code altered and streamlined the law of real estate. Water law, however, it left largely intact.[9]

---

[6]Murata (1979: 5); Francks (1984: 32). Note, however, that Hayami & Yamada (1991: 261) claim that the area of irrigated land increased 56% from 1880 to 1930.

[7]*Mimpo [Civil Code]*, Law No. 89 of 1896; Law No. 9 of 1898 (Articles 4 and 5). For more detailed analyses of the doctrinal permutations to Japanese water law, see, e.g., Yasuda (1933); Nishizaki (1927).

[8]Land became formally alienable in the Meiji period, see Dajokan fukoku No. 50 of 1872, through deeds authorized by Okura sho tatsu No. 25 of 1872.

[9]Only a few Civil Code provisions touched on water rights, see, e.g., Civil Code, § 219, and only a few other statutes did so, see, e.g., *Kasen ho [Rivers Act]*, Law No. 71 of 1896 (control of rivers, especially flood control); *Kochi seiri ho [Farm Land Rationalization Act]*, Law No. 82 of 1899 (rationalization of layout of paddy fields); *Suiri kumiai ho [Water Collectives Act]*, Law No. 50 of 1908 (regulation of water collectives).

Because this chapter focuses on the customary common law of water rights, it does not discuss this legislation or the cases construing it. Such statutes (and the administrative apparatus they impose) are important to a full understanding of Japanese water law, however, and readers interested in the statutes should consult, e.g., Yasuda (1933); Kato (1973); Watanabe (1951).

## 2.1 Irrigation

In large part, therefore, the water law at the close of the nineteenth century was indigenous customary law.[10] It was a law that recognized private claims to water flow based on use: by steady use, one who diverted and used water acquired a right against all others. Granted, details varied from village to village. But in most communities, the customary law protected hydraulic investments by privatizing the water flow itself – by granting current users of water an enforceable right to its continued use.

Early Meiji period (1868–1912) courts generally followed this traditional law and enforced customary private interests in water flow.[11] Yet when the Diet passed the Civil Code in the 1890s, the courts initially appeared unsure of what to do. Juxtaposing the common law against the Code, some courts seemed to find a conflict – and applied their understanding of the Code. The Code spoke of "rights" and "title" to land, grand terms applied grandly. To landowners it seemed to give a general right to do with their land as they pleased.[12] Because it also said virtually nothing about water, some courts held that landowners with access to water could use it as they wished.

In March 1896, for example, the Supreme Court held that title to land gave its owner the absolute right to use any percolating water.[13] The plaintiffs were farmers who had traditionally irrigated their fields with water flowing from the defendant's land. By using the water to irrigate new rice paddies, the defendant had now made the plaintiffs' traditional use impossible. Because the plaintiffs asserted a customary right to the water and the defendant a fee simple interest in the land from which it flowed, the case seemed to present a conflict between custom and the Code. The court chose what it apparently thought the more modern rule and held for the defendant. Title to land, it wrote, extends to the water

---

[10]See *Horei [Choice of Law Rules]*, Law No. 10 of 1898, § 2; Dajokan fukoku No. 103 of 1875, § 3; see also Shiho sho tatsu No. 9 of 1879. Some of this customary law had developed in the Tokugawa courts, but much had developed in the informal adjudicatory mechanisms of the local villages and water collectives (Kato, 1985: 258–9). For a historical account of Tokugawa water law, see Kitamura (1950).

[11]See, e.g., Ito v. Hanaoka, ll Daihan minroku (1st series) 1111, 1139 (Daishin'in [Supreme Court] Feb. 28, 1879) (presumption that customary rights govern water disputes).

[12]See Civil Code, § 207 (title to land extends to everything above and below the surface).

[13]Nakanobo v. Yoneda, 2-3 Daihan minroku lll (Daishin'in [Supreme Court] Mar. 27, 1896). Although the Civil Code did not take effect until 1898, one draft (based on the Napoleonic Code) had already been enacted in 1890. See Law No. 28 of 1890. That draft was rescinded and replaced by the Prussian-based draft before it ever took effect. See Law No. 89 of 1896.

below. Owners may do with such water as they please, and the customary rights of others matter not.[14]

Nevertheless, the courts almost immediately restricted this approach to water underground.[15] By October 1896, the Supreme Court made clear that it would decide disputes over water above ground by the rules that had governed irrigation disputes for centuries: customary water use created an entitlement to that body of water.[16] In turn, the content of the entitlement depended on the use: the one who first used the water could continue to use it to the exclusion of all others, in the frequency and quantity of that customary use. A farmer who irrigated one field for three hours each day during certain months, for instance, could enforce his right to do so. He could not, however, enforce any claim to irrigate his field for longer periods or during other months. Effectively, the court bifurcated the law between underground and above-ground water flow. The courts recognized few customary entitlements to the former, but almost all customary entitlements to the latter.

The defendants in an October 1896 case, for example, were apparently an upstream riparian family that had opened a new paddy field by diverting water from a stream. The plaintiffs were thirteen downstream farmers. Although by custom they had used the water for their own paddies, the defendants' new use threatened to transform those paddies into dry fields. The court held for the plaintiffs. "By ancient custom," it explained, riparian owners may use flowing water only to the extent they do not damage the traditional use of others.[17]

[14]See also Kiyono v. Takauchi, ll Daihan minroku 1703, 1706–7 (Daishin'in [Supreme Court] Dec. 20, 1905) (owner of land has right to use underground steam); Japan v. Kashima, 10 Daihan keiroku 429, 434–5 (Daishin'in [Supreme Court] Mar. 7, 1904) (owner of fee simple interest has right to dig well on his or her property regardless of village custom to contrary; criminal case); Sakaguchi v. Rokugawa, 4-10 Daihan minroku 24, 29 (Daishin'in [Supreme Court] Nov. 18, 1898) (customs "contrary to reason" are unenforceable); Yamawake v. Yamamoto, 4306 Horitsu shimbun 17, 18 (Daishin'in [Supreme Court] July ll, 1938) (title to land gives right to subterranean water, subject to contrary custom).

[15]Even that subterranean water, courts sometimes explained, was subject to some customary limits on its use. See, e.g., Kagawa v. Kagawa, 23 Daihan minroku 202, 204–5 (Daishin'in [Supreme Court] Feb. 6, 1917) (holding for customary user of water that flowed from springs on land owned by defendant); Kagawa v. Kagawa, 21 Daihan minroku 886, 888 (Daishin'in [Supreme Court] June 3, 1915) (title to land from which water percolates gives rights which remain subject to contrary customs); Yoshizawa v. Horie, 1204 Horitsu shimbun 31, 32, 5 Horitsu hyoron min 1254, 1255 (Kobe D. Ct. Sept. ll, 1916) (same).

[16]Yoshida v. Komori, 2-9 Daihan minroku 19, 21 (Daishin'in [Supreme Court] Oct. 7, 1896). But see Japan v. Kashima, 10 Daihan keiroku 429 (Daishin'in [Supreme Court] Mar. 7, 1904) (owner of fee simple interest has right to dig well on his or her property regardless of village custom to contrary; criminal case).

[17]Yoshida v. Komori, 2-9 Daihan minroku at 21.

In February 1899, the Supreme Court reiterated this adherence to custom.[18] Again, the defendant was a dry-field farmer who had converted his fields into irrigated paddies. He could properly do so, he claimed, because the water he used flowed through his land. Yet in using that water, he apparently prevented eighteen downstream established paddy farmers from irrigating their own lands. Customary water use, the court held, created an enforceable right to its continued use. The defendant could use the water only to the extent that he did not reduce the amount available to the downstream users. In enjoining him, the court explained:

True, riparian owners may generally use whatever water flows in a river or stream. By established national custom, however, they may not use that water freely if other established users already use that water to irrigate rice paddies. On the contrary, they may use it to develop new paddies only if they do not thereby damage the existing use of the downstream riparian users. This custom is one we recognize in court.[19]

This deference to custom took a variety of forms. The most common cases were ones where upstream riparian owners destroyed the viability of existing downstream paddies by irrigating what had previously been dry fields. Almost uniformly, the courts upheld the downstream users' customary rights.[20]

---

[18]Kasuga v. Miyahara, 5-2 Daihan minroku 1 (Daishin'in [Supreme Court] Feb. 1, 1899).

[19]Id., at 4–5.

[20]In addition to the cases cited in the text, see, e.g., Kagawa v. Kagawa, 23 Daihan minroku 203, 204–5 (Daishin'in [Supreme Court] Feb. 6, 1917) (customary use prevails regardless of character of use); Shiga v. Hosokawa, 22 Daihan minroku 2341, 2344 (Daishin'in [Supreme Court] Dec. 2, 1916) (same); Kagawa v. Kagawa, 21 Daihan minroku 886, 888 (Daishin'in [Supreme Court] June 3, 1915) (title to land from which water percolates gives rights which remain subject to contrary custom); Kano v. Shirashima, 15 Daihan minroku 6 (Daishin'in [Supreme Court] Jan. 21, 1909) (court finds for thirty-two farmers against developers of new paddies on basis of customary rights noted in village contract of 1756); Kajishima v. Kawase, 12 Daihan minroku 507, 510 (Daishin'in [Supreme Court] Apr. 4, 1906) (upstream owner cannot redirect stream to detriment of downstream owner; though Civil Code, § 219, governed this matter, court notes that same rule applied prior to adoption of the Civil Code); Yoshida v. Inagaki, 11 Daihan minroku 1328 (Daishin'in [Supreme Court] Oct. 11, 1905)(court finds for upstream waterwheel user against downstream builder of dam); Akamatsu v. Yoshikawa, 1396 Horitsu shimbun 28 (Kobe D. Ct. Feb. 3, 1918) (court finds for prior user on basis of custom); Yoshizawa v. Horie, 1204 Horitsu shimbun 31, 32, 5 Horitsu hyoron min 1254, 1255 (Kobe D. Ct. Sept. 11, 1916) (title to land from which water percolates gives rights which remain subject to contrary custom); Kobayashi v. Yazawa, 494 Horitsu shimbun 7, 8–9 (Nagano D. Ct. No date) (customary use gives rise to right, but such use not found here); Komatsu v. Yamada, 319 Horitsu shimbun 21, 24 (Nagano D. Ct. Nov. 24, 1905) (court finds for forty-one villagers against upstream developer from whose land the stream percolated).

Yet custom could also include the right to injure other parties. In 1902, for instance, the Supreme Court declined to hold fourteen defendants liable for flooding the fields of fifty-three plaintiffs.[21] The defendants had maintained a water-storage pond for irrigation, but the pond had leaked. Because the defendants had used the pond long enough for that use to constitute custom and the plaintiffs could not prove that they had been unusually careless, the court refused to award damages.[22]

Although the disposition of individual cases proceeded easily enough, the courts had trouble fitting customary water rights into the conceptual categories the Civil Code provided. Recall that the Code rarely referred to water rights. As a result, the courts eventually articulated a form of privatization distinct from the "ownership" concepts they applied to land. As the Supreme Court put it in 1900:

Never in our nation's history have individuals owned flowing streams. Instead, custom has granted riparian owners and other residents only the right to use the water. Since they use it jointly, they have the right to use it only to the extent that they do not injure each others' rights.[23]

If not ownership in form, however, this customary law was a form of privatization nonetheless. As the earlier discussion makes clear, holders of customary surface water rights could not only divert the water, they could consume it. If they wished, they could even sell their rights to third parties. Their rights to water flow differed from their rights to other scarce resources primarily only in the way the courts limited their water rights to the water they actually used. Simple diversion, for example, would not do.[24]

[21]Nishimura v. Nakao, 8-5 Daihan minroku 69, 74 to 75 (Daishin'in [Supreme Court] May 16, 1902); see also Arima v. Mitsuishi, 4836 Horitsu shimbun 14, 15–16 (Nagano D. Ct. Feb. 3, 1943) (where defendant's paddy irrigation had damaged plaintiff's downhill home every previous year, defendant was not liable when it damaged it again this year).

[22]The court reached this result despite language in the Civil Code dictating a standard close to strict liability in this case. See Civil Code, § 216. The court explained that community custom expressed the terms of an agreement between the parties.

[23]Yamaguchi v. Kojima, 6-2 Daihan minroku 90, 91 (Daishin'in [Supreme Court] Feb. 26, 1900) (emphasis added); see Kai v. Kataoka, 6-7 Daihan minroku 89, 92 (Daishin'in [Supreme Court] Mar. 19, 1900) (riparian owners have right to use flowing rain water to extent they do not damage rights of others); Sakaguchi v. Rokugawa, 4-11 Daihan minroku 24 (Daishin'in [Supreme Court] Nov. 18, 1898) (custom gives right to use water, not to own it).

[24]Sakaguchi v. Rokugawa, 4-10 Daihan minroku 24, 29 (Daishin'in [Supreme Court] Nov. 18, 1898) (right to use water does not extend to right to control use of flow-off); Shiga v. Hosokawa, 22 Daihan minroku 2341, 2344–5 (Daishin'in [Supreme Court] Dec. 2, 1916) (right to use water limited to amount deemed necessary); Yasuda (1933: 47–75).

## 2.2   Hot springs

The courts also enforced the new rules governing subterranean water in the other principal area of private water rights: the law of hot springs. In part, the Japanese public treasured these baths for their medicinal qualities. They also enjoyed them as recreation – so much so that one early-nineteenth-century bestseller revolved entirely around the ribald antics at a neighborhood bathhouse (Shikitei, 1809). Because of this popularity, hot springs were economically valuable. They constituted an important attraction at many vacation resorts, and access to them determined many a rural inn's success. Most veins of steam, however, supported only a few baths. As a result, innkeepers who drilled new steam wells could often destroy their older competitors.

Cases raising the right to drill new wells appeared in the courts by the turn of the century.[25] In almost all cases, the source of the dispute was social and technological change: with the advent of the railroad, increasing numbers of urban Japanese could vacation in rural hot springs resorts, and increasingly they demanded private baths. The plaintiffs in these disputes were often bathless innkeepers who relied on a local public bath to attract patrons. The defendants were new upscale hotel developers or wealthy vacationers – in either case, people who hoped to pipe the steam indoors.

To these disputes, the courts generally applied the new Japanese law of subterranean water: landowners could generally exploit underground water freely. To this rule, however, most courts noted a caveat: landowners could not draw underground water or steam if local custom prohibited them from doing so. Although custom varied from community to community, courts did occasionally recognize that it might limit new steam wells. In some communities, for example, custom seems to have prohibited new users from drilling for steam unless they acquired the permission of the village or purchased a right to draw steam from existing users.[26]

Consider the dispute that split the seaside community of Kinosaki.[27] The springs in this hamlet enjoyed a repute for medicinal value that dated,

---

[25]See, e.g., Kiyono v. Takauchi, ll Daihan minroku 1702, 1707 (Daishin'in [Supreme Court] Dec. 20, 1905) (landowner has right to use underground vein of steam; customary law claim rejected on the facts), *aff'g*, 311 Horitsu shimbun 9, 10–11 (Miyagi Ct. App. No date) (same).

[26]See generally Kawashima, Shiomi & Watanabe (1964); Kawashima (1960); Waza (1960). But see Watanabe (1962) (premodern Japanese communities held hot springs in common and did not privatize the resource)

[27]Kinosaki Village v. Kataoka, 4249 Horitsu shimbun 5 (Kobe D. Ct. Feb. 7, 1938). The facts in the text are taken from this opinion, Kawashima, Shiomi, & Watanabe (1964), and general geographical guides.

by popular account, to a visit by an ailing seventh-century emperor. By the turn of the twentieth century, the town had 2,300 residents, and its springs fed six rock pools. To cater to tourists, the villagers operated over sixty inns. The more religious of these visitors prefaced their jaunts to the baths with a pilgrimage up to the local "Hot Springs Temple." Others went straight to the public pools. None of inns had their own baths.

In 1910, the railroad arrived. Vacationers from the metropolitan centers of Kobe, Kyoto, and Osaka could now visit Kinosaki with ease. Imbued with Western or aristocratic sensibilities, many of them preferred not to bathe with the hoi polloi. The wealthiest piped steam into their villas. Those a bit poorer (if still rich by local standards) demanded new hotels with private facilities. At first, the villagers welcomed the urban money, whatever they thought of urban scruples. Later, however, they changed their minds. In pumping the steam indoors, the new hotels and villas threatened to leave the public pools dry. The pool that cured the emperor of centuries past was apparently about to disappear; certainly about to follow were the sixty-odd bathless inns that depended on the public pools for their survival.

The economic changes split the town. Villagers ostracized the owner of one of the new hotels and boycotted merchants who dealt with him. Their children harassed his children. Eventually, the villagers even tried to cut off the electricity to the town and use the confusion to storm the hotel. But the dispute also proceeded in the courts. In 1933, the town of Kinosaki filed suit against the hotel. It argued that by custom the underground vein of steam belonged to the villagers in common and was not appropriable and, alternatively, that local custom banned all unauthorized indoor hot spring outlets.[28]

The court disagreed with the town on both points. First, it held that a vein of steam generally is not an object owned separately from the land through which it passes. Rather, a landowner acquires with his or her land the right (as with other water rights) to exploit any steam underground, subject to local customary limits on that use. Second, the court held that local custom did permit landowners to pump steam indoors. In a sense, the town had sued too late. Although rapid development did not begin until the railroad arrived in 1910, some people had already begun to pipe steam indoors by the 1880s. That practice continued, and (whatever the custom before 1880) by the 1930s so many people had indoor steam that no effective ban remained. By the time the villagers realized the damage private bathing caused, any customary ban had disappeared.

[28]Kinosaki buttressed its argument with a host of policy arguments, some stressing the drastic economic effect that private bathing would bring, others citing the practices in other countries. See Kinosaki v. Kataoka, 4249 Horitsu shimbun at 7.

Such was how the law left Kinosaki.[29] Yet the vacationers did not leave. Instead, they came in droves. By the 1960s, the town attracted 1,500,000 visitors per year. Entrepreneurs transformed the nearby mountains into a ski resort, and ran cable cars up to the venerable Hot Springs Temple. They could cater to the tourists because they could use technology to enlarge the capacity of the springs. By using the new pumping and drilling techniques, they apparently increased the total volume of steam dramatically. With such technology, the town could support many more baths.

What the hotel owners seemingly recognized and the villagers did not was that Kinosaki competed for tourists on a nationwide resort market. Increasingly, those tourists demanded private baths. Late-night "hot springs guides" on Japanese television may still feature nubile models bathing in the out-of-doors, but Japanese increasingly request baths in their homes and hotels. With modern sensibilities entrenched, no town banning private bathing was likely to attract many visitors.[30]

## 2.3   Holdups

Although this law may have been reasonably clear, it occasionally let newcomers "holdup" existing users. The problem derived from two sources: the difficulty of acquiring a customary claim, and the largely unrestricted nature of subterranean water rights. Consider each in turn.

The customary-use test was was usually one of priority in time. But not always — for being ahead of another user did not necessarily create a customary right. Instead, Japanese courts assigned prior users a right only if they had used the water long enough for that use to have become customary.[31] As technological change accelerated the pace of economic activity, the distinction became crucial. Where farmers had irrigated their fields for decades, custom usually protected their use. Few industrial developers, however, could claim such long use. Yet many had built large facilities that required a stable water supply. Many factories, for instance, depended on hydraulic power but could not claim a customary right to the necessary water. If newer users lowered the water level, they could find their investments worthless.

---

[29]Although the plaintiffs appealed, the parties eventually settled out of court. The settlement, reproduced in Kawashima, Shiomi, & Watanabe (1964: 393), recognized the right to pipe the steam indoors.

[30]Occasionally, the traditional users of the hot springs won. See, e.g., Japan v. Masaki, 3453 Horitsu shimbun 15 (Daishin'in [Supreme Court] Aug. 10, 1932). More commonly, however, the plaintiffs alleging improper drilling of hot springs outlets lost.

[31]See, e.g., Kobayashi v. Yazawa, 494 Horitsu shimbun 7, 8–9 (Nagano D. Ct. No date) (plaintiff farmers' claim to water rejected where they could not show customary right). By contrast, in American prior appropriation states, rights vest when one puts water to a beneficial use.

Nor did the nominal transferability of water rights solve this problem.[32] Suppose farmer A had a customary right to 50 percent of a stream's water flow and the rest was unclaimed. B, a new factory, needed 50 percent of the water. Although B could purchase A's 50 percent, A and B would agree on a price only if A's use were less productive than B's. Since 50 percent of the water was unused, however, the efficient solution required only that both projects have a net positive value. Ultimately, this problem derived from B's inability to purchase the unused rights. Because the unused 50 percent had no customary user, B could not purchase rights to it. If B could not induce A to sell A's rights, B could only begin using the other 50 percent and hope that no one would usurp it before B's use had acquired customary status.

The dilemma is one which inheres in all regimes that leave scarce resources unowned until used, and initially assign users less-than-secure claims to the resource. Unless a regime gives claimants a quick and secure way to acquire unused rights, it necessarily makes resource-specific facilities less advantageous. Where the economy grows only gradually, the problem may remain minor. Where it grows rapidly the problem can become critical. Only through administrative rather than judicial efforts, though, did Japan eventually begin to come to terms with the problem.[33]

The courts' subterranean water rule created similar problems. The courts may have developed this rule in their eagerness to apply the "modern" Civil Code. If they did, however, in doing so they destroyed much of the security that water users would otherwise have enjoyed. The plaintiffs in one 1929 case, for instance, had farmed paddy fields.[34] In the spring of 1923 the defendants opened their own paddies nearby. To irrigate these new paddies, the defendants dug a well – and thereby exhausted the plaintiffs' access to well water. Because the defendants used underground water rather than water above ground (and no community custom specifically banned wells), the Supreme Court allowed them to proceed. By the logic it had now been applying for over two decades, the plaintiffs lost.[35] In fact, however, the problem was worse than this example suggests: because surface and substerranean streams often merge, any regime that permits unlimited use of the latter can also exhaust the former. Even if riparian users have a customary right to river flow, they can protect

---

[32]In fact, both practical and theoretical problems plagued the sale of water rights from agricultural to non-agricultural users.

[33]For a discussion of the administrative mechanisms that eventually developed, see Watanabe (1973: 150–1).

[34]Fujikawa v. Nakamura, 3000 Horitsu shimbun 10 (Daishin'in [Supreme Court] June 1, 1929).

[35]The plaintiffs argued that the "abuse-of-rights" principle applied, but the court did not discuss the point. Id., at 10.

themselves from competing users only if they buy all the land above the subterranean streams that flow into the river.

These problems essentially involved "holdups:" unless users (1) owned all the land above the underground streams feeding their water source and (2) either owned the land on which they had dug a well or had a customary right to flowing water, others could threaten to cut off their water by diverting streams or drilling wells. A newcomer could extract payoffs (quasi rents) from earlier users, in other words, by threatening to block their water and render their water-dependent investments worthless. Once peasant A had built a paddy, each peasant B owning land above the water source upon which A depended could serially threaten to divert the water. In doing so, each B could try to extort from A an amount up to the present value to A of irrigating his or her paddy. Those holdup opportunities based on the difficulty in acquiring customary rights had been present in premodern law as well (though the slower rate of economic growth may have kept the problem less visible). Those based on the underground water rule, however, were opportunities that the Meiji courts may have created in trying to adopt the Civil Code.

### 2.4   *The abuse-of-rights doctrine*

In part to solve these holdup problems, Japanese judges turned to and transformed the European doctrine of "abuse of rights."[36] Continental judges had created the concept to ameliorate various no-liability rules implicit in their civil codes.[37] During the first decades of this century, Japanese courts developed it into a sophisticated doctrine that imposed liability in a variety of new situations. In water-law cases, they used it to protect people with significant water-dependent investments against more recent users who made those earlier investments untenable by aggressively exploiting underground water. They used the abuse-of-rights doctrine, in other words, to limit the scope of a landowner's rights to underground water. In the process, they effectively transformed Japanese water

---

[36]Courts explicitly acknowledged European antecedents in such cases as Osaka Arukari, K.K. v. Tomura, 22 Daihan minroku 2474, 2477 (Daishin'in [Supreme Court] Dec. 22, 1916). Early cases generally classified by Japanese scholars as abuse-of-rights cases include Sonoda v. Sonoda, 7-6 Daihan minroku 47, 51 (Daishin'in [Supreme Court] June 2, 1901) (abuse of household head's rights); Japan v. Iida, 10 Daihan keiroku 122, 124 (Daishin'in [Supreme Court] Feb. l, 1904) (abuse of parental right); [No names given], 7-6 Hoso kiji 70 (Tokyo Ct. App. June 6, 1907) (abuse of creditor's rights). One of the earliest cases explicitly to refer to "abuse of right" is Uchida v. Uchida, 10 Daihan minroku 1190, 1192 (Daishin'in [Supreme Court] Sept. 29, 1904) (abuse of parental right).

[37]For a general discussion of the abuse-of-rights doctrine in Europe, see, e.g., Bolgar (1975); Cueto-Rua (1975).

law into a regime remarkably like the American prior-appropriation regime.

That prior-appropriation regime had itself developed in response to problems the traditional Anglo-American water-law regime had created in the relatively water-scarce American West. England and many eastern states had maintained regimes under which landowners could generally exploit underground water freely,[38] but could use above-ground water only if their land abutted a watercourse and then only within circumscribed limits. Under the "natural-flow" doctrine used in some jurisdictions, they could use this water only if they did not noticeably diminish the quantity of the remaining flow (with exceptions for prescriptive rights and domestic uses).[39] Under the "reasonable-use" doctrine used elsewhere, they could reduce the net flow, but only if their use was one that courts considered "reasonable."[40] Under either doctrine, landowners could use the above-ground flowing water only by virtue of the riparian character of their land. Whether they had used the water in the past did not matter, and any attempt to sell their water rights separately from their land was ineffective.

These traditional English and eastern rules presented the western states with at least two problems. First, a landowner's largely unrestricted right to use subterranean water created the same holdup opportunities that the rule posed in Japan. Second, the natural-flow and reasonable-use regimes prevented people from making full use of watercourses. To solve these problems, many western states adopted a "prior-appropriation" regime: those who first diverted and beneficially used water – whether above or below ground – acquired a right to it transferrable and enforceable against all others.[41]

The result of the Japanese case law was a regime that closely resembled this western American water-law regime. As the discussion above makes clear, the Japanese customary-use doctrine for watercourses (except for the difficulty of acquiring the initial customary right) tracks this prior-appropriation rule closely. As the discussion below will show, even the Japanese subterranean-water rule of unlimited use (as close as it initially seems to the English and eastern rule) begins to look like the prior-appropriation regime once one accounts for the abuse-of-rights doctrine.[42]

---

[38]See, e.g., Acton v. Blundell, 152 Eng. Rep. 1223 (1843); Epstein (1979: 1232–4).
[39]See, e.g., Mason v. Hill, 110 Eng. Rep. 692, 698–701 (1833).
[40]See, e.g., Stratton v. Mt. Hermon Boys' School, 216 Mass. 83, 103 N.E. 87 (1913).
[41]For an example of the dissatisfaction with the riparian doctrines, see Coffin v. Left Hand Ditch Co., 6 Colo. 443, 446 (1882).
[42]Arguably, a closer comparison would be to the Californian "correlative rights" doctrine. See Katz v. Walkinshaw, 141 Cal. 116 (1902).

This abuse-of-rights doctrine first appeared in a water dispute in 1916.[43] Readers should by now recognize the facts. The defendant had tried to increase his irrigation capacity by expanding his water storage pond. In the process, he had reduced the water available to the twenty-one plaintiff farmers. Because the defendant filled his pond with underground water rather than river water, the customary-use doctrine did not protect the plaintiffs. In the course of evaluating the defendant's actions, however, the court invoked a new principle: even if water-using plaintiffs do not have a superior right to the water flow, a rival user may not ignore their use if doing so would be "abusive." The court stated the principle as grandly as it did vaguely:

One's rights extend only to actions that do not damage the stability and development of the nation. Actions that violate either the public order or good morals cannot constitute the exercise of a right.[44]

No matter how solid a defendant's rights to water, in other words, he or she may not use the water if doing so would infringe "the public order or good morals." Such use would, according to the court, constitute an "abuse of ownership rights."[45]

What use violated the public order was somewhat less clear, though the extent of the plaintiff's damages was a critical element. Consider a 1930 case.[46] The defendant, a Tokyo subway company, was extending its tracks through the heavily populated merchant quarters in the northeastern corner of the city. During the course of the work, its contractor destroyed the water source for a neighboring bathhouse's well. Because the subway could (according to the subterranean water rule) do as it pleased with any water it struck in digging the line, the bathhouse owner seemed unprotected under established water law. The court found for him nonetheless. The damage he suffered, it explained, exceeded the scope of the injuries that a community could expect its citizens to bear. Accordingly, the subway company was liable as principal for the actions of its agent, the contractor. Despite its right to lay the subway line, its exercise of that right in a way that destroyed the plaintiff's well constituted abuse.[47]

[43] Yoshizawa v. Horie, 1204 Horitsu shimbun 31, 5 Horitsu hyoron min 1254 (Kobe D. Ct. Sept. ll, 1916).

[44] Yoshizawa v. Horie, 1204 Horitsu shimbun at 32, 5 Horitsu hyoron min at 1256.

[45] Id. In the case at bar, the court denied the plaintiffs' petition on the grounds that they had not suffered substantial damages. Id.

[46] Arai v. Tokyo Chika Tetsudo, K.K., 3172 Horitsu shimbun 9 (Tokyo D. Ct. July 4, 1930).

[47] Id. at 12. With respect to more minor inconveniences, the court was less sympathetic. It awarded no damages, for example, for the increased traffic on the neighboring streets caused by the construction activities. This was, it explained, "activity within limits generally perceived as reasonable in a social setting." Id. at 14.

But it is in another case, the most famous abuse-of-water-rights case, that the court best articulated this doctrine. The dispute involved an elegant surburban Tokyo restaurant complex named Komatsuen (Small Pine Garden).[48] The villa had opened for business in 1932. It surrounded a Japanese garden with trees, a fountain, and ponds stocked with carp. Beyond the garden, it overlooked a river and a golf course – itself something of an aristocratic curiosity in 1932. To maintain water in the garden, the owner sank two wells.

Nearby, the defendant operated a trout farm. Because trout thrive only in flowing streams, he needed an enormous amount of water and over the course of 1933 and 1934 dug six wells. Predictably, one of the plaintiff's wells dried up completely, and the water in the other dropped perilously low. She complained to the defendant and sank a third well, but the defendant ignored her pleas. Instead, he expanded the scope of his operations and drilled his wells deeper still. All three of the plaintiff's wells then went dry. Her gardens died, her clientele disappeared, and her restaurant went out of business.

Because the defendant owned the land on which he dug his wells, the plaintiff seemed without legal recourse. To hold the defendant liable, however, the Supreme Court invoked the abuse-of-rights doctrine: landowners who harm others by causing "socially unreasonable" damages abuse their rights and are liable in tort.[49]

## 2.5   Ambiguities

Unfortunately, by outlining the law so systematically one can exaggerate its clarity. For all its logical rigor, water law in imperial Japan remained ambiguous in several respects. First, courts never made clear how long one had to use water to acquire a customary right. Some authorities suggested forty years, others twenty. The only certainty was that it involved a very long time and imposed a correspondingly large risk on the entrepreneur.[50]

Second, by its very nature, water never lent (and still does not lend) itself to precise claims. Water rights purport to entitle users to consume

---

[48]The case history is Honda v. Samejima, 3913 Horitsu shimbun 5 (Tokyo D. Ct. Oct. 28, 1935); Samejima v. Honda, 4262 Horitsu shimbun 12 (Tokyo Ct. App. Feb. 24, 1938); Samejima v. Honda, 4301 Horitsu shimbun 12 (Daishin'in [Supreme Court] June 28, 1938).

[49]4301 Horitsu shimbun at 14.

[50]See, e.g., Japan v. Tajima, 18 Daihan keiroku 567, 569 (Daishin'in [Supreme Court] May 6, 1912) (forty years); Tsuchiya (1966: 267) (twenty years). As a factual matter, proving a customary right could sometimes be extraordinarily difficult. In hot springs cases, for example, plaintiffs seldom succeeded in proving any customary ban on indoor baths.

water in varying amounts in different weather and during different seasons. No matter how straightforward the law may seem, those rights remain notoriously hard to measure.

Third, a few courts severely limited what one could do with water rights and how one could protect them. Although most courts in Japan (as in many American prior-appropriation jurisdictions) allowed people to sell their rights,[51] a few held transfers unenforceable.[52] Likewise, although most courts seemed willing to protect plaintiffs through injunctive remedies,[53] contrary cases also appeared.[54]

Finally, for all the prominence of the customary-rights doctrine, a few courts failed to apply it. Some courts instead considered how much each party had invested in maintaining the water supply.[55] Others considered what each party planned to do with the water. Like some American

[51]See, e.g., Nagano Shogyo, K.K. v. K.K. Nihon Kangyo Ginko, 19 Daihan minshu 1611 (Daishin'in [Supreme Court] Sept. 18, 1940) (rules for making transfer of hot spring rights enforceable against third parties); Furihata v. Okamura, 3873 Horitsu shimbun 5, 6 (Daishin'in [Supreme Court] Jul. 17, 1935) (hot spring rights are transferrable as rights separate from the land); Nozawa v. Ogiura, 1-1 Daihan minroku 83, 86 (Daishin'in [Supreme Court] Feb. 6, 1895) (hot springs can be sold without recordation); Nagano Shogyo, K.K. v. Nihon Kangyo Ginko, K.K., 4517 Horitsu shimbun 12, 13 (Tokyo Ct. App. Oct. 16, 1939) (hot spring rights are transferrable as rights separate from the land).

[52]See, e.g., Watanabe v. Watanabe, 1126 Horitsu shimbun 23, 24 (Tokyo Ct. App. Nov. 19, 1915) (water rights run with land and cannot be transferred independently); see also Shiga v. Hosokawa, 22 Daihan minroku 2341 (Daishin'in [Supreme Court] Dec. 2, 1916) (illustrating difficulty of selling rights for new purpose).

[53]See Japan v. Masaki, 3453 Horitsu shimbun 15 (Daishin'in [Supreme Court] Aug. 10, 1932) (injunctive right); Yoshida v. Inagaki, 11 Daihan minroku 1326, 1331 (Daishin'in [Supreme Court] Oct. 11, 1905) (one riparian owner uses waterwheel in way contrary to custom that destroys upstream owner's ability to use his own waterwheel; court permits upstream owner to enjoin downstream owner's use in such fashion); Nozawa v. Ogiura, 1-1 Daihan minroku 83, 100 to 101 (Daishin'in [Supreme Court] Feb. 6, 1895) (right to mineral springs is *bukken* [*in rem*] – thereby implying under Japanese law that injunctive rememdy is likely); Kawanabe v. Kimura, 3 Horitsu hyoron min 223, 224 (Tokyo Ct. App. May 9, 1914) (injunction granted against builder of dam); see also Yasuda (1933: 412, 433–42) (both injunctive remedy and damages available); Kobayashi (1979: 208–9) (although contrary views exist, weight of scholarship supports granting of injunctive right).

[54]See Yamaguchi v. Kojima, 6 Daihan minroku 90, 92 (Daishin'in [Supreme Court] Feb. 26, 1900) (holding rights to flowing water not *bukken*; hence, by implication, no injunctive remedy); Watanabe v. Watanabe, 1126 Horitsu shimbun 23, 24 (Tokyo Ct. App. Nov. 19, 1915) (same). But see Japan v. Masaki, 3453 Horitsu shimbun 15, 16 (Daishin'in [Supreme Court] Aug. 10, 1932) (rights to underground water give rise to *saiken* (tort) claim, but injunctive remedy is nonetheless available). Apparently some scholars also argued that water rights were public rights (*koken*) rather than private rights (*shiken*) – with the result that injunctive remedies were available but damages were not. See Yasuda (1933: 30–1).

[55]See, e.g., Sakaue v. Kohana Village, 7 Daihan minroku (1st ser.) 6, 14 (Daishin'in [Supreme Court] Oct. 3, 1881); Yasuda v. Kuwabara, 9-1 Daihan minroku 226, 232–4 (Daishin'in [Supreme Court] June 22, 1883).

courts, a few Japanese courts even systematically favored agricultural uses over more modern developmental projects.[56] Most courts applied the customary rights doctrine, in short, but not all.[57]

### 3 EFFICIENCY IN WATER LAW

For all these troubling ambiguities, customary Japanese water law remained in most ways a regime that tended to promote relatively efficient outcomes. A regime's efficiency depends, of course, on both the supply of and demand for the scarce resources at stake, and the regime's own administrative costs – as the standard justifications for the different water-law rules in the eastern and western American states illustrate. By such criteria, the imperial Japanese regime fit its society well. The regime privatized water flow. A user acquired with time a right, transferrable and enforceable against newcomers. True, judges never made the nature of the customary right quite clear, they seldom recognized customary claims to underground water, some hesitated to enforce sales of water rights, and a few even ignored customary rights entirely. From all the cases, however, one theme stands out: courts usually defined and enforced private claims to water flow.

Where water is scarce, a system that refuses to enforce such private claims creates at least two well-known potential problems. First, such a regime may permit the excessive use of the resource (Epstein, 1985: ch. 15; Cheung, 1970; Hardin, 1968). During several earlier periods in Japanese history, for example, communities recognized no private claims to water. Predictably, people fished by draining lakes and poisoning rivers (Yasuda, 1933: 4). Second, as noted earlier, a regime that keeps a scarce resource in common may let newcomers "hold up" earlier users who invest in resource-specific facilities. Each newcomer can extract payoffs from earlier users, in other words, by threatening to block the resource and render the users' investments worthless.

Because scarcity is always relative to demand, water is scarce in Japan. Japanese eat white rice, and irrigated paddies are the most productive way to grow it. Water is not scarce year-round; total annual rainfall is quite heavy. But water is scarce during several of the critical spring and summer growing months – during the time farmers need it most for these paddies. Given this demand for rice and the use of irrigated paddies to grow it, enforceable private rights to water flow are critical. On the whole, the Japanese legal regime effectively enforced those rights.

[56]Compare Cowell v. Armstrong, 210 Cal. 218, 290 P. 1036 (1930), with Yasuda (1933: 88–9).
[57]See, e.g., Sakaguchi v. Rokugawa, 4-10 Daihan minroku 25, 29 (Daishin'in [Supreme Court] Nov. 18, 1898) (customs "contrary to reason" are unenforceable).

## 4 CONCLUSION

Water is scarce when most needed in Japan. As a result, few entrepreneurs – peasants or otherwise – would invest substantial sums in agricultural improvements without some continued entitlement to the water upon which they depend. Imperial Japanese law privatized that water flow. It assigned to one who used the water by custom the right to enforce that claim against most new users. If a user had invested in water-dependent facilities but either he or she had not used the water long enough to acquire a customary right, or a newcomer had a superior legal claim (based on ownership of a well, for example), the law protected the earlier user through a common-law notion of "abuse of rights."

Granted, Japanese land and water law had inefficient details. During the earliest years of Japanese history, it required the government regularly to redistribute real estate. During the seventeenth through the nineteenth centuries, it declared land inalienable. People circumvented the rule, but the mechanics of circumvention necessarily raised the cost of transfers. And modern tenant "protection" law remains responsible for much of the frenetic chaos of Japanese urban land use. Water law too has had its problems. By its very nature, water is not an asset easily metered, verified, or transferred. As a result, the law never gave users as secure an interest in water as it did in most scarce assets.

Notwithstanding those inefficiencies, the law of land and water in Japan for the most part did protect private claims to scarce resources. To early modern economic growth in Japan, agricultural investment mattered crucially. To agricultural investment, stable claims to land and water mattered crucially. Largely, the Japanese government provided those stable claims.

# 3

## Externalities: Smoke and noise

### INTRODUCTION

In any world where people cannot bargain with each other costlessly (which is to say, in any world that counts), a court that would promote efficient growth will need to resolve disputes over conflicting uses of property. Typically, it will face the problem when one person develops property in a way that lowers the value of the property next door. In Chapter 2, I discussed related issues in water use. Here, I turn to the problem of pollution.

Although observers sometimes suggest that the imperial Japanese government let entrepreneurs externalize the costs of their activity by polluting freely, the observers are wrong. Notwithstanding the many ambiguities in the law, the government did not let entrepreneurs freely pollute. Instead, if an entrepreneur harmed others through inefficient activity, the courts held the entrepreneur liable in tort. In the process, they necessarily encouraged efficient levels of growth.

To explore how imperial Japanese courts handled the externalities to industrial production, I first summarize the economics of pollution (Section 1; readers familiar with law & economics may safely skip to Section 2). I then explain Japanese tort law (Section 2), and discuss its implications for economic growth (Section 3).

### I   LAW AND EXTERNALITIES

To explore the relation between pollution law and efficient growth, consider a simple example from Polinsky (1983: 16). Posit one factory F, one neighbor N, production volumes that range from 0 to 3 units per day, and hypothetical profits to F and harm to N given by Table 3.1.

Ask first what the efficient level of production might be: what level will maximize aggregate social welfare? Necessarily, the efficient level is the

43

Table 3.1. *Hypothetical polluting*
*factory – profits and harm*

| Production | F profits | N harm |
|---|---|---|
| 0 | $    0 | $    0 |
| 1 | 10,000 | 1,000 |
| 2 | 14,000 | 9,000 |
| 3 | 16,000 | 36,000 |

Table 3.2. *Hypothetical polluting factory – marginal profits*
*and harm*

| Production | F marginal profits | N marginal harm |
|---|---|---|
| 0 | — | — |
| 1 | $10,000 | $1,000 |
| 2 | 4,000 | 8,000 |
| 3 | 2,000 | 27,000 |

*Note:* Calculated from values given in Table 3.1.

level beyond which any additional (i.e., marginal) gains to F produce larger offsetting losses to N. Some production is clearly efficient. In producing 1 unit, F earns profits of $10,000 but imposes costs on N of only $1,000. As a result, the socially optimal level of pollution here is not zero. It is positive. Just as clearly, however, full production is inefficient. In producing 3 units, F earns profits less than the costs it imposes on N. But is the efficient level then 1 unit or 2?

To find the efficient level of production, convert the total profits and losses in Table 3.1 into Table 3.2, the marginal profits and losses involved. In going from 0 to 1 unit, the *net* marginal gain is positive ($10,000–1,000), but in going from 1 to 2 and from 2 to 3, the net marginal gains are negative ($4,000–8,000 and $2,000–27,000). The efficient production level is thus 1 unit.

The role that a legal regime plays in inducing parties to reach this efficient level is more subtle than one might think. Suppose, for example, that F and N can costlessly bargain and negotiate. If so, then the law will have no efficiency implications at all. Regardless of the law, F and N will bargain to the efficient solution out of self-interest.

To see this potential legal irrelevance (called the Coase [1960] theorem), take the above example again. If the law holds F liable for all harm it imposes on N, F will still produce the first unit, for in producing 1 unit it earns profits large enough to compensate N without incurring a loss. It will not produce more than 1, for in moving to 2 units it earns additional profits of $4,000 but incurs additional liability of $8,000.

By contrast, if the law lets F freely pollute, F will still produce only 1 unit. Because F retains all profits it earns, it will clearly produce the first unit. But suppose F decides to increase production to 2. N will now find it profitable to pay F up to $8,000 to hold production at 1. If N does pay F between $4,001 and $7,999 to hold production at 1, both F and N benefit: F prefers that payment to the extra $4,000 profits it would otherwise earn; N prefers the payment to pollution costs of $8,000.

Now suppose the F and N face high bargaining and negotiating costs. If a polluting factory harms many people, for example, the victims may find it so expensive to organize that they cannot effectively bargain with the factory. If so, then should the law not force F to compensate them, F will not hold production at 1. It will instead produce at inefficiently high levels.

In this context, an efficient legal regime is one that induces F, in the presence of such bargaining and negotiating costs, to produce 1 but only 1 unit. Such a regime is not necessarily one that requires F to compensate neighbors for all damages. It is, however, one that requires F to compensate neighbors for damages resulting from inefficiently high levels of production. Toward that end, most economically advanced societies maintain either a "strict liability" or a "negligence" regime. Both tend toward efficiency. Under the former, F compensates N for all harm N suffers as a result of F's activity. If F produces 1 unit, F pays N $1,000; if it produces 2 units, it pays N $9,000; and if F produces 3 units, it pays N $36,0000. As just discussed, under this regime F will produce 1 unit and no more.

Under a negligence regime, F compensates N only if its production is "unreasonable," and courts gauge that reasonableness (sometimes explicitly, sometimes implicitly) by reference to the efficient level of production.[1] At production levels of 1 unit or less, the marginal gains to F exceed the marginal costs to N. Accordingly, production is "reasonable" and F ownes N nothing. At production levels of 2 units or more, F's marginal gains fall short of N's marginal losses. Production is unreasonable, and F owes N damages. Under this regime as well, F will produce 1 unit and no more.

Strict liability and negligence do have differing wealth implications, of course. Under strict liabiltiy, F compensates N for the harm it causes even when it produces at optimal or subobtimal levels. Under negligence, F compensates N only if it produces at excessive levels.

[1]The classic American statement is Learned Hand's formula in United States v. Carroll Towing Co., 159 F.2d 169, 173 (2d Cir. 1947): the tortfeasor is liable if but only if the benefit to the tortfeasor is less than loss to the victim times the probability of the loss.

Although the efficiency implications of negligence and strict liability can also differ, they do not differ in a way that causes one regime systematically to dominate the other. Instead, their relative efficiency depends primarily on how readily courts can ascertain crucial bits of information: the harm from pollution, the benefits to the polluting firm, and the costs (whether to the factory or to the victim) of mitigating the harm.[2] Although their economic effects thus can differ, that difference will generally fall far short of the difference between either regime and the generally much less efficient no-liability regime.

## 2 JAPANESE TORT LAW

### 2.1 *Negligence*

Imperial Japanese courts – like most of their American contemporaries (Posner, 1986: 56) – generally (but not always) held polluters to a negligence standard. The rule followed from the basic (if cryptic) language of § 709 of the Civil Code: "Any person who intentionally or negligently infringes the rights of another shall compensate that person for any damages he or she causes."[3]

By way of illustration, take one of the most famous of all Japanese tort cases: a 1919 case involving a pine tree.[4] The national railroad had double-tracked the line past this tree. Because it switched its trains at this double-tracked area, it blew more smoke on the tree than on most trees along its tracks. Yet this was not just any tree. At least by legend, it was the tree against which the sixteenth-century warlord Takeda Shingen (celebrated in Kurosawa's *Kagemusha*) had once rested his banner. When the smoke killed the tree, the owner sued.

In holding the government liable, the Supreme Court first clarified the basic principle: even if one owns property in fee simple, one cannot necessarily use it as one pleases, for how one uses it affects how others can enjoy their own property:

One must exercise one's rights within the bounds established by law. Suppose one person exercises his rights in a way that exceeds those bounds and intentionally or negligently infringes another person's rights. Depending on the extent of the infringement, under the case law of this Court he has committed a tort.[5]

---

[2]For careful discussions of many of these issues, see Landes & Posner (1987); Posner (1986: chs. 3, 6); Shavell (1987).

[3]*Mimpo [Civil Code]*, Law No. 89 of 1896; Law No. 9 of 1898.

[4]Koku v. Shimizu, 25 Daihan minroku 356 (Daishin'in [Supreme Court] Mar. 3, 1919), *aff'g* 1461 Horitsu shimbun 18 (Tokyo Ct. App. July 16, 1918).

[5]25 Daihan minroku at 362.

The crucial question, therefore, is the scope of those legal bounds: Just how much smoke could a train (or factory) emit without becoming liable to the neighbors? In the same elliptical manner, the Court continued:

Because modern social life is communal, anything one does can harm someone else. When it does, that harm does not necessarily mean that one has infringed that other person's rights. After all, given the communal character of life, victims must accept the fact that they may be harmed by what someone else does. Instead, one exceeds the proper bounds of one's rights and infringes the rights of a victim when one causes harm that exceeds a certain level – when one causes harm which exceeds the level that, according to social norms, victims must be willing to endure.[6]

Just what were the levels that, according to social norms, a victim had to be willing to endure? The formula itself seemed to imply that the issue depended only on the harm the victim suffered. It did not, for the Court considered several other factors: the benefits accruing from railroads, the *ex ante* likelihood of the harm, and the cost of any measures that might have prevented the harm. Here, (1) given the use of the track as a switching facility, the railroad should have known that adjacent trees would suffer extra harm, and (2) the railroad could readily have prevented that harm by relocating the track or by installing a wall. Because it could cheaply have prevented the foreseeable damage, it was liable in tort.

As in the United States, courts in Japan used a cost-benefit analysis that often bordered on a crude guess. Many courts tried to phrase the guess in moral terms instead, and some missed it entirely. Nonetheless, over the decades, three basic elements of the common-law calculus emerged. First, the extent of the expected harm mattered. As in the pine tree case, that harm depended on social and geographical context. For example, take the plaintiff who sued the city of Yokohama over vibrations from the city gas plant. The court explained:

From our own investigation and that of the court below, we find, as the appellant [plaintiff] contends, that the appellee did cause vibrations on the appellant's land and house by operating the machinery. . . . Given that we all live communally, however, one cannot expect to be able to exercise one's rights free of all adverse influence.[7]

It then proceeded to make explicit what the pine tree case had left unsaid:

To determine whether an action infringes a person's rights, we must consider and weigh all the circumstances of the case. We cannot merely measure objectively the impact of the action itself. For example, fireworks may be fine if used within the quiet boundaries of a farm, but can infringe the rights of others if used near a crowded city.

---

[6] 25 Daihan minroku at 362–3. Note that the test closely resembles that which governed the abuse of water rights. See Chapter 2.

[7] Fuse v. Yokohama, 9 Horitsu hyoron min 495 (Tokyo Ct. App. May 26, 1920).

The harm from the contested action depended on context, and its legality depended on that harm. Second, the size of the expected benefit mattered. In calculating the benefit in the Yokohama gas case, for example, the court asked whether private entrepreneurs captured the entire benefits or whether there were larger gains as well.

Third, the cost of preventive measures mattered. In another railroad case, the Supreme Court faced the issue of how much the railroad should invest in safety. The plaintiff argued that it should have hired round-the-clock watchmen at all crossings. On the basis of costs, the court disagreed. The accident at issue could have been avoided either if the railroad had hired a watchman or if the plaintiff had been more careful. Given the time of the accident (11 P.M.), a watchman would not have been cost-effective. Far more efficient, the court implied, to demand that the public be careful. "[The] duty to reduce dangers is not a duty only of railroad managers." Rather, it is a duty that all members of the public share.[8]

Similarly, take a 1926 land-use case.[9] The plaintiff ran a tuberculosis sanitarium near the beach. He ran a good sanitarium and, being successful, wanted to expand it. When a patient offered him the adjoining land at ¥5 per tsubo (about four square yards), he agreed. Unfortunately, the patient died before they could complete the sale. Control over the land then passed to the defendant, the patient's son-in-law.

This defendant now demanded ¥63 per tsubo. When the plaintiff refused, the defendant began to harass him. On the land next to the hospital, he built a large storage shed within a foot of the boundary. Given the large size of the lot, he had no reason to put the shed so close except to harass. Harass it did, for the building cut off air and light, crucial ingredients in a tuberculosis sanitarium. To build the shed, the workmen manipulated huge sheets of corrogated steel, an ear-shattering process. To protect the wood, they coated it with creosote, a noxious preservative.

Throughout the process, the workmen did their best to encourage the plaintiff's patients to leave. "We'll cook you to death in there," they yelled at the patients. "If you can walk, go to [the competing] Iida Hospital."[10] In the end, the plaintiff lost business and two of his patients died. When the court asked the defendant why he had built the shed so near the boundary, he could claim only that the plaintiff's patients dumped garbage out their windows.

The court found for the plaintiff. Its analysis was simple. First, the

[8]Koku v. Kusuda, 5 Daihan minshu 833 (Daishin'in [Supreme Court] Dec. 11, 1926).
[9]Ishida v. Kanamori, 2648 Horitsu shimbun 10 (Annotsu D. Ct. Aug. 10, 1926).
[10]2648 Horitsu shimbun at 14.

garbage issue was a nonstarter. "If the plaintiff's patients dumped garbage, the defendant could have solved the problem by placing a wall or other appropriate installation along the boundary."[11] Second, the defendant earned no gains from locating the shed so near the hospital. Indeed, he "had no need at all for an establishment of this sort."[12] Third, in locating it where he did, the defendant imposed enormous losses on the plaintiff. Effectively, the defendant played a hold-up game: because the plaintiff had few ways to expand his operation, he hoped to extract from him a large portion of the value of the hospital itself.[13] Because the defendant earned no other benefits from the shed, and because the shed imposed large losses on the plaintiff, the court held that the defendant used his property unreasonably and owed the plaintiff damages.

## 2.2   Strict liability

Although the imperial Japanese courts often held polluters liable, the law they applied remained ambiguous. The ambuiguity was not whether firms could freely pollute at inefficient levels. They could not. The ambiguity was whether they were liable even if they polluted at efficient levels. Effectively, the ambiguity was whether they answered to a strict liability or a negligence regime.

The most famous industrial pollution case involved the Osaka Alkali Company. In the course of manufacturing fertilizer, the firm discharged sulferic fumes that killed nearby wheat and rice crops. Facing those losses, thirty-seven neighboring farmers sued the firm. By 1915, their case was before the Osaka Court of Appeals. The company argued that the court should not hold it liable if it had used the best available technology – that if it used the best technology, it necessarily could not be negligent. Rejecting negligence for a standard closer to strict liability, the Osaka Court of Appeals held for the plaintiffs.

The appellant [defendant] company produces sulfuric acid and refines copper, activities characteristic of the chemical industry. Directors of such a company should realize that the [sulfuric] gas will leak from its facilities. They should also realize that the leaking gas will harm neighboring people, animals, and crops. Indeed, if they do not realize these facts, they are unreasonably – and negligently – lax in researching the consequences of their activities.

Accordingly, the appellant as tortfeasor must compensate the appellees [plaintiffs] for the damages they suffered. The appellant claims that it used the best methods available to modern engineers to prevent its gas from escaping. That use, it argues, should immunize it from liability. Yet, so long as it discharged gas that

---

[11]2648 Horitsu shimbun at 15.   [12]2648 Horitsu shimbun at 15.
[13]For a fuller discussion of these issues, see Chapter 2, Sections 2.3–2.4.

damaged the appellees' crops, it caused the appellees' damages. If so, then whether or not it could have prevented its gas from leaking, it is liable.[14]

This was not the only opinion to apply a standard close to strict liability in pollution cases. In October 1916, the Osaka Court of Appeals published another opinion holding a fertilizer firm liable for discharging acidic fumes. This defendant apparently did not claim that it could not have prevented the discharge; it claimed only that preventing it would have been unprofitable. Although the court's result could fit within a neligence regime, its language suggested (consistent with strict liability) that cost was never a defense:

As noted above, the appellee [defendant company] has chosen to use a method for producing fertilizer and sulfuric acid that involves the production of dangerous gases. It has done so in an area next to rice paddies. Necessarily, therefore, it has a duty to take adequate measures to prevent the discharge of those gases and any harm to the rice. . . . Lowering the level of the gases discharged to levels that would not have damaged the rice was not impossible. Instead, it would simply have caused the appellee occasionally to incur losses.[15]

Two months later, however, the Supreme Court reversed the Court of Appeals in the *Osaka Alkali* case (if the Supreme Court ever heard the second fertilizer case, it did not publish the opinion). Japanese tort law, it insisted, was a negligence regime. Accordingly, a polluter who took reasonable precautions was not liable:

Suppose someone, whether in the chemical industry or anyone else, damages another through its business activities. Provided that he took reasonable precautions (judged by the nature of the activity), he is not liable in tort for those damages.[16]

This conflict between strict liability and negligence recurred several times during the pre-War years. The negligence cost-benefit analysis, for example, appeared in a 1926 Tokyo District Court opinion on the externalities to railroad operations.[17] The plaintiffs lived next to the defendant's tracks and complained of the noise, the lack of privacy, and the trash people threw from the trains. The court analyzed their claimed elements of damage separately. On the one hand, the government had licensed trains for the greater good of society, and trains are always noisy.

[14]Osaka Arukari K.K. v. Tamura, 1047 Horitsu shimbun 25, 28 (Osaka Ct. App. July 29, 1915).

[15]Hirakuni v. Taki, 1193 Horitsu shimbun 24, 26 (Osaka Ct. App. Oct. 24, 1916).

[16]Osaka Arukari K.K. v. Tamura, 22 Daihan minroku 2474, 2479 (Daishin'in [Supreme Court] Dec. 22, 1916). Upon remand, the Osaka Court of Appeals held that the defendant had not taken reasonable precautions (its smokestacks were too short) and held it liable. Osaka Arukari K.K. v. Tamura, 1659 Horitsu shimbun 11, 13 (Osaka Ct. App. Dec. 27, 1919).

[17]Onishi v. Keihin denki tetsudo K.K., 2684 Horitsu shimbun 5 (Tokyo D. Ct. Sept. 30, 1926).

For their damage from the noise, therefore, the defendant train company was not liable. On the other, the defendant could have cheaply protected the plaintiffs' privacy and solved the trash problem by building a wall. For failing to do so, the court now held it liable.

Something closer to strict liability reappeared in a 1931 Osaka District Court opinion.[18] The plaintiff owned land next to a construction site. There, the defendant built the Kobe branch of the Industrial Bank of Japan. To do so, it used a steam hammer and dug an eighteen-foot-deep hole only $3\frac{1}{2}$ feet from the plaintiff's building. Because of the vibration and the loss of lateral support, the plaintiff's building began to tilt dangerously and cracks appeared in many of its walls. In holding the defendant liable, the District Court apparently followed the *reversed* opinion of the Osaka Court of Appeals case. The defendant was liable, it reasoned, even if it had used the best available construction technology, and even if placing buildings this close was inevitable in modern cities. This much harm from a construction project, it explained, was harm greater than the levels that, "according to social norms, victims must be willing to endure."[19]

Nonetheless, the Supreme Court demanded negligence in these externalities cases, and for most practical purposes the law was what the Supreme Court said it was.[20] Consider an irrigation pump operated by the city of Hiroshima. One dry summer, the city ran it day and night for three months. Because of the noise and vibration, the plaintiff (who owned an inn nearby) lost business. He sued, and in 1918 the Hiroshima Court of Appeals held the city liable under a simple analysis that considered only his damage: "The Imperial Constitution makes clear that the property rights [*shoyu ken*] of Japanese citizens may not be violated unless the violation is both pursuant to law and necessary for the public good."[21] Nothing in the analysis suggested that the city was negligent, but the court held it liable anyway. On appeal, the Supreme Court reversed: "if a party used the best methods for installing the machine, it is not liable under § 709 even if it caused damage to other people's proper-

---

[18]G.K. Toyo shokai v. K.K. Obayashi gumi, 3339 Horitsu shimbun 4 (Osaka D. Ct. Nov. 12, 1931). The case was brought under § 716 of the Civil Code, which holds contractors liable for actions by subcontractors (as was the case here) where the contractors act negligently.

[19]I found no appellate opinions in this case.

[20]This point holds even when (as may have been the case in the Kobe IBJ branch case discussed immediately above) parties do not appeal a lower court decision that violates Supreme Court precedent – for rational litigants will settle such a case not by the lower court judgment but by reference to the decision that the Supreme Court would render if they *did* appeal.

[21]Kikawa v. Hiroshima shi, 1479 Horitsu shimbun 24, 25 (Hiroshima Ct. App. Oct. 19, 1918).

ty."[22] As in the *Osaka Alkali* case, it demanded a more rigorous negligence analysis, and a defense for using the best available technology.

### 3  IMPLICATIONS

All this raises serious doubts about the standard accounts of pollution in pre-War Japan. Most writers implicitly criticize the imperial courts for two phenomena: (1) many pre-War industrial and commercial installations polluted the air and the water, and harmed their neighbors through noise and vibrations, and (2) the victims of these activities generally collected no compensation. As the discussion above should make clear, both facts are perfectly consistent with a relatively efficient legal regime.

First, under any Kaldor-Hicks efficient regime, factories and other installations will pollute. The economically optimal level of pollution (whether air, water, noise, or vibration) is seldom (if ever) zero. Instead, pollution is economically undesirable only when it imposes costs on society greater than the gains it produces to the polluter (and others). Any legal regime that limits pollution to lower levels reduces aggregate economic welfare.

Second, under an efficient negligence regime, polluters will compensate victims only when they miscalculate. At root, under a negligence regime compensation is an out-of-equilibrium phenomenon. In equilibrium, polluters will calculate the legal standard correctly and pollute at a level just below the point at which they would be liable. Victims will receive no compensation, but the result will be relatively efficient nonetheless. The point may seem harsh to late-twentieth-century scholars accustomed to elaborate safety nets and redistribution schemes. That harshness, however, should not cloud the basic point: that a system with large amounts of pollution and large numbers of uncompensated victims can still foster growth at rates that maximize aggregate economic welfare.

Pollution levels were high in imperial Japan, and modern Japanese no longer tolerate those levels. Fundamentally, though, such complaints say nothing about the efficiency of the imperial regime. Japanese today are richer than ever before and, for at least two reasons, the economically efficient level of pollution falls with income. First, the efficient level of environmental attractiveness rises with per capita income because beauty and comfort are luxury goods: people willingly pay more for beauty and

[22]Hiroshima shi v. Kikawa, 1590 Horitsu shimbun 16, 17 (Daishin'in [Supreme Court] May 24, 1919). On remand the Court of Appeals held the city liable on the grounds that it had failed to take reasonable measures. Kikawa v. Hiroshima shi, 2027 Horitsu shimbun 15 (Hiroshima Ct. App. June 22, 1922). Faced with that finding of negligence, the Supreme Court affirmed. Hiroshima shi v. Kikawa, 3 Daihan minshu 295 (Daishin'in [Supreme Court] June 19, 1924).

comfort at high incomes than at low. Second, the efficient level of health and safety rises with income too because the observed value of human life correlates with income: people willlingly pay more at high incomes to avoid the risk of injury or death than they do at low incomes.[23] Fundamentally, levels of pollution that generate the same amount of profits, that desecrate the same natural beauty, and that kill the same number of people can be inefficient at higher incomes yet efficient at lower.

### 4  CONCLUSION

Although imperial Japanese courts enforced a property rights regime, they generally did not allow people to use their property in ways that inefficiently harmed others. If an owner used property in a way that earned returns smaller than the costs imposed on others, the owner was liable to the people harmed. Ambiguity and error existed in large measure, to be sure. Yet neither the ambiguity nor the error should obscure the basic point: imperial courts did not promote growth at all costs. With ambiguities and errors to be sure, they promoted it at relatively efficient levels.

[23]On valuing human life, see generally Friedman (1982); Viscusi (1992: 30).

# 4

## *Markets: Children*

### INTRODUCTION

As Thomas Hardy told it, Michael Henchard sold her in a tavern at a wayside fair. He was poor, drunk, unhappy, and unhappily married. He owned her. "I don't see why men who have got wives and don't want 'em, shouldn't get rid of 'em as these gipsy fellows do their old horses," he explained (Hardy, 1886). If a passing sailor wanted her, well for five guineas he could have her.[1]

From time to time, scholars have told similar tales of Tokugawa (1600–1868) Japan. The late Takeyoshi Kawashima (1950a,b), professor of civil law at the University of Tokyo and probably the best-known legal sociologist in Japan, claimed Tokugawa men routinely sold their wives and children or rented them long-term. It was endemic to the brutality of Asiatic patriarchal feudalism, he explained. During the early Tokugawa period "peasants frequently sold their family members into temporary servitude," echoes historian Mikiso Hane (1972: 170–1). "In reality this resulted in permanent enslavement, because the contract could not be dissolved until the debt was repaid, and this the impoverished peasants could seldom do. . . . [I]ndentured servants [had] terms of service [that] might run from ten years to a lifetime."

One might have thought the sold children would resist. According to most scholars, though, out of ideological conformity or cultural docility they eventually complied. Living as they did within a hierarchical and familistic world, they thought working in a place like a brothel for the sake of the family "a supreme example of filial self-sacrifice" (Hendry, 1986: 21). Within the household, such scholars continue, the

---

[1]Note that according to modern scholars (e.g., Thompson, 1991; Thompson, 1988: 91), the women "sold" in Britain probably often left their husbands because they hated them. They agreed to the deal as their best alternative in a world without ready divorce, and often arranged to be "bought" by their lovers.

54

male members dominated the female. The elder members dominated the younger. And because of the ideology "in the air," the female and younger members usually did as they were told. For the good of the house, for greed, or perhaps from sheer folly, fathers worked the other members on the farm, rented them under long-term contracts, and sold them into slavery.

In fact, work-age children did resist, and by the mid–eighteenth century largely ran their own lives. Notwithstanding the ideology in the air, work-age children (whether male or female) obtained an effective property right in their own labor. Given the generally greater efficiency of free labor over bound, the fact had important – and positive – consequences for economic growth in Japan.[2] For purposes of the analysis in this book, the point is simple but crucial: by the middle of the eighteenth century, laborers in Japan generally controlled their own work lives.

To explore these issues, I collected about 1,000 contracts for the sale or rental of humans: straightforward sales contracts, adoptions for cash, indentured servitude agreements, and loans tied to security interests in human beings. By tracing the use of these various contracts, I unravel the way ostensibly subordinate family members used their labor market potential to obtain control over their own labor. I begin by reconstructing the contractual arrangements themselves (Section 1). I show that by the mid–eighteenth century, sales contracts, pledge contracts, and long-term indenture contracts had largely disappeared (Section 2). I argue that the reason for the disappearance lies in the growing market for non-agricultural labor. By making it possible and profitable for workers to abscond, this market destroyed the ability of most workers and their parents to transfer long-term "property rights" in the workers' labor. I also explore the apparent absence of any contracts for infants (Section 3). Peasants did not use contracts to sell them, I suggest, because infants in early modern Japan (like infants elsewhere for much of history) fetched a market price close to zero. I conclude by exploring the relations among cultural norms, the non-agricultural labor market, and the ability of parents to control their children (Section 4).[3]

---

[2]The issue touches both on Oliver Williamson's (1985) work on the relation between external markets and internal hierarchies, and on Gary Becker's (1991: 14) analysis of how "bargaining within marriages takes place in the shadow of competition in marriage markets." See also Folbre (1994: 86) ("The growth of markets for labor . . . has weakened patriarchal property rights"). For a recent empirical study of how markets constrain opportunism within firms, see Fishback (1992).

[3]The relative altruism of parents toward other family members remains a controversy in economics and economic history: see Parsons & Goldin (1989) (pervasive non-altruism); Nardinelli (1982) (parents demanded higher wages when their children were beaten in factories); Becker (1991: 8–9) (evolutionarily adaptive character of parental altruism).

## I THE CONTRACTS

### 1.1 *The data*

I base this study on 1,016 contracts found in sixty-three sources.[4] To assemble the data set, I collected all relevant contracts or records of contracts that I could find in published sources. I thus included all contracts I located that were written between 1601 and 1860, that dealt with the sale or rental of humans, and that concerned periods of at least six months.

Several basic qualifications are in order. First, for reasons that will become clear, I would have preferred to measure the accessibility of urban centers from the place of contracting. Unfortunately, that much specificity proved unworkable. Note, though, (1) that the places of contracting remained predominantly rural throughout the period, and (2) that (for better or for worse) they included a wide variety of domains across the country. Second, I would have preferred to know the age of the worker involved. Unfortunately again, most sources do not give that information. Third, these 1,016 contracts obviously represent a small sample of all employment contracts actually written. That sampling, however, was not done by me. It was done by the vagaries of floods, fires, worms, and the historians and archivists upon whose efforts I have relied. To be sure, these processes introduce potential biases. When they do, I address them in the course of the analysis.[5]

### 1.2 *Indentures*

The contracts in this data set took one of four forms: indentures, pledges, sales, and adoptions. Indentures were the most common. Under an indenture contract, worker W agreed to work for a given term, and employer E paid wages in exchange. During most of the Tokugawa period, E paid the promised wages at the outset. For straightforward incentive reasons, some employers added discretionary bonuses later.[6]

In most of these contracts (as well as in the pledges, sales, and adop-

[4]In some cases only partial records of the contracts were available. Where critical aspects of the contracts are missing, I exclude them from the set. The sources appear in the References preceded by an asterisk.

[5]One of the clearest cases of bias caused by academic fashions derives from the recent fascination with prostitution. Because of this interest, several studies have uncovered relatively large numbers of prostitution contracts (e.g., Usami, 1986, 1993). Since very peculiar considerations drive the terms of these contracts (discussed in Chapter 6), I have in places explicitly distinguished prostitution from non-prostitution contracts.

[6]Hidemura (1950b: 120); Ishii (1961: 189; 1967: 136); Shitanaka (1959: 226–7). On the use of "freedom dues" in the West, see Grubb (1992b); Galenson (1989a: 57).

tions), the principal parties were E and the head H of W's household (generally W's father). The reason is straightforward: Tokugawa law and custom dictated it, and local authorities often required parties to clear the contract with them at the outset (Miyamoto, 1948: 112). Indeed, to obtain that clearance many of the parties also recited that they had negotiated the contract to enable them to pay taxes they owed.[7] Granted, under the federal legal system in effect, the law of the Tokugawa shogunate applied only to the Tokugawa domains – land producing about one-quarter of the country's total crops. Yet Tokugawa law frequently served as the model elsewhere. Although the lords of the other domains did not do so consistently, they often copied Tokugawa decrees.[8]

Under these contracts, H generally agreed to guarantee W's performance and to make good E's loss if W absconded.[9] Usually, H added extra guarantors as well. Given that few peasants would have made good guarantors, E may not realistically have expected these guarantors to make E whole. Instead, E may have demanded guarantors because a worker's *in*ability to provide them signaled (however imperfectly) that he or she may have absconded in the past, and was in any event a bad risk.

The timing of the payments in these contracts presents a puzzle, for the parties had strong incentives to have E pay the cash wages at the end. Between the workers and the employers, the workers were the more mobile and numerous. Necessarily, they were the less constrained by reputational sanctions; necessarily, they were more likely to abscond than the employers were to refuse the promised wages. All else equal, therefore, most parties should have negotiated contracts in which the workers worked first and the employer paid last. And indeed, in the West most indentured workers (other than those indentured for trans-Atlantic carriage) did perform first (Grubb, 1992b).

In the longer-term (six- to eight-year) contracts that the peasants negotiated at the start of the Tokugawa period, the reason for the odd timing seems straightforward: cash-constrained peasant parents apparently coupled loans with their children's labor contracts.[10] Nonetheless, with the far more common short-term contracts (the one- or two-year arrangements), the puzzle remains: here too E almost always paid the cash wages

---

[7]Kaneda (1927: 1125, 1443–52); Murao (1977: 232–3); Nakada (1943: 381–4, 390); Yoshida (1977: 189).

[8]Ishii (1948: 395; 1964: 161–2); Maki (1977: 175); Murao (1977: 48–50, 185, 220); Yoshida (1977: 53–5).

[9]For the contractual resolution of these issues in the case of one servant who absconded in 1759, see the documents collected (and translated) at Henderson (1975: 135–6).

[10]In some cases, the long terms may have reflected investments specific to the employment relationship. Those investments, however, would only explain the length of the contract – not the payment of all cash wages at the start of the term.

in advance. Granted, perhaps all peasants wanted loans, even if only of one or two years. Yet Western peasants were presumably cash-constrained too. Notwithstanding, unlike Japanese peasants they almost always received their cash wages at the end of the year. Some reason for the difference thus seems appropriate.

The explanation for the apparently perverse Japanese timing probably lies in the way the Tokugawa government limited access to courts. In order to make litigation practice consistent with its official neo-Confucian hierarchical premises, the government generally let employers sue their workers but banned workers from suing their employers.[11] If W absconded, E thus could sue and – depending on the quality of the guarantees – recover. If W worked for a promised period and E refused to pay, W had no legal recourse. Faced with these legal asymmetries *ex post*, the parties negotiated compensating asymmetries *ex ante*: effectively, they required E to post a large bond with H (or W).

### 1.3 Pledges

The second most common contracts were pledges. They included three very different groups of contracts. In the first (Type A), the household head H borrowed money from employer E and pledged family member or servant W as security. If H defaulted on the loan, E obtained W as a hereditary servant (effectively, as a slave).

Many peasants probably negotiated these pledges to circumvent the Tokugawa ban on sales. Several times during the seventeenth and eighteenth centuries, the government issued edicts banning the sale of humans.[12] Yet just as they circumvented the parallel ban on land sales, peasants learned to circumvent the ban on human sales. In 1643, the Tokugawa government had banned the sale of agricultural land.[13] After it did so, peasants who wanted to sell land simply pledged it. Even if the government refused to enforce contracts to sell land, it enforced security interests in land. Accordingly, if S wanted to sell land to B, S borrowed from B an amount equal to the sale price, gave B a security interest in the land, and defaulted (Yoshida, 1978: 2). With humans, some peasants adopted the same strategy: the household head sold servants and family members by borrowing money, creating security interests, and defaulting.

In the second type of pledge contract (Type B), H borrowed money from E and sent W to work for E during the term of the loan. If H repaid

---

[11]For a discussion of these legal provisions, see Henderson (1974: 70–5); Ishii (1961: 189); Kaneda (1927: 1325); Maki (1970: 462; 1977: 57).

[12]The edicts are detailed in Maki (1970: ch. 1, sec. 3). The government enforced the ban most commonly against kidnappers. Id., at 84, 89.

[13]E.g., Ishii (1964: 161); Maki (1970: 49); Murao (1977: 212–13).

the principal at the end of the loan, E relinquished W. If H defaulted, H forfeited W to E. Effectively, W's service during the loan term constituted interest.

In the third type of pledge (Type C), H sent W to work for E during the term of the loan, but the value of that service exceeded the market interest on E's loan to H. Hence, it reduced (often to zero) the amount H repaid at the end of the term. If H did not have the funds to repay any residual principal, H could do one of two things: H could renew the contract with E and use additional work by W to reduce further the amount payable, or H could borrow the amount payable to E from a third party, and pledge W's work to the third party.

To W, pledge C had radically different consequences from pledges A or B. Under A or B, if H defaulted, W became a hereditary servant. Effectively, by defaulting H sold W in perpetuity.[14] Sometimes, that was probably just what H and E intended. Under C, even if H defaulted, W worked for only a limited term of years. Because W's work reduced the principal amount of the loan, the pledge functioned as a disguised indenture agreement.

As with sales, peasants probably negotiated indentures in pledge form to avoid Tokugawa regulatory restrictions. During the seventeenth century, the Tokugawa government limited the indenture contracts workers and employers could negotiate. Several times, for example, it banned them from contracting for periods of more than ten years – before it permanently repealed that ban in 1698.[15] Workers who wanted longer terms may thus have disguised their contracts as secured loans.

Moreover, in several domains the local government capped the wages private-sector employers could pay (Nakabe, 1974: 106–7; Yoshida, 1977: 188–93). In the labor market, these governments (and the samurai they employed) competed against private employers for hired servants. Gradually, that competition raised market wages. In response to the competition, some domainal governments capped wages. In response to those caps, some private employers probably disguised the wages they paid as loans.

In Table 4.1, I classify the contracts by function. I list as "pledges" only those contracts that posed for W a genuine risk of being transferred to

---

[14]Of course, if at the end of the term under the second type of contract H did not have the principal, H could pledge W to E or a third party for the same amount. Because W's work did not reduce the principal, however, W at that point was no closer to freedom than when he or she started.

[15]Initially, the ban was on contracts of more than three years. See generally Maki (1970: ch. 1, sec. 3). Within Edo (Tokyo), the government during the early part of the Tokugawa period also banned indentures of under one year, but Maki (1970: 69–70; 1977: 82–8) argues that the ban primarily applied only to samurai. See generally Yoshida (1977: 57–66; 1978).

Table 4.1. *Pledge, indenture, and sales contracts*

| Date | Number of observations, followed by percent in parentheses | | |
|------|--------|-----------|------|
| | Pledge | Indenture | Sale |
| 1601–20 | 8 (47) | 0 (0) | 9 (53) |
| 1621–40 | 6 (50) | 3 (25) | 3 (25) |
| 1641–60 | 32 (67) | 6 (13) | 10 (20) |
| 1661–80 | 24 (52) | 14 (30) | 8 (18) |
| 1681–1700 | 9 (43) | 8 (38) | 4 (19) |
| 1701–20 | 14 (27) | 38 (73) | 0 (0) |
| 1721–40 | 4 (10) | 35 (83) | 3 (7) |
| 1741–60 | 1 (1) | 95 (99) | 0 (0) |
| 1761–80 | 4 (9) | 43 (91) | 0 (0) |
| 1781–1800 | 0 (0) | 165 (100) | 0 (0) |
| 1801–20 | 2 (1) | 135 (96) | 3 (3) |
| 1821–40 | 1 (1) | 95 (97) | 2 (2) |
| 1841–60 | 5 (2) | 217 (94) | 10 (4) |

*Notes:* Pledge contracts are: (1) those contracts in which the borrower pledges to transfer a human should the borrower default on the loan, but where the pledged human does not work for the lender in the interim (Type A); and (2) those contracts in which the borrower pledges a human to work for the lender during the term of the loan, but where that labor does not reduce the principal amount of the loan (Type B).

Indenture contracts are: (1) employment contracts for specified lengths of time; and (2) contracts-denominated pledges where the labor of the pledged human reduces the principal amount of the loan (Type C).

Sales are: (1) contracts denominated sales and (2) adoptions in which the transferor receives compensation.

Only contracts for terms of six months or longer are included.

*Sources:* See material in References preceded by an asterisk.

another party as a hereditary servant (Types A and B). Pledge agreements that created indentured servitude instead (Type C), I list as indenture contracts.

## 1.4 Sales and adoptions

Of two other contractual arrangements, the records disclose a smaller number. Both were transfers in perpetuity. Under one scheme, H straightforwardly sold W to E. Under the other, E "adopted" W from H, but paid H for the privilege. The probable reason for the adoption is again straightforward: Tokugawa law allowed adoptions but (from time to time) banned sales. Accordingly, those who wished to sell a child could

Table 4.2. *Contractual substance, by sex*

| Date | Part A: Contract length (mean term in years, n in parentheses) | | | Part B: sales and pledges | | | |
|---|---|---|---|---|---|---|---|
| | Male | | Female | Sales | | Pledges | |
| | Male | | Female | M | F | M | F |
| 1601–20 | * | | * | 4 | 5 | 2 | 6 |
| 1621–40 | * | | 8.4 (5) | 1 | 2 | 2 | 4 |
| 1641–60 | 6.7 | (23) | * | 2 | 8 | 23 | 9 |
| 1661–80 | 7.7 | (25) | 8.2 (9) | 4 | 4 | 14 | 10 |
| 1681–1700 | * | | 6.2 (10) | 3 | 1 | 2 | 7 |
| 1701–20 | 5.1 | (21) | 4.5 (30) | 0 | 0 | 6 | 8 |
| 1721–40 | 3.9 | (24) | 4.0 (14) | 0 | 3 | 3 | 1 |
| 1741–60 | 1.9 | (66) | 1.5 (28) | 0 | 0 | 0 | 1 |
| 1761–80 | 2.9 | (42) | 3.8 (6) | 0 | 0 | 2 | 2 |
| 1781–1800 | 2.1 | (122) | 2.6 (29) | 0 | 0 | 0 | 0 |
| 1801–20 | 1.6 | (99) | 1.0 (24) | 2 | 1 | 2 | 1 |
| 1821–40 | 2.0 | (68) | 1.8 (14) | 0 | 2 | 0 | 1 |
| 1841–60 | 3.1 | (56) | 3.4 (77) | 1 | 9 | 5 | 0 |

*Notes:* Part A: The mean length is for all contracts in Table 4.1 that specify a term. Female contracts exclude contracts for prostitution. Contractual terms were rounded to nearest year before being aggregated. Asterisk indicates four or fewer observations.
  Part B: Sales and pledges are as defined in Table 4.1.
*Sources:* See material in References preceded by an asterisk.

denominate the transaction an adoption. Table 4.1 lists both straightforward sales and adoptions for cash as "sales."

### 2. CONTRACTUAL TERMS

Tables 4.1 and 4.2 identify two central puzzles. First, over the course of 260 years, indenture contracts eventually replaced sales and pledges (though with a mysterious jump for the last period). Second, over the same period, the mean length of the contractual terms steadily declined (though with the same odd jump at the end). I consider the first puzzle in Section 2.1, and the second in Section 2.2.

### 2.1 *Sales and pledges*

After 1740, contracts where W faced a significant risk of sale largely disappeared. Workers, families, and employers substituted rental agreements for sales and pledge contracts. Whether for men or for women (the

*r*

data show no real difference by sex) they abandoned slavery for indentured servitude.[16]

*Urban growth*. The explanation for the decline in the use of sales contracts is simple: sales contracts declined because of an increase in a basic form of post-contractual opportunism (Klein, Crawford, & Alchian, 1978; Williamson, 1979) – namely, running away. In turn, the incidence of that opportunism increased because of the growth in the non-agricultural labor market. During the seventeenth century, the Japanese population grew from 12 million to 28 million (Hayami & Miyamoto, 1988a: 44), and the urban centers captured much of that growth. Peasants flocked to the largest of the cities, and by the mid–eighteenth century Edo (Tokyo) boasted a population of over one million and Osaka and Kyoto of over 400,000 each (Hauser, 1983: 149). Many others, however, flocked to the regional centers scattered over the entire country – to the 200–odd castle towns and what Gilbert Rozman calls the "hundreds of local and regional port cities, post towns, and small commercial and craft centers" (1986: 318–21). Urbanization was rapid, and it was pervasive. Over two Tokugawa centuries, the urban population grew nearly 400 percent (Rozman, 1973: 285). By the end of the Tokugawa period, 12–13 percent of the 30–2 million lived in cities of at least 10,000, and 16–17 percent in towns of at least 3,000 (Rozman, 1986: 323).

With this increase in the cities and towns, the demand for non-agricultural workers grew apace. As shortages developed, brokers who placed workers by the day appeared. Indeed, over 400 brokers appeared in Edo alone (Steenstrup, 1991: 144; Saito, 1987: 70, 113). As workers arbitraged their services, wage differentials among markets declined (Saito, 1978). And as lucrative by-employment opportunities appeared, even many families in the farm villages came to earn the bulk of their income from non-agricultural work (Smith, 1969).

To the new towns and cities, adolescent boys and girls could now run and find work. With their "highly variegated life, very large populations, and the drama and excitement of the bustling amusement and business centers," writes Robert Smith (1963: 417), the cities "provided a large measure of anonymity." "Although people in the castle towns register on the city records," complained contemporary political theorist Ogyu Sorai (1722: 15), "they can freely leave their establishment or switch to anoth-

[16]Nor does this seem an artifact of sample bias. One would expect families to retain a document that gave them title to their hereditary servants – and this may explain why larger numbers of sales survive from the seventeenth century than indentures. It could also explain why so many pledge contracts survive – for the borrowers may have defaulted on these contracts and transferred workers who became the family's hereditary servants. The point does *not* explain, however, why the number of sales and pledges dramatically declined by the mid-1700s.

er. Because they came to the city from elsewhere, they have no relatives around and no one knows their history." Indeed, by the mid–nineteenth century, a quarter to a third of all Edo residents had been born elsewhere (Hayami, 1992: 255).

For both men and women, mobility was a fact of life. In one province in the eighteenth century, reports Mark Fruin (1973: 3), towns and villages "recorded migration-related population changes of as much as 20 percent in one year." Akira Hayami (1992: 101) finds a similar phenomenon: during the latter half of the Tokugawa period, half of the men and 62 percent of the women left the village he studied for a job at least once during their life. Of those who left, only 44 percent of the men and 55 percent of the women ever returned.[17]

*Agricultural labor contracts.* For the Japanese men and women bound for life or at least many years, the new urban labor markets promised large returns to absconding.[18] Because of the economics of agricultural labor contracting, at the outset of the Tokugawa period these workers would have found it hard to find work if they absconded. The landlords on large farms needed nonfamily workers only during peak seasons. To obtain that peak-season help, the landlords faced a choice. They could either hire help on the spot market at high wages during times of peak demand, or hire workers on contracts that extended beyond those peak months and pay them their total product over the contractual term.

To avoid holdups, most Japanese landlords chose contracts at least a year long. Given the limited transportation facilities, they hired their help in small (and necessarily "lumpy") labor markets. Like landlords in many other agricultural societies, if they sought help only when their crops stood ripe and the frost was but a few days away, they ran tremendous risks.[19] Because everyone needed to harvest their crops at the same time, they could easily fail to find help. If they failed, they lost their crops. Even if they found someone, the worker (depending on the availability of other help) could potentially extract wages that captured much of their revenue

[17]Although legislation often purported to ban migration, most such decrees were highly porous. See Fruin (1973: 14; 1980); Hayami (1971: 67 n.2); Hayami & Uchida (1971); Murao (1977: 124–5).

[18]On the use of the risk of absconding to explain the decline of bound labor in other societies, see Barzel (1989: 83–4); see also Bloch (1975: ch. 2) (discussing risk in the Middle Ages).

[19]On the use of annual agricultural contracts elsewhere, see Bardhan (1984: ch. 5) (India; also citing evidence from Denmark, Sweden, Germany, Egypt, Chile); Karsten (1990) (Britain and United States); Kussmaul (1981) (England); Roback (1984: 1171–3) (postbellum South). On the eventual disappearance of such contracts in New England, see Rothenberg (1992: ch. 7). Bardhan (1984: 76) notes that these contracts are particularly useful in economies – like Tokugawa Japan – facing relative labor shortages.

for the year. To avoid these bargaining problems, they hired help during slack seasons on contracts of at least a year. Perhaps to split the risks of year-to-year crop fluctuations with their workers, they generally negotiated the contracts before either party knew whether that year's harvest would be fat or lean.[20]

Because employees could not sue a defaulting employer (Section 1.2), landlords who negotiated annual contracts had to pay their employees their wages at the outset. This, coupled with the necessarily uncertain character of contractual guarantees from poor peasants, meant they would generally hire only those workers whom they could effectively force to work.[21] Absent that coercive power, workers had an incentive to collect room and board and wages during the slack seasons and then quit.

Now consider a simple example. Suppose peasant father F sold his 17-year-old son S to wealthy landlord E. Suppose too that all jobs in the areas to which S could realistically escape were agricultural. In such a world, if S tried to escape, he would have had a very hard time locating anyone willing to hire him.[22] No new employer would advance him a year's wages without guarantors. Yet because he had already left his father and guarantor liable on his labor contract once, no one would likely guarantee his work. Being a demonstrably bad risk, he would have found work only if he could locate a rare farmer who needed extra help by the day.[23]

Suppose, by contrast, that S worked in an area with a large non-agricultural labor force. S now had a greater incentive to abscond. As industrial and commercial work is seldom seasonal, employers can dis-

---

[20]The argument in the text does not explain why peasants chose one-year contracts instead of contracts that started in (for example) March and lasted only through October. Presumably, they did so because peasants in societies like Tokugawa Japan without well-developed credit markets tend to prefer contracts that pay them room and board over the winter months as well as the summer. Note that husbandry contracts in the West, too, were generally negotiated in the spring (Grubb, 1992b).

[21]This need for specific enforcement would also arise (though less severely) even if employers paid employees by the day (indeed, much of the employee's compensation – room and board – was effectively paid by the day). The need for specific enforcement would arise because otherwise the employee had an incentive to work during the slack season on a one-year contract in which he or she collected each month one-twelfth of his or her expected marginal product for the year (much more than his or her marginal product for the slack months) and then quit.

[22]Because runaways earlier would have had trouble finding work (there were fewer spot-market jobs available), it had been less important in Japan than in some other societies that potential employers maintain a cartel against hiring runaways. See Engerman (1994); Bloch (1975: 52).

[23]By the end of the Tokugawa period, the transportation improvements would have reduced the earlier holdup problems by letting both workers and employers compete in a larger labor market. As a result, even spot-market agricultural contracts would have become more feasible.

pense with advance wage payments, guarantees, and formal long-term contracts. Instead, they can hire workers on at-will contracts.[24] S might still suffer a handicap on the market. After all, by absconding (or by refusing to divulge his past) he necessarily signals some unreliability. Depending on how easily his potential employer can monitor his work, however, that employer might yet find it profitable to hire him.

Because F had guaranteed his performance to E, S would still impose a large loss on F by absconding. To date, most scholars have assumed that ideology or religion prevented children like S from absconding – that ideology and religion induced them to sacrifice their personal welfare for the sake of the family. Yet perhaps more skepticism is in order. F did, after all, sell S into slavery. By all logic, S ought to care less about F than most sons care about most fathers.

Indeed, notwithstanding any ideology or religion, many peasant children faced with the new non-agricultural jobs in the cities and towns did escape and leave their parents liable on their contracts. By the middle of the Tokugawa period, workers fleeing their contracts crowded the cities (Murao, 1977: 124–5). Court documents detail their exploits, village registries record their absence, and absconding prostitutes became the theater's stock in trade.[25] Contemporary philosopher Ogyu Sorai (1722: 14) spoke for many aristocrats when he complained that "indentured servants now often steal and abscond. Loyal ones have grown rare." Those who absconded were not just peasants: in a single year in eighteenth-century Edo, samurai employers filed 600 complaints against their absconded valets, and from 1837 to 1867, 44 (13%) of the employees of the one prominent Edo dry goods store absconded (Leupp, 1992: 86–8).

Runaways pose a problem for bound labor contracts in any society, of course, but the ethnic homogeneity in Japan compounded the problem. Compare the antebellum United States. The American slaves could not easily abscond, for they were a different race from most freemen.[26] The indentured servants from Europe were the same race, but often could not speak English. Moreover, these indentured servants in North America worked under short enough contracts that they were probably free before they did learn the language: four-year contracts during the seventeenth and eighteenth centuries, and two-year ones by 1821. Because they often received large "freedom dues" at the end of their contract, even in the

[24]Or, if for official reasons they chose to sign the standard indenture contract, the employer and employee could agree to name fake guarantors, parties, etc. – a phenomenon noted by Ogyu Sorai at the time (1722: 15). On the use of short-term contracts in the cities, see Saito (1987: ch. 2) (noting differences between Osaka and Edo).

[25]Hayami (1971: 1 n.2); Keene (1961); Maki (1970: 241 n.6); Nakabe (1974: 106); Yoshida (1977: 205). Hayami (1992: 276) finds that about 12 percent of the workers in his village study may have absconded on their contracts.

[26]See, e.g., Engerman (1973: 61); Hicks (1969: 133); Barzel (1989: 83).

eighteenth century they effectively repaid a past debt only during the first two years of their service (Grubb, 1992a: 171, 180–1; 1994a: 4, 10; 1994b).

By contrast, being physically and linguistically indistinguishable from free workers, Japanese servants could escape into the chaotic and largely anonymous cities with relative ease. Yet at the start of the Tokugawa period they still found themselves bound to employers for extremely long periods: life for some, six to eight years for many of the rest. Eyeing at-will non-agricultural jobs in the new towns and cities, many of these workers now absconded.

Given all this, the risk that a worker might abscond would have changed (and apparently did change) agricultural contracting practices radically. Suppose employer E buys seventeen-year-old daughter D from her father F. To the extent D can credibly threaten to escape, E will need regularly to pay D herself a large portion of the wage D could earn elsewhere if she left. E will need to pay D this wage whether or not he already paid F for D. That purchase price is sunk, and largely irrelevant to whether D will stay.

Necessarily, however, if E will need to pay D directly a large portion of the wage D could earn elsewhere, he will pay F less for D *ex ante*. More precisely, when E buys D, he will pay F D's present-valued lifetime productivity, *less* the present value of all payments he expects to pay D directly. If he must pay D her potential wage elsewhere, he will pay F only D's lifetime earnings less that wage elsewhere. Effectively, the non-agricultural labor market will drive the sales price of children down, potentially even to levels approaching zero.

Suppose now that parents vary in their willingness to sell their children (e.g., that they vary in their affection or in the value they obtain from using their children at home). If so, then some parents will necessarily have a higher reservation price for their children than others. As the market price for children falls (because of the increasingly large runaway risk), more and more parents will withhold their children from the market. Effectively, therefore, the sale of children may have disappeared in Tokugawa Japan because (1) the urban labor market prevented parents from transferring an enforceable property right in their offspring, and (2) that inability to transfer an enforceable right drove down the price of children to levels at which almost no parents were willing to part with them.

*Hereditary servants.* This logic may explain a further curiosity in Tokugawa history: during the period, hereditary servants disappeared.[27] Where such men and women had been common in 1600, by the early

[27]Fruin (1973: 34); Maki (1970: 98–100); Nakabe (1974: 104).

eighteenth century they had all but vanished from most communities. "The number of temporary servants has recently jumped," Ogyu Sorai observed in 1722 (30). "Hereditary servants have vanished from the samurai houses. Even in the rural farmhouses, few remain." Unless owners encouraged their hereditary servants not to reproduce – a thesis no one has argued[28] – such a decline necessarily implies that owners freed them on a wide scale. That they would do so presents a puzzle: people rarely throw away valuable assets, and slaves in most societies are significant capital assets.

Perhaps, however, by the middle of the eighteenth century Japanese hereditary servants were no longer very valuable. If they could credibly threaten to abscond, they could successfully demand a large portion of their wage elsewhere. If they did, their value as capital assets would have fallen substantially.[29] Paying slaves is not uncommon, after all. To motivate them, owners in many societies have paid them substantial wages (Fogel & Engerman, 1974: 239; Barzel, 1989: 79–81). The more readily a slave can run away, however, the higher the wage an owner will need to pay to induce the slave to stay and work. In Tokugawa Japan, that dynamic would simultaneously have caused two phenomena: it would have lowered the value of hereditary servants as capital assets, and raised the wealth of the hereditary servants themselves. Inevitably, it would have increased the frequency with which owners and hereditary servants found manumission mutually beneficial.[30]

## 2.2 Contractual length

Recall Table 4.2A: the mean terms of indenture and pledge contracts. The terms start long (six to eight years) but decline steadily to one or two years by the end of the eighteenth century. Again, the phenomenon ap-

[28]Although if slaves *were* less valuable one would expect owners to work less hard to encourage them to reproduce – a point consistent with the argument here that the value of the slaves fell drastically.

[29]Thomas Smith (1959: 109) argues that hereditary servants vanished because the sources of hereditary servants disappeared as the village came into contact with newer forms of employment. "After all," he explains, "why should a family sell the persons of members when their labor could be more profitably sold instead." Smith leaves two fundamental problems unaddressed: (1) why should labor contracts necessarily yield more if sold in annual segments than if sold for life, and (2) why should the disappearance of sources for *new* hereditary servants cause the progeny of *old* hereditary servants to disappear from the rolls?

[30]Note that manumission need not explicitly take the form of a cash-for-freedom deal: "If you pay me X, you can go free." Instead, it can (and in Japan apparently often did) take the form of an implicit understanding that accomplished the same result: "If you work faithfully for me for Y years, I will help you set up a modest household of your own."

plies to both sexes: by the nineteenth century, only prostitution and apprenticeships – both relatively unusual arrangements – involved long-term contracts.[31] Men and women did not now work outside the home for *total* periods that were progressively shorter. Instead, where they had earlier worked under a series of fewer but longer contracts, they increasingly worked under a greater number of successive shorter-term contracts. Two reasons for this shortening of contractual terms suggest themselves – one involving changes in the market and one involving sample bias. Take each in turn.

*Market changes.* Perhaps the mean contractual term declined for the same reason that sales disappeared: once a market in non-agricultural labor developed, workers became a bad credit risk. Once workers could cheaply escape, employers would no longer advance them or their parents several years' wages except in highly discounted form. At those discount rates, the parents and workers evidently preferred to eliminate much of the runaway risk by negotiating one-year contracts instead. Accordingly, employers hired workers for the shortest term possible, given the technological constraints of agriculture. That term, in most cases, was one year.[32]

Evidence consistent with this hypothesis appears in the age of the workers hired for long-term contracts: over the course of the period, not only did the mean length of all contracts fall to one or two years, but the mean age of the workers hired for the longest-term contracts fell to ages twelve or thirteen (Table 4.3). All else equal, if workers generally became bad risks for long terms, employers would hire them for such terms only (1) when the efficiency reasons for the terms (e.g., the need to pay for any training received) were greatest, (2) when the adverse-selection problems were least, and (3) when the employees found it hardest to escape. All factors tend to point toward children at the start of their careers: ages twelve or thirteen.

First, these younger workers had less training, and took longer to pay for any training they received.[33] Employers who hired such workers often

---

[31]On the reason for the use of long-term contracts in prostitution, see Chapter 6. On the use of such contracts in apprenticeships, see Saito (1987: ch. 2).

[32]Should they choose to hire on the spot market instead of under annual contracts, that too became more feasible over time – since the improvements in transportation enabled employers to reach beyond the local village for their labor services.

[33]These children hired under long-term contracts were at the beginning of their careers. In general, peasant children left home for work in their early teens, returned in their mid- to late twenties, and then married. Hayami & Uchida (1971: 232–3, 238–9). For evidence that the longer-term contracts were negotiated with the need for extensive training in mind, see Ichikawa (1961: 139); Ishii (1961: 173–4). For other data showing that the length of the indenture correlated inversely with age over the relevant range, see Yamazaki (1961: 201).

Table 4.3. *Mean age of male workers, by length of contract*

| | Mean age, followed by number of observations in parentheses | | |
|---|---|---|---|
| Contractual term | 1601–1680 | 1681–1760 | 1761–1840 |
| $x \leq 2$ years | * | 29.7 (6) | 29.4 (43) |
| $3 \leq x \leq 5$ years | 28.5 (11) | * | 20.8 (16) |
| $x \geq 6$ years | 19.1 (16) | 12.0 (6) | 12.7 (6) |

*Notes:* Ages are as noted in the contracts. By custom, a newborn baby, was considered one year old, and gained a year each New Years Day. Prostitution contracts are excluded. Female contracts are excluded because of small numbers. Term lengths are as defined for Table 4.2.
*Four or fewer observations
*Sources:* See material in References preceded by an asterisk.

needed to train them extensively before they became productive. If they invested substantial time in that training, however, they were less likely to recoup the room and board they gave unless they kept the children for several years. Without long-term contracts, twelve-year-olds were likely to find employers who would train them only if their parents subsidized their employment. Older children could pay for any training they received more quickly, and were more likely to have the requisite training anyway.

Second, the youngest children presented the smallest adverse-selection problems. Parents (and the child himself or herself) had relatively imperfect information about how productive an eleven-year-old might be. About an eighteen-year-old who had worked at home for several years, they had far better information. Potential employers, however, often had coarse information about both children. As a result, parents (and the child) had an incentive either to keep high-quality older children at home or to rent them under a succession of single year contracts. Only thus would they earn returns equal to the child's true marginal product. If parents offered an eighteen-year-old child under a ten-year contract, employers necessarily had reason to suspect that the child was relatively less productive. Only with much younger children could they avoid that risk.[34]

Third, the youngest workers were less able successfully to abscond, for they were less likely to have the "street smarts" necessary to succeed on

[34]This adverse selection is partially (but only partially) offset by the guarantees in the indenture contracts.

their own.[35] Even an employer who could not stop a twenty-year-old from escaping might yet be able to keep a twelve-year-old child. For all these reasons, therefore, peasants stopped negotiating long-term contracts for the older workers. Instead, they primarily used them only for the younger children – only those who needed several years to pay for the training they received, who presented smaller adverse-selection problems, and who could not easily escape.

*Data bias.* Perhaps, however, the Table 4.2A decline in contractual terms reflects a bias in the surviving data rather than any change in the length of contracts negotiated. In general, families may have preserved long-term contracts more carefully than short-term contracts (after all, a longer contract represented a larger cash investment). They may have made little effort to safeguard one-year contracts, but worked hard to safeguard their contracts with their long-term workers. Because of these different preservation strategies, perhaps a larger percentage of long-term contracts survives than short-term contracts.

Perhaps, then, the average duration of *surviving* contracts does not decline because the average duration of the *negotiated* contracts declined. Instead, it declines because the long- and short-term contracts had different survival rates. More precisely, perhaps the data reflect the fact that survival rates probably increased more steeply from 1601 to 1860 for short-term contracts than for long-term contracts.

Plausible as it may sound, the hypothesis probably does not explain the data. To see why, take the number of surviving long-term (six or more years) non-prostitution contracts:

| Years | 1601–1680 | 1681–1760 | 1761–1840 |
|---|---|---|---|
| Contracts: | 37 | 28 | 32 |

If people negotiated long-term contracts as often in 1860 as in 1601, then the number of surviving long-term contracts should at least keep pace with the population. In 1650, Japan had a population of 17 million. By 1720 it had a population of 31 million, and in 1800 it was still 31 million (Hayami & Miyamoto, 1988a: 4). If workers concluded as many long-term contracts per capita in the last two periods as the first, and if the same percentage of long-term contracts survives from 1601 as from 1840, then nearly seventy contracts should survive for each of the later

[35]Intuitively, one also might have thought that female children would find it harder to survive on the street than male children would. In fact, other historical records indicate that female workers did regularly abscond, and Table 4.2 shows no real differences in sex in the willingness of the parties involved to negotiate longer-term contracts.

periods. If (more plausibly) contracts of all sorts are much more likely to survive the 156 years from 1840 to 1996 than the nearly 400 years from 1601 to 1996, then far more than seventy long-term contracts should survive.

### 2.3 Alternatives

*Ideology.* Consider now three other explanations for the disappearance of sales contracts and the decline in the mean length of indentures and pledges. Most commonly, observers invoke Henry Maine's (1906: 173–4) famous transition from status to contract (e.g., Ishio, 1975: 437–61). In the seventeenth century, the rich preferred hired help for whom that function was their fixed status. As time passed, they learned to think contractually and began renting their help instead. Even the perceptive Thomas C. Smith (1959: 116) merely advances an ideological change to explain the shortening of contractual terms: "This drastic shortening of the employment period," he writes, "reflects the fact that labor was being slowly lifted out of the context of the social group and recognized as having an economic value independent of social relations." Unfortunately, describing a shift does not explain it, and "explaining" an economic shift by positing an ideological shift is usually less an explanation than a description.

*Incomes.* For the sake of argument, however, take a couple of the more obvious alternatives.[36] For example, perhaps peasants abandoned sales and long-term contracts because their incomes increased. During the Tokugawa period, average peasant incomes did rise (Hanley & Yamamura, 1977). If peasants in 1600 sold their children out of desperation, then an increase in income should have caused a decrease in sales. Promising as the hypothesis may seem, however, two factors militate against it.

First, higher incomes do not explain why *existing* slaves disappeared. The full puzzle, recall, is not just why peasants stopped negotiating sales contracts. It is also why existing hereditary servants disappeared, and that phenomenon the rising incomes hypothesis does not answer. By contrast, the labor market hypothesis above suggests that the new non-agricultural jobs in the cities facilitated manumission by simultaneously raising the wealth of hereditary servants and lowering their value.

[36] Alternatively, one could try to explain the contractual shifts by positing the development of financial innovations that enabled landless peasants to obtain credit without using human mortgages. The explanation does not work: although the sophistication of rural financial markets did increase during this time, even by the late nineteenth century landless peasants still had access to almost no credit.

Second, because peasant incomes continued to vary over a broad range during the period, some peasants remained desperately poor. Necessarily, therefore, even if an increase in peasant incomes might have reduced sales contracts it should not have eliminated them. According to Table 4.1, though, sales all but disappeared by the mid–eighteenth century. Even from the desperate years of the Temmei famine (1782–7) when 130,000 to 200,000 people died, no sales or pledges survive.[37] By contrast, if peasants everywhere were by then within a few days' walk of a modest urban center, then anyone who bought a sixteen-year-old or rented one long-term risked losing the child to the city. Unable to distinguish the likeliest runaways in advance except by age, employers were likely to demand an extremely high discount rate before agreeing to long-term arrangements for any but the youngest adolescents.

*Technology.* Alternatively, perhaps peasants abandoned sales and multi-year contracts because changes in agricultural technology reduced the variance to agricultural yields. Suppose, for instance, that they had earlier negotiated the longer-term contracts (whether sales or multiyear indentures) to mitigate the risks associated with year-to-year variations in the harvest. Suppose further that improvements in agricultural technology decreased these fluctuations. If so, then the later peasants should have negotiated the long-term contracts less frequently than the earlier. Unfortunately, this hypothesis too leaves two gaps.

First, like the rising incomes hypothesis, technological change does not explain why existing hereditary servants disappeared. Although it explains why peasants negotiated fewer longer-term contracts, it does not explain why the existing hereditary servants vanished. Second, the hypothesis does not explain the contracts the peasants actually negotiated. In negotiating contracts where the employer paid several years' wages in advance, early Tokugawa peasants created enormous moral-hazard (runaway) problems. If they had wanted primarily to reduce the risk from harvest fluctuations, these problems were entirely unnecessary. To avoid them, they simply could have negotiated multiyear employment contracts but paid each year's cash wages separately at the start of each year. That they did not negotiate such contracts suggests, therefore, that they were addressing something else entirely.

---

[37]On famine mortality, see Kokushi (1988). For the five years preceding the famine years the mean length of the contracts with stated terms (22 contracts) was 3.6 years; for the famine years and the five succeeding years, the mean length (89 contracts) was 2.9 years. During and immediately after the famine, in other words, the length of the contracts negotiated *fell*. Note, of course, that during famines the *demand* for agricultural laborers would probably decline.

## 3  INFANTS

In 1978, Elisabeth Landes and Richard Posner proposed a radical experiment in American adoption practice: allow adoption agencies to pass a portion of the adoption fee onto the birth mother, even when the amount exceeds her maintenance and medical expenses. Doing so would reduce, they argued, many of the more egregiously inefficient aspects of modern adoption. Curiously, however, apparently none of the contracts in Table 4.1 involves a newborn – virtually no evidence of Landes-Posner contracts survives.[38] Again, two explanations suggest themselves.

First, the phenomenon could reflect data bias rather than the underlying market. Perhaps peasants did transfer newborns for cash, but left no contractual evidence of their deals.[39] Although the data set itself does not disprove this hypothesis, two considerations militate against it. First, I know of no allusions to such transactions either in contemporary literary accounts or in the Marxist histories that try so hard to show the destitution to which Tokugawa peasants fell. Extant accounts instead detail the ways peasants abandoned their babies while others rescued them – transfers at a price of zero. Second, Table 4.1 suggests that peasants eagerly documented the ways they sold or rented older children. If they transferred infants for cash too, all else equal one might expect some of the contracts to survive. Apparently, none does.

Instead, perhaps peasants negotiated no baby-sale contracts because the market price of babies approached zero. Even in the antebellum South, newborn slaves had a market value of only 4 percent of their peak adult price (Fogel and Engerman, 1992b: 472 n.9). Given the apparent low sales price of Japanese adults by the mid–eighteenth century, perhaps infants just fetched an extremely low price. Recall, in this regard, that Tokugawa peasants had neither effective birth control nor safe abortion technology. Birth control involved little more than abstinence, and most abortions involved either toxic drugs or dangerous mechanical ploys (Sakurai, 1993; Shitanaka, 1959–60: 210). Faced with these choices, many peasants – according to demographic studies – killed their babies instead (Smith, 1977: 83–5; Mosk, 1978, 1979).

That peasants routinely killed "surplus" babies (both girls *and* boys) itself implies that infants commanded a market price near zero. All else

---

[38]Ishii (1978: 556) does include an 1812 contract for the sale (denominated an adoption) of a two-year-old boy.

[39]Thomas Smith (1977: 68) notes that adoptions recorded in village registries were almost exclusively of males over age twelve; in his study, Fruin (1973: 155) finds no adoptees under age fifteen.

equal, one might ask, why kill your baby if you can sell it for cash? Or why pay much for your neighbor's baby (except to ensure adequate prenatal care) if you can obtain an abandoned one for free? Perhaps, therefore, peasants seldom sold babies because babies had little market value; they seldom negotiated elaborate contracts for babies because the low economic value of the asset transferred did not justify the transactions costs of contractual draftsmanship.[40]

If infants in Japan did have a zero market price, the recent proposals to let adoptive parents pay birth mothers may be largely artifacts of modern birth control, abortion technology, and information about prenatal care. Babies may indeed warrant nontrivial positive payments where professional couples defer childbirth until their mid thirties, where parents who do not want children use the pill, where inadvertently pregnant mothers safely and cheaply abort in the first trimester, and where adoptive parents realize the importance of prenatal care. Landes and Posner advanced their proposal in such a world – but for most of history the world has been very different. In Tokugawa Japan, couples married in their twenties and practiced little effective birth control. Rather than abort, they often brought their children to term, and killed or abandoned those born at inconvenient times or those of inconvenient sex.

## 4 LABOR MARKETS AND FAMILY NORMS

Indirectly to be sure, the analysis above (Section 2) also suggests tentative conclusions about the way the external market shaped internal family organization. For if this analysis explains the gist of why long-term contracts disappeared, then it also suggests – indirectly yet necessarily – that most scholarly accounts of Tokugawa Japan have exaggerated the power that parents had over their children. To date, most scholars have assumed that the real parties to these contracts were the employers and the heads of the workers' households. Even Thomas Smith (1959: 115) finds in these contracts evidence "of the enormous power of the peasant family over its members." The family head (generally the father) received the money, Smith writes, and "was apparently thought . . . able to guarantee" a child's performance.[41] He decided which children would

---

[40]Because the adoptive father could register the baby as his own, even without a sales contract he could still protect his "title" to the newborn.

[41]Smith (1959: 115 n.k) adds in a footnote that the fact that the worker sometimes signed the contract "suggests a slight loosening of the family head's control," and notes in passing a point consistent with the analysis above – "that the expanding labor market makes [this] entirely understandable."

work where for how long. He negotiated the contracts and he kept the money.[42]

Fundamentally, though, function did not follow form in Tokugawa contracts. Instead, form merely followed regulatory and customary dictates. Tokugawa law and custom required the parties to draft labor contracts as though the household head negotiated the terms and pocketed the money (Ishii, 1961: 181; Miyamoto, 1948: 112). The parties largely complied, and included appropriate contractual recitals. Ultimately, the contractual text tells us nothing about any control household heads exercised.

*Parental control.* Granted, in some cases the parents did control the transaction. In the sale contracts, for example, they probably negotiated the deal and took the money. So too in the indentures for six-year-old children. But contracts involving very young children were always rare, and by the middle of the Tokugawa period sales contracts had virtually disappeared. Most contracts instead concerned indentured arrangements for teenagers and workers in their twenties. The important questions concern these.

Indirectly but necessarily, the analysis above implies that by the mid–eighteenth century many of the workers in these run-of-the-mill contracts exercised significant control over their own lives. Recall first that sales and long-term contracts seem to have disappeared because the growing market in non-agricultural labor destroyed employer E's ability to enforce his property right in worker S's labor. Because E no longer could readily prevent S from absconding, he refused to advance S's father F several years' cash wages except at an unacceptably (to F or S) high discount rate. Accordingly, E, F, and S negotiated contracts for the minimum technologically feasible unit. With agricultural contracts, that unit was one year.

Consider how Tables 4.1 and 4.2 would look if father F in 1750 could still have prevented his son S from absconding. If F had had that power – either by force or by normative authority – he would have been able to continue to persuade E to accept sales and long-term indenture arrangements. Presumably, if some parents wanted to trade their children's long-term service for cash advances in 1650, some still wanted to do so in 1750. Yet if F in 1750 could still control S, then E would not have much

---

[42]Smith (1959: 116) cryptically claims that the "drastic shortening of the employment period reflects the fact that labor was being slowly lifted out of the context of the social group and recognized as having an economic value independent of social relations." Unfortunately for Smith, this does not follow. After all, why would parents in the early seventeenth century rent their children for long terms unless they recognized the economic value to the child's labor independent of the child's social relations?

feared that S would abscond. Similarly, if S in 1750 were not so heartless as to abscond and leave F liable for several years' cash wages, then E would not have feared that S would abscond. Instead, in either case E could have relied on S to stay. Accordingly, if some parents wanted to sell their children long-term, E could safely have bought the children. Notwithstanding, by 1750 E, F, and S abandoned such contracts.

Hence the necessary conclusion, indirect as it may be: By the middle of the eighteenth century parents could no longer reliably control their sons and daughters. Perhaps precisely because a father's real control had grown so attenuated, the parties themselves often came to ignore his role. Noted Ogyu Sorai in 1722 (15), "the household heads they recite in the contracts often have no address. In fact, they often are merely fictitious names."

*Parental expropriation.* The proposition that by 1750 many children kept much of the cash they earned (or gave it to their parents with the implicit understanding that they received it back with interest when they established their own household) again follows − indirectly but necessarily − from this logic. If, by the mid eighteenth century, son S *could* profitably abscond, father F generally had to let S keep much of the money. Otherwise, S often *would* abscond. Recall that the fathers were liable on their sons' contracts. Even when absconding left their families liable for several years' cash wages, many children willingly ran to the city. S, Tables 4.1 and 4.2 thus imply, often did as F said only if F made it worth his while. Unless S found it worthwhile not to leave home, and even if leaving home left F liable on the contract, S left. If E had to pay S the wage S could earn elsewhere to keep him, so did F.

In effect, a father who expropriated the money his children earned substantially raised the risk that they would abscond, even when they worked under a succession of one-year contracts. Necessarily, in deciding whether to abscond, S weighed the extra wages he could earn at a new job against the risk of punishment he incurred by absconding and the social dislocation he suffered. To explore the implications of this calculus for whether F could keep the cash S earned, assume S earned market cash wages of 4 *ryo* a year.

Suppose first that S kept any cash he earned. If he absconded from a one-year contract, he could expect to gain at most 4 *ryo*: he could pocket the 4 *ryo* he received in advance from his rural employer $E_1$, and earn an extra 4 *ryo* from urban employer $E_2$ under an at-will contract. If he instead absconded from a ten-year contract he could expect (at a 10 percent discount rate) gains of up to 27 *ryo*: he could pocket the 27 *ryo* $E_1$ paid him up-front, and over time earn extra cash wages under an at-will contract from $E_2$ with a present value of 27 *ryo*. Effectively, through absconding he increased his net cash income by up to 27 *ryo*. Unless the expected costs to absconding were much higher under ten-year contracts than one-year contracts,[43] he would have had a substantially greater incentive to abscond under a ten-year contract.

Suppose now that S worked for $E_1$ under a succession of one-year contracts, but that F kept all cash wages S earned and that S expected this to continue for the next ten years. If S stayed with $E_1$, he earned cash wages of zero, for F levied an annual income tax of 100 percent. If he absconded, he earned cash wages from $E_2$ with a present value of 27 *ryo*. Effectively, and precisely because of F's expropriative conduct, S had the same incentive to abscond as he would have had if he were working under a ten-year contract: by absconding, he increased his net cash income by up to 27 *ryo*.

*Ideology.* But early modern peasants were not like this, readers will protest. Such an ahistorical and a-ideological approach misses the way Tokugawa peasants saw the world. Integrated into family networks, they would not have found it profitable to abscond. Trapped by cultural notions of filial piety, most would not even have tried.

Not so. That norms and ideology tightly bound peasants to their family is a claim that Tables 4.1 and 4.2 (and the large anecdotal evidence of absconded servants) potentially contradict. Once a market for non-agricultural labor developed, E no longer advanced several years' wages. Notwithstanding any familistic ideology, E apparently could no longer trust his workers to stay. Notwithstanding any norms of filial piety, many sons and daughters apparently ignored their parents and pursued their selfish interests instead.

At least as important as the fact that many of the peasants did abscond is the fact that many of the rest could credibly threaten to abscond. For if peasants could credibly threaten to leave, then in equilibrium relatively few would. In equilibrium, most sons and daughters would stay in their jobs. They would stay because their parents (1) knew they could profitably leave, (2) knew that they might indeed leave if the parents did not let them keep most of the money they earned, and (3) therefore let them keep that money. Indirectly to be sure, Tables 4.1 and 4.2 testify to the probable establishment by the middle of the Tokugawa period of precisely that equilibrium.

---

[43]Presumably they were somewhat higher, since E would invest more resources in searching for workers who absonded with 27 *ryo* than for workers who absconded with 4 *ryo*.

## 5  CONCLUSION

From the seventeenth century to the nineteenth, Japanese parents, children, and employers radically changed the labor contracts they negotiated. In the early seventeenth century, some parents still sold their children into hereditary servitude. Within a century, they had stopped, and employers who had owned such servants had freed them. In the early seventeenth century, some parents still rented their children under indenture contracts spanning several years. Within a century, they had stopped this too.

Japanese parents, children, and employers changed the contracts they negotiated, I argue, because of changes in the labor market they faced. By the mid–eighteenth century, workers could readily negotiate at-will contracts in towns and cities. Where farmers needed yearly contracts to assure themselves workers during peak seasons, urban employers did not. Instead, they could hire large numbers of workers informally. If they wished, they could then dispense with contracts, advance payments, and guarantors.

Because urban employers offered informal at-will contracts, by the mid–eighteenth century rural servants could profitably abscond. Because they could abscond, rural employers could not profitably offer the contracts they once offered. Because they could no longer enforce any property right to their workers' product, employers and parents no longer bought and sold children outright or rented them under long-term contracts.

Curiously, none of the surviving contracts explicitly concerns the transfer of an infant for cash. Notwithstanding the theoretical efficiency of Landes and Posner's famous arrangement, Japanese peasants did not use it. They probably did not do so, however, because infants in Tokugawa Japan – like infants in most of the world for most of history – were not a scarce commodity. Lacking effective and safe contraceptive and abortion technology, peasants routinely abandoned or killed extra infants. As a result, most adoptive parents had little reason to transfer substantial amounts of cash to the birth parents.

The most startling implications in this study follow from the analysis in Section 2 indirectly: If by the mid–eighteenth century employers could not enforce a property right in their workers, then many parents could not control their children either. And if their parents could not control them, then many children probably chose the jobs they took, kept much of the cash they earned, and generally ran their own lives.

In the end, the labor market itself shaped the internal organization of the family, constrained domestic exploitation, and conferred real autonomy on work-age children. By the mid–eighteenth century, many peasant children who found themselves in circumstances not to their liking absconded. Many more did not abscond, but even they apparently used the threat of absconding to their private advantage. That implication follows (indirectly) from the contracts themselves: by the mid–eighteenth century, employers, parents, and children negotiated contracts that seemed to reflect an awareness that an exploited child could easily abscond. In effect, the *external* labor market shaped the *internal* dynamics of the family. Scholars have detailed how competitive markets mitigate exploitation within firms. According to the data from Japan, the same markets mitigate it within the family as well.

The more general implications follow directly: Because sellers could only transfer their *own* labor, Japan no longer incurred the deadweight losses commonly associated with slavery. If A (e.g., a father) can sell the labor of B (e.g., a son, a slave), substantial social losses follow — for (given constant monitoring and policing levels) sold workers have weaker incentives than free workers to exert effort (Barzel, 1989: ch. 6). A society without such sales sacrifices occasional gains from trade, to be sure. Crucially for the chapters that follow, however, it also avoids significant deadweight losses.

# 5

## Autonomy: Family law

### INTRODUCTION

Markets shape families. The real estate market shapes the way people pass property across generations. The capital market affects the investments parents make in their children. The marriage market influences the jobs children take and the promises they make prospective spouses. The labor market limits the extent parents control their children (Chapter 4).

The law shapes markets. Japanese law shaped the markets for water and land by defining the property rights involved (Chapter 2). In the process, it promoted agriculture. It shaped the labor market by enforcing (at least by the late nineteenth century) a worker's property right to his or her own labor (Chapters 6, 7). In the process, it enabled people to negotiate contracts that mitigated informational asymmetries and promoted their private best interests.

And the law also shapes directly the families that operate within these markets. In Japan, claim scholars, the law imposed on families a rigidly "exploitative" regulatory scheme. According to most observers, through the Civil Code[1] it made the eldest male in each generation head of the family. To him, it gave all the property and the power to determine how the other family members lived. Children, sisters, younger brothers, and his widowed mother all did as he said. In effect, any independence the Tokugawa labor market gave children and siblings (detailed in Chapter 4) the imperial Civil Code undid.

Scholars also argue that the law gave a husband (and his natal family) nearly autocratic control over his wife. He could test her before marrying her. He made all the important family choices. And he could divorce her on nearly a whim. By contrast, she made decisions only at his sufferance, could divorce him only for the most egregious misconduct, and lived her

---

[1]*Mimpo [Civil Code]*, Law No. 89 of 1896 (effective 1898).

80

life in perpetually subservient status. "The difficult, almost cruel conditions that many young wives had to endure," concludes historian Mikiso Hane (1982: 69), "often led to suicide or a nervous breakdown."

Notwithstanding this elaborate academic orthodoxy, imperial Japanese family law did *not* have the exploitative features usually ascribed to it. On the law, the observers are simply wrong. Family heads could not control other members in the ways usually described. Husbands and their families could not dominate wives as typically claimed; and fathers did not have to leave all property to their oldest sons. Free labor is generally (obviously not always) more productive than bound, and the imperial Japanese courts carefully protected the freedom of family members against fathers, husbands, and older brothers. People generally produce most efficiently when autonomous, and the law jealously guarded their autonomy. The point is vital to this book's thesis: the independence that the Tokugawa labor markets conferred partially and implicitly on individuals, the imperial courts confirmed more expansively and explicitly. In imperial Japan, individuals controlled their own lives.

To illustrate these themes, I briefly summarize the extant scholarship (Section 1). I then explore the ability of a family head to decide where other family members lived (Section 2), and the power he had over whom those members married (Section 3). I examine whether the law mandated primogeniture (Section 4). And I conclude by studying the control husbands and their families had over wives (Section 5).

## I   SCHOLARS AND PATRIARCHY

Scholars of pre-War Japan routinely argue that the imperial Civil Code helped institutionalize patriarchy. By structuring families along authoritarian lines, it even facilitated militarization.[2] A quick summary of these orthodox accounts (I include more detailed references below) would proceed as follows.[3] The Civil Code imposed on indigenous peasant and lower-class families a samurai ethic. In the process, it restructured such families along rigidly hierarchical and patriarchal lines. Effectively, it institutionalized a family system that brutally subordinated large parts of the Japanese population. Once again, Takeyoshi Kawashima's (Kawashima, Nagai, & Bennett, 1962: 108) polemics dominate the scholarship:

[2]E.g., Fuse (1984: 2) (the patriarchal family under the Code "was a key channel for inculcating the ideology of the imperial state"); Miyake (1991: 270) ("The implementation of the Meiji Civil Code [1898] gave final legal substance to an ideology that functioned to sustain the patriarchal family as the basic unit of the ruling order of the state").

[3]The most notable exception to this summary is Smith & Wiswell's (1982) fine ethnographic study. They describe a radically egalitarian village where family heads and husbands had little power over other adults.

The family system as it is prescribed in the [pre-war Civil] Code is part of the family system of the *samurai* class, and it must be said that the *samurai* family system is a functioning part of the family institutions of our society. . . . In this [*samurai*] family system, the relationship between parent and child, and between husband and wife, is a relationship of one-sided dominance and submission, of the one side having only powers, and the other side merely duties.

The Civil Code focused, most scholars continue, on a concept of the family that Japanese call *ie* (sometimes translated "house"). This institution is not one most Western readers would readily recognize. Neither the nuclear nor the extended family, it was a "stem family" – an organization that transcended its present members through history and spanned generations through the eldest son. According to most observers, property in pre-War Japan effectively belonged to this stem family, and the oldest son (as head of the family) managed it. Other children (whether young or old) were members of this family, and the eldest son managed them too. As Hiroshi Oda (1992: 232) wrote, "The head of the family had the power to designate the place where family members should live, to control their choice of marriage-partner and to expel them from the family when necessary."

Superficially, the Code does seem to confirm parts of this description. It did recognize the stem family. It did define family heads. It did provide that the oldest male of each generation generally served as that head. It did seem to let him decide where the other members would live and whom they would marry. If they disobeyed him, it did seem to let him expel them from the family. And in formulating inheritance rules, it did seem to give him all the property.

As explained below, however, in several ways this account misdescribes pre-War Japan: it describes rules the Code never included; it ignores the way the courts enforced the Code; it misses how the Code let people bargain around its legal provisions; and it misstates the way markets themselves constrain the bargains people reach. To illustrate these problems, consider initially two of the more important powers that the head supposedly wielded – the powers over residence and marriage.

## 2 THE POWER OVER RESIDENCE

### 2.1 *The issue*

Scholars of Japan routinely claim that the family head could tell other members where to live. As University of Tokyo law professor Yoshiyuki Noda put it, "The head could arbitrarily determine the place of residence of members of his family, and those who did not obey him could be excluded from the family."[4] To Noda's credit, the Code (§ 749) did specify that "members of a house may not determine their place of residence, if the head of the house objects to their choice." Unfortunately, writers like Noda apparently take the recitation at face value – and at face value they miss the law's effect.

Simple logic should make one wonder. By the late Tokugawa period people migrated extensively (see Chapter 3). Given those habits, it would seem odd if the newly appointed heads used their power to stop that migration. Under the Code, those heads also had a duty to support destitute members of the family (§ 747; see Section 2.3). Given that potential liability, it would seem just as odd if they prevented family members from moving to better-paying jobs.

In any case, the conventional account of the law is wrong: the head could *not* force other members to live where he wished. Two years into the Civil Code, the Supreme Court made the point clear. The head in the case had ordered a family member to return home. She refused, and the court let her stay where she was:

Suppose a head notifies a family member [that she should return]. If she refuses to comply, he has the right to refuse her further support and to remove her from the house registry. He does not have the right to force her to return home.[5]

In short, a head could do two things: he could apparently (but only apparently – see Section 2.2) condition family membership on a member's agreeing to live where he wished, and he could apparently (see Section 2.3) condition his economic assistance on that compliance. If a member lived where he ordered, he had to support the member financially. If a member chose to live elsewhere, he could apparently expel him or her and refuse further support.

To explore how much effect these putative rights to expel and to refuse support might have had, suppose that my sister lives alone in New York City, and I (as an overly protective older brother) am worried. I want her back in Chicago, but what can I do? Most obviously, I can tell her that if she agrees to live in the servants' quarters above our garage, I will pay her $20,000 a year. If she agrees, I must pay her the money. If she refuses, she

---

[4]Noda (1976: 200–1); see also George (1965: 510) ("Members could not fix their place of actual residence against the will of the head of the house and could be ordered upon reasonable notice to move their residence wherever the head directed").

[5]Watanabe v. Watanabe, 6-3 Daihan minroku 65, 68 (Mar. 13, 1900); see also Nagahama v. Nagahama, 6-3 Daihan minroku 1 (Daishin'in [Supreme Court] Mar. 1, 1900) (enforcing the right of family head to condition support on living where specified).

can stay where she is and I can keep the money. Nothing in American law mandates this arrangement, but nothing prohibits it either.

Surprisingly, my arrangement differs little from any arrangement an older brother would have negotiated under the imperial Civil Code. In imperial Japan, too, siblings could have negotiated deals like mine. The only real differences were two fold. First, as eldest brother and household head, under the imperial Civil Code I potentially had a duty to support my sister if she lived where I specified (§ 747). By contrast, under American law, I need support her only if I agree in advance to do so. Second, under the Code, if my sister refused to live where I specified, I could try to expel her from our official family registry (§ 749 [c]). Under American law, I have no registry from which to expel her.

As a result, these residence rules raise three questions basic to the issues in this chapter: (1) how freely could a family head expel members for violating his orders; (2) how substantial was his financial duty to support them; and (3) how badly did family members want to stay in their stem family. In the rest of this section, I address these questions in turn.

## 2.2   The power to expel

Notwithstanding the language of the Code, by 1901 the Supreme Court held that a head exercised his power to expel under stringent constraints. The case concerned a stepmother. Alleging that the family head (her stepson) had grown abusive, she left his house. When he ordered her back and she refused, he dropped her from the registry. She sued, and the court ruled in her favor:

A family head's power under § 749 is the power to do what is necessary to order the affairs of his house. In exercising that power, a head must operate within the realm dictated by the Code's legislative purpose. He does not have an unlimited right to exercise that power [to expel members]. He cannot exercise his power without reasons, in other words, solely on a whim.[6]

Because the stepson proferred no valid reason for demanding that his stepmother return, in expelling her he abused his right as family head.

Over the next several decades, the courts repeated the point many times: family heads could remove members from the registry only under extremely limited circumstances – only when "necessary" to manage

[6]Saito v. Saito, 7-10 Daihan minroku 80, 83 (Nov. 21, 1901).

family affairs.[7] In most cases, the courts interpreted "necessity" narrowly to cover only financial need. Where an economically strapped head was supporting the others, they explained, he could properly insist that they live in his house.

In a few – but only a few – cases, the courts stretched "necessity" to other exigencies. Where one brother ran a usury operation, the Supreme Court held that the family head could order him home. He was jeopardizing the family's good name, and the head could order him home to protect it.[8] Where the presence of one family member destroyed the collective peace of the household, another court held that the head could order her to live elsewhere for the good of the family.[9]

Yet when a head ordered members to move for reasons other than financial exigency, the courts usually balked. In one 1937 case, for instance, a family member lived with a married man. In order to stop the affair, her family head told her to move. According to the Supreme Court, in doing so he abused his power.[10] The more typical cases involved widows and daughters-in-law who wanted either to live independently or to live in their natal homes. And the most touching cases involved war widows who had large statutory death benefits from the government. In almost all these cases, the courts held that the women could live where they pleased and the head could not expel them.

As an example, take one plaintiff who had married the defendant head's second son. She and her husband had lived apart from his family, and when he left for the Russo-Japanese War she returned to her natal home. Once her husband died in battle, the defendant ordered her to move to *his* house. When she refused, he dropped her from the registry. She sued to void her expulsion, and the Osaka Court of Appeals granted her petition. The defendant had ordered her home only to capture her

---

[7]See generally, e.g., Suginohara (1940: ch. 1). Cases on point not cited elsewhere include Furutani v. Furutani, 3203 Horitsu shimbun 16 (Daishin'in [Supreme Court], Oct. 28, 1930); Sonoda v. Sonoda, 7-6 Daihan minshu 47 (Daishin'in [Supreme Court] June 2, 1901); Nozaki v. Nozaki, 3111 Horitsu shimbun 7 (Nagasaki Ct. App. Mar. 28, 1929); Iwabuchi v. Iwabuchi, 2865 Horitsu shimbun 10 (Tokyo Ct. App. Apr. 9, 1928); Yuhara v. Yuhara, 2489 Horitsu shimbun 9 (Tokyo Ct. App. Oct. 13, 1925); Kusuda v. Kusuda, 2020 Horitsu shimbun 15 (Nagasaki Ct. App. July 10, 1922); Yamaji v. Yamaji, 1264 Horitsu shimbun 23 (Osaka Ct. App. May 5, 1917); Arisawa v. Arisawa, 725 Horitsu shimbun 22 (Nagoya Ct. App. May 21, 1911); Nakamoto v. Nakamoto, 3795 Horitsu shimbun 12 (Osaka D. Ct. Dec. 18, 1934); Horie v. Horie, 3111 Horitsu shimbun 9 (Tokyo D. Ct. Apr. 7, 1930); Yamazoe v. Yamazoe, 201 Horitsu shimbun 7 (Osaka D. Ct. Mar. 17, 1904).

[8]Yasuda v. Yasuda, 26 Daihan minroku 1623 (Daishin'in [Supreme Court] Nov. 2, 1920).

[9]Anhiru v. Anhiru, 1042 Horitsu shimbun 23 (Tokyo Ct. App. May 24, 1915).

[10]Yamamoto v. Yamamoto, 16 Daihan minshu 418 (Daishin'in [Supreme Court] Apr. 8, 1937).

widow's war benefits. That, it held, was not a "necessity" within the scope of § 749.[11]

For at least two reasons, one should not think such family heads unreasonably crass. First, they could rightly note that a widow who lived with her parents would probably share the benefits with them – the soldier's parents-in-law. Probably, most soldiers would have preferred that any benefits payable upon their death went to their own family instead. By requiring the widow to live in her marital family, the heads ensured that result. Second, the heads could note that a widow and her children were members of the head's family. As such, the heads potentially owed them a legal duty of support (Civil Code, § 954). Should a widow squander the cash, she and her children could then legally demand (subject to the limits in Section 2.3) that he support them.[12]

Notwithstanding such arguments, the courts routinely found for the widows. Effectively, they held that the women could live where they pleased, that they could keep their death benefits, and that their in-laws could not drop them from the registries. As the Yamagata District Court put it in yet another war benefits case:

A head does not have an absolute right to remove a family member from the registry. Instead, he may exercise his right only when necessary to maintain the peace and order of the house. As a result, he may not remove a member when he has no proper reasons to do so. He may not remove someone when he acts only on his own emotions or in his own self-interest.[13]

When a family head expelled members out of spite, courts were just as hostile. As a typical example, consider a 1917 Supreme Court decision.[14] The family head had died, and left a wife and a son by an earlier wife. The son (as the new head) wanted to cut all ties with his stepmother. As the first step in that scheme, he ordered her to live with him. He knew she would refuse. That refusal would, he apparently reasoned, give him grounds for expelling her.[15] Not so, said the Supreme Court. "His order that she move into his home is an unfair order that a family member has

---

[11]Ikeda v. Ikeda, 493 Horitsu shimbun 17, 17 (Osaka Ct. App. Mar. 26, 1908).

[12]See Nakaoka v. Nakaoka, 3773 Horitsu shimbun 5 (Oct. 1, 1934).

[13]Saito v. Saito, 2550 Horitsu shimbun 11, 11 (Yamagata D. Ct. Mar. 18, 1926). Other cases involving war benefits include Kurita v. Kurita, 1602 Horitsu shimbun 18 (Tokyo Ct. App. June 6, 1919); Uda v. Uda, 459 Horitsu shimbun 8 (Nagasaki Ct. App. Sept. 28, 1907); Toyama v. Toyama, 438 Horitsu shimbun 8 (Nagasaki Ct. App. June 15, 1904); Sakamoto v. Sakamoto, 4176 Horitsu shimbun 4 (Kofu D. Ct. No date, journal issue dated Sept. 20, 1937).

[14]Yamaji v. Yamaji, 23 Daihan minroku 1223 (Daishin'in [Supreme Court] Aug. 17, 1917).

[15]Although he (as stepson) would still be liable for her support, as explained in Section 2.3.

no duty to obey."[16] Because his stepmother could validly ignore his strategically spiteful order, he could not drop her from the registry.

## 2.3  The duty of support

For all the controversy it caused, the head's duty to support the members of his house was minimal.[17] First, under the law he needed to provide only the minimum amount that would keep the members alive. As one court put it, "a recipient [of the statutory support] can demand from the obligor only that amount which he or she needs for the future, and only if the recipient cannot survive either on his or her own financial resources or by the fruits of his or her labor."[18] The duty was not a duty to equalize resources within the family. It was a duty to keep the other members from starving, and little else. As a corollary, the courts held, able-bodied men and women in their twenties necessarily collected nothing.[19]

Second, the head's duty to support was a duty he owed only if he had sufficient resources. As the Tokyo Court of Appeals explained in 1901, "members of a family are entitled to demand support from their family head only when the head as obligor has the resources to support them."[20] Inability in practice meant immunity under the law. Absent resources to share, the head had no legal duty to share.

Moreover, in most cases a family head could not avoid his support liability by expelling a family member anyway. Under the Civil Code, a variety of blood relatives owed support to each other. As obligors, they were liable in the following order (Civil Code, §§ 954, 955):

(1) Spouses
(2) Lineal descendants
(3) Lineal ascendants
(4) Family heads
(5) Children-in-law, if the parents-in-law are in the same family
(6) Siblings

Suppose now that head H expelled son S from his house. H would no

---

[16]Yamaji v. Yamaji, 23 Daihan minroku at 1226. See also Kurita v. Kurita, 25 Daihan minroku 1929 (Daishin'in [Supreme Court] Oct. 30, 1919).

[17]Civil Code, §§ 747, 954; see Makino (1908: ch. 8); Matsumoto (1962).

[18]Izumi v. Izumi, 498 Horitsu shimbun 9, 10 (Kyoto D. Ct. Apr. 4, 1908) (quoting § 959). See also Tanaka v. Tanaka, 10 Daihan minroku 1075 (Daishin'in [Supreme Court] July 18, 1904); Sumizane v. Sumizane, 7–9 Daihan minroku 11 (Daishin'in [Supreme Court] Oct. 3, 1901); Kawamura v. Kawamura, 56 Horitsu shimbun 10 (Tokyo D. Ct. Sept. 21, 1901).

[19]See, e.g., Izumi v. Izumi, 498 Horitsu shimbun 9 (Kyoto D. Ct. Apr. 4, 1908); Kawamura v. Kawamura, 56 Horitsu shimbun 10 (Tokyo D. Ct. Sept. 21, 1901).

[20]Kozaka v. Kozaka, 25 Horitsu shimbun 7 (Tokyo Ct. App. Feb. 21, 1901); see Hozumi (1933: 708).

longer owe S support under clause (4). Crucially, however, the categories of siblings and lineal descendants and ascendants were based on biology rather than the family registry (Hozumi, 1933: 450, 561; Makino, 1908: 471–2). As a result, because as biological father H owed S a prior support obligation under clause (3) anyway, he escaped no liability. The same held true for any daughters, parents, or grandparents he expelled. If he expelled his siblings, he lowered his priority from clause (4) to clause (6), but still did not necessarily escape liability. The only liabilities he could avoid by expelling a member were liabilities to people toward whom he was not otherwise locked in a status listed in §§ 954 and 955: primarily daughters- and sons-in-law, and parents-in-law in other families.[21]

From time to time, observers have argued that family heads had power because the others needed their help in starting their careers. "Even though they usually leave the household eventually," note Beardsley, Hall, & Ward (1959: 236) in their classic account, "they need money from the household to get properly married or to establish themselves elsewhere." What matters here, however, is that any such power was unrelated to Civil Code – and no different from any power I have over a sister in New York.

First, Beardsley et al.'s family head had no legal duty to help the others start their careers. Like my sister in New York City, Beardsley et al.'s sisters and younger brothers could only rely on their older brother's goodwill. Second, if Beardsley et al.'s older brother was richer than the others, he was richer because of parental preferences, not because of the law. As explained in Section 4, the pre-War Civil Code never mandated primogeniture. If they so chose – and subject only to those limits described in that section – parents could split their wealth among their children.

## 2.4 The desire to stay in the family

Because a family head had only limited power to expel (Section 2.2) and because expulsion imposed only a minimal financial cost on those who were expelled (Section 2.3), the sole remaining issue is how badly members wanted to stay in their stem family. If expelled, a family member automatically started his or her own independent legal family (Civil Code, § 742). Effectively, therefore, the issue is whether most people strongly wanted to stay in their original family.

This is a crucial question to test. If most men stayed in their stem family as subordinate members (most women left it when they married), then heading a small independent family might have been stigmatizing. On the other hand, if most men (other than the oldest brother) left their stem family to start their own legal family anyway, then they would not have

[21]Stepparents were generally treated as parents under the Code. See Civil Code, § 728; Hozumi (1933: 56–67).

cared as much whether their head expelled them.[22] According to census data, virtually all adult males did leave their stem families.

The data appear in Table 5.1. Unfortunately, the national government seems not to have published the number of family heads in the country, and neither did most prefectural governments. Necessarily, therefore, the data are partial. Nonetheless, a few prefectures did divide their population into family heads and members, and the table summarizes these data. Note that it covers several diverse prefectures (from urban Osaka to rural Shizuoka) and spans several decades (from 1885 to 1921).

Consider now two back-of-the-envelope estimates. First, if most adult younger brothers stayed on the registers of their stem families, then the number of physically independent households should significantly exceed the number of legal family heads. In fact, this does not occur. By dividing the number of legal family heads by the number of physically independent households, one obtains the following percentages:

| Prefecture | Heads/Households |
|---|---|
| Chiba | 103.9% |
| Nagasaki | 100.4 |
| Osaka | 81.5 |
| Shizuoka | 98.9 |
| Yamaguchi | 100.0 |

Apparently, almost every physically independent household was a legally distinct family.

Second, if many younger brothers stayed in their original stem family, the number of adult males should significantly exceed the number of male family heads. In fact, this does not occur either. Note that males would seldom head their own houses before their mid-twenties, and that most would probably resign their headship by age sixty. Because the Osaka census data divide the population by age, note the male age distribution (Osaka, 1914: 58–9):

| Age | Number |
|---|---|
| 0–25 | 439,191 |
| 25–60 | 368,176 |
| 60 and over | 60,827 |

---

[22]One could also start one's own family voluntarily by Civil Code, § 743 (a). Although one needed the head's consent to do so (id.), any refusal to consent was governed by the usual abuse-of-right standard. See Tsuzuki v. Tsuzuki, 3924 Horitsu shimbun 9 (Tokyo Minji D. Ct. Oct. 11, 1935). According to Nakane (1990: 219), even during the Tokugawa period, "the system decreed that younger sons move out and establish their own *ie*" upon marriage.

89

Table 5.1. Legal family heads and members, and physically independent households, in selected prefectures

| Prefecture | Family heads | | | Family members | | | Households | Date |
|---|---|---|---|---|---|---|---|---|
| | Male | Female | Total | Male | Female | Total | | |
| Chiba | 237,014 | 16,980 | 253,994 | 536,468 | 751,233 | 1,287,701 | 244,562 | 1921 |
| Nagasaki | 167,069 | 16,505 | 183,574 | 336,900 | 391,228 | 728,128 | 182,859 | 1913 |
| Osaka | 347,175 | 60,127 | 407,127 | 536,846 | 806,233 | 1,342,079 | 499,923 | 1914 |
| Shizuoka | 247,536 | 14,478 | 262,014 | 584,494 | 790,429 | 1,374,923 | 264,906 | 1919 |
| Yamaguchi | 193,275 | 6,932 | 200,207 | 266,456 | 433,157 | 699,613 | 200,208 | 1885 |

Sources: Chiba ken chiji kanbo (ed.), Chiba ken tokei sho [Chiba Prefectural Statistics] (Chiba: Chiba ken, 1925), pp. 46, 48–9; Nagasaki ken (ed.), Nagasaki ken tokei sho [Nagasaki Prefectural Statistics] (Nagasaki: Nagasaki ken, 1913), pp. 33, 39; Osaka fu (ed.), Osaka fu tokei sho [Osaka Prefectural Statistics] (Osaka: Osaka fu, 1916), pp. 39, 60–1; Shizuoka ken chiji kanbo (ed.), Shizuoka ken tokei sho [Shizuoka Prefectural Statistics] (Shizuoka: Shizuoka ken, 1919), pp. 39, 61; Yamaguchi ken (ed.), Yamaguchi ken tokei sho [Yamaguchi Prefectural Statistics] (Yamaguchi: Yamaguchi ken, 1885), pp. 90, 92.

Recall from Table 5.1 that there were 347,175 male family heads in Osaka. If there were only 368,176 males between the ages of twenty-five and sixty, then – as a rough estimate – 94 percent of all twenty-five to sixty-year-old males must have legally headed a family. Apparently, most adult males did *not* stay in their stem family as subordinate members. Instead, upon becoming adults (probably upon marrying) they left their original family and formed their own, independent family.

The Yamaguchi data also let one test the eagerness of younger sons of different social classes to leave the stem family. In its 1885 census, Yamaguchi prefecture divided its population by commoners and (former) samurai.[23] If, as so many observers claim, the stem family were a strong samurai tradition, then perhaps younger brothers in samurai families would more likely have stayed in their stem family than younger brothers in commoner families.[24] If so, then (adjusted for family size), the fraction of households headed by non-family heads should be larger among samurai than among commoners. Similarly, the fraction of men who did not head families should also be larger among samurai than among commoners. In fact, neither phenomenon occurred.

Consider first the number of male family heads, male family members (of all ages), and physically independent households for the samurai and commoner groups:

|          | Male Heads | Male Members | Households |
|----------|------------|--------------|------------|
| Samurai  | 15,621     | 20,448       | 16,129     |
| Commoner | 177,654    | 246,008      | 184,078    |

Note that the samurai and the commoners had about the same size households: 4.4 members among the samurai, and 4.5 members among the commoners.

According to these data, both samurai and commoner younger brothers left their stem families to form their own independent families. The ratio of male family heads to households was 96.9 percent for samurai, and 96.5 percent for commoners. The ratio of male family heads to male family members (of all ages) was 76.4 percent for the samurai, and 72.2 percent for the commoners. At least in Yamaguchi, the samurai – those people whose family patterns the Civil Code supposedly imposed on everyone else – left the stem family as readily as anyone else.

[23] Yamaguchi (1885: 90, 92). According to the census, there were no aristocratic families in Yamaguchi.

[24] Nakane (1990: 221) argues that during the Tokugawa period many younger samurai sons "remained in their natal household in the unpromising status of *heyazumi*, one who is permitted to occupy a room."

### 3  THE POWER OVER MARRIAGE

Although scholars routinely assign the head the power to control marriages in the family, in fact he had no such power. The misunderstanding probably arises from § 750 (a) of the Civil Code:

In order for a family member to marry or to enter an adoptive relationship, he or she must obtain the consent of the family head.

Scholars apparently stop reading with subsection (a), for subsection (b) provided:

If a family member marries or enters an adoptive relationship in violation of the previous subsection, the head may, within one year of the date of such marriage or adoption, expel such member from the family or refuse his or her reentry into the family.

The implication is obvious but crucial: the head did not have the power to veto marriages. Rather, he had the power to expel members who married without his consent (a power, Section 2 suggests, with little substance).[25] Even over his opposition, a couple could properly register their marriage. When they did, the registrar was to warn them that they lacked that consent, but – crucially – to proceed with the registration (Civil Code, § 776; see Hozumi, 1933: 154).

This system gave family heads very little control over marriages, for children generally left their family upon marriage anyway. Most women who married joined their husband's family (Civil Code, § 788), and most younger sons who married started their own legal family (Section 2.4). The point was not lost on contemporaries. "Depending on the situation, this expulsion and reentry refusal right is a terribly weak system," observed University of Tokyo law professor Shigeto Hozumi (1933: 156). If the expelled spouse would otherwise have succeeded to the family's headship, it had some bite. "Otherwise, if a house member is already independently established and does not need the head's support, he or she will feel no pain from the expulsion. Indeed, he or she may even feel as if the air is cleared and that he or she has been liberated" (id.).

This does not mean men and women could marry as they pleased. Until they reached the statutory age – thirty for men, twenty-five for women – they could marry only if *both* of their parents consented.[26] If they submitted their marriage application without their parents' consent, the registrar – contrary to his practice when they lacked their head's consent – refused it (Civil Code, § 776). If he mistakenly accepted it, their parents could

---

[25]If he consented to the wedding, he could not later withdraw his consent at the time of registration. See Hayashi v. Hayashi, 2 Daihan minshu 696 (Daishin'in [Supreme Court] Dec. 27, 1923).

[26]Civil Code, § 772 (a); see Hozumi (1933: 290–1); Fukushima (1962).

later void the marriage (§ 783). Because the family head generally was the father (Section 2.4), of course, he usually did have a veto. Crucially, though, he had the veto only because he was a father, not because he was a family head. He had no more power than his wife, and the stem family with its elaborate rules of headship necessarily had almost no effect on marriage patterns at all.

## 4 PRIMOGENITURE

### 4.1 *Introduction*

According to most scholars, the pre-War Civil Code required that all property pass from the oldest male of one generation to the oldest male in the next. "Primogeniture," Joy Hendry (1986: 16) writes, "was institutionalized in the Meiji Civil Code." Oda (1992: 241) claims that "[i]n the pre-War period, the 'house' and all the property contained in it were inherited by the eldest son. The younger sons and daughters had no rights whatsoever to the estate." Robert Smith (1983: 34) more carefully (and rightly) notes that the property did not necessarily pass to the oldest son, but does argue that by law the entire estate passed to a single child, whichever it might be: "it was the genius of the civil code that it required impartible inheritance." And University of Tokyo professor Tadashi Fukutake (1982: 26–7) flatly declares that "with the Meiji Civil Code primogeniture became the law of the land."

### 4.2 *Family heads*

These accounts misstate the law. If the head of a family so chose, he could readily and legally split his estate and leave up to half of his assets to people other than his oldest son. Notwithstanding the many easy references to primogeniture in the literature, the easy references are wrong. The Civil Code did *not* require primogeniture. It merely let people leave their property to their oldest son if they so chose.

Take several examples. First, suppose family head H had four sons, A, B, C, and D. Absent special circumstances, A (the oldest) would become the next head (Civil Code, § 970). If A were a daughter and B a son, B would become the next head (id.). And if A were a son but died before H died or resigned the headship, A's oldest son (if any) would become the next head (§ 974). So far – but only so far – the usual accounts are right.

Suppose now that H died intestate (died without leaving a will). Under § 986 of the Civil Code, the next household head (A, in this example) would take all the property of H. If H resigned from the headship before he died, his property would again pass to A (Civil Code, § 964[a]). The intestate rule was thus one of impartible inheritance. Crucially, however, it was only the intestate rule.

Suppose that H did not want to leave everything to A. The Code did let him transfer property to his other children. The mechanisms were simple: he could either devise property to his other children by will, or transfer property to them through *inter vivos* gifts (gifts made while still alive).

To be sure, H could not leave his younger children as much as he left succeeding head A. If he tried, under § 1130 of the Code A could "take against the will." By the terms of this section, he could demand up to half of H's estate (calculated by adding back in *inter vivos* gifts to his other children – Civil Code, §§ 1032–1033), regardless of the terms of the will. Suppose H died with an estate of ¥1,200. If by will he left it to his four sons in equal portions, A could demand ¥600 rather than the ¥300 he would take by will. B, C, and D would then receive ¥200 a piece, notwithstanding H's attempt to leave them ¥300 each. The same limits applied if H tried to divide his estate equally while still alive.

Should H choose to do so, therefore, he could leave his younger children up to half of his estate. He could do this either by will or by gift. Wills were easy to write,[27] and *inter vivos* gifts were easy to make. For anyone with substantial property, neither the trouble of writing a will nor the trouble of making a gift would have deterred him from splitting his estate. To the extent some Japanese did leave all their assets to their oldest son, therefore, they did not do so because the Civil Code required it – for the Code did not require it. They did so because that was what they wanted to do.

### 4.3    Family members

For people not heads of a family, the Civil Code actuually banned primogeniture. Suppose M, a family member not a head, died leaving a husband (the family head), four children, and two parents. If she died intestate, all of her property passed to her children in equal portions (Civil Code, § 994). None passed to her husband or parents, and the sex and birth order of her children made no difference (§ 1004).[28]

Although a non-head could also dispose of his or her property by will, the law allowed some of the descendants to take against the will. Specifically, the decedent's lineal descendants could together demand up to one-half of the decedent's estate (§ 1131). Consider two simple examples.

---

[27]For the rules that governed the writing of wills, see Civil Code, §§ 1067–1075.
[28]This discussion ignores minor complications not relevant here – e.g., that illegitimate children received half the portions of legitimate children (§ 1004).

1. M dies with an estate of ¥1,200, a "dear friend," and four children. She tries to bequeath her entire estate to her friend. Under the Code, her friend can take only ¥600, and her four children can demand ¥150 each.

2. M dies with a ¥1,200 estate, and four children. Believing in primogeniture, M bequeaths all her property to oldest son A. Notwithstanding that will, A can demand only ¥600. B, C, and D can then collect ¥200 each.

Even if a family member with several children wanted to pass all of his or her property to his or her oldest son, the law forbad it.

## 5  THE POWER OF HUSBANDS

### 5.1  *Trial marriages*

*Introduction.* Scholars frequently note how late people registered their marriages in pre-War Japan, and stress how exploitative this practice was. After the bride and groom performed the religious wedding ceremony, they explain, the pair moved to the husband's home. They then waited several years to record the marriage, often until the woman gave birth. Until they registered it, they were not legally married (Civil Code, § 775), and the wife was effectively on trial. If her husband's family did not like her, they sent her home, no questions asked.

As University of Tokyo professor Yozo Watanabe (1963: 365) put it, "[i]f the report [to the family registry] is postponed for some time after the ceremony, the interval can be used as a trial period; and if the new wife should not fit in with her husband's family, she can be expelled from it unilaterally and without the possibility of judicial recourse."[29] Writes Hendry (1986: 22), "marriages often were not legally registered until after a period of adjustment, perhaps until a baby was due to be born, so the [bride], or indeed [an adopted son-in-law], could be sent home without legal recourse."

*Strategy and law.* These accounts miss what courts actually did, for the law *did* give the spurned bride or groom legal recourse. If a groom's family tried to use the pre-registration period as a trial, they did so at their peril. If they rejected the bride, she could sue for breach of contract to marry.[30] The rule is not the rule of a few isolated, idiosyncratic opinions. It is a rule courts repeated many times, at all levels of the judicial hier-

---

[29] Watanabe elsewhere more carefully qualifies this statement (e.g., 1963: 366 nn. 7, 9).
[30] For general discussions, see, e.g., Coleman (1956); Iwata (1935); Bai (1992).

archy, from the Supreme Court in Tokyo to the District Court in Hakodate.[31]

Because the Civil Code provided that a marriage did not take effect until registered, the very earliest courts did treat unregistered relationships inconsistently. Sometimes, they awarded a spurned spouse-to-be contract damages,[32] sometimes tort.[33] Sometimes, they simply declared the relationship unprotected.[34]

By the mid-1910s, however, the courts had made the rule clear: spurned prospective spouses could recover significant sums (see "Damages"

[31]In addition to the many cases cited elsewhere in this discussion, see Miyashi v. Sagara, 3544 Horitsu shimbun 18 (Daishin'in [Supreme Court] Mar. 27, 1933); Okubo v. Yoshida, 11 Daihan minshu 1525, 3451 Horitsu shimbun 12 (Daishin'in [Supreme Court] July 8, 1932); Okaku v. Ushiyama, 3345 Horitsu shimbun 15 (Daishin'in [Supreme Court] Nov. 27, 1931), *aff'g* 3257 Horitsu shimbun 13 (Tokyo Ct. App. Mar. 23, 1931); Ikegami v. Nozaki, 2670 Horitsu shimbun 7 (Daishin'in [Supreme Court] Feb. 26, 1927); Nohara v. Yoshizawa, 25 Daihan minroku 1010 (Daishin'in [Supreme Court] June 11, 1919); Kiyama v. Sadaishi, 25 Daihan minroku 693 (Daishin'in [Supreme Court] Apr. 23, 1919); Fujimoto v. Ishida, 21 Horitsu hyoron min 560 (Tokyo Ct. App. Apr. 7, 1932); Kuroda v. Iwaki, 20 Horitsu hyoron min 1102 (Tokyo Ct. App. July 14, 1931); Okuma v. Okuma, 19 Horitsu hyoron min 419 (Tokyo Ct. App. Dec. 23, 1929); Noguchi v. Noguchi, 2574 Horitsu shimbun 14 (Tokyo Ct. App. May 1, 1926); Komiya v. Komiya, 2452 Horitsu shimbun 5 (Tokyo Ct. App. Aug. 10, 1925); Sugina v. Ono, 10 Horitsu hyoron min 94 (Tokyo Ct. App. Dec. 14, 1920); Tsubota v. Hamana, 9 Horitsu hyoron min 492 (Tokyo Ct. App. Apr. 14, 1920); Nakamura v. Takubo, 9 Horitsu hyoron min 264 (Tokyo Ct. App. Mar. 8, 1920); Yoshizawa v. Nohara, 8 Horitsu hyoron min 282 (Tokyo Ct. App. Jan. 30, 1919); [No names given], 2 Horitsu hyoron min 271 (Tokyo Ct. App. Mar. 8, 1913); Hazama v. Tomiyama, 4780 Horitsu shimbun 17 (Shizuoka D. Ct. Feb. 5, 1942); Harada v. Mizuno, 21 Horitsu hyoron min 1142 (Tokyo D. Ct. Nov. 17, 1932); Tsukamoto v. Yonehara, 21 Horitsu hyoron min 339 (Osaka D.C. Nov. 27, 1931); Kobayashi v. Kanazawa, 3312 Horitsu shimbun 12 (Osaka D. Ct. Aug. 6, 1931); Ishida v. Morimoto, 20 Horitsu hyoron min 552 (Tokyo D. Ct. Mar. 6, 1931); Hayashi v. Inukai, 18 Horitsu hyoron min 634 (Ogaki Ward Ct. Dec. 18, 1928); Ishizuka v. Someya, 13 Horitsu hyoron min 293 (Tokyo D. Ct. Aug. 3, 1923); Hataya v. Iwase, 10 Horitsu hyoron min 1330 (Chiba D. Ct. Oct. 15, 1921); Yoshida v. Ito, 9 Horitsu hyoron min 264 (Tokyo D. Ct. Mar. 30, 1920); Ono v. Yamauchi, 8 Horitsu hyoron min 197 (Tokyo D.C. Mar. 10, 1919); Kawano v. Sakai, 7 Horitsu hyoron min 334 (Tokyo D. Ct. May 15, 1918); Ando v. Noguchi, 1135 Horitsu shimbun 29, 5 Horitsu hyoron min 267 (Tokyo D. Ct. Mar. 6, 1916).

[32]See, e.g., Fujita v. Harigatani, 383 Horitsu shimbun 6 (Mito D. Ct. June 11, 1906).

[33]See, e.g., Kuroki v. Suzuki, 17 Daihan minroku 16 (Daishin'in [Supreme Court] Jan. 26, 1911).

[34]See, e.g., Hiramatsu v. Ide, 17 Daihan minroku 169 (Daishin'in [Supreme Court] Mar. 25, 1911); Fujii v. Takeda, 3 Horitsu hyoron min 398 (Tokyo Ct. App. July 25, 1914), *aff'g* 841 Horitsu shimbun 13 (Tokyo D. Ct. No date, journal issue date of Feb. 10, 1913); Ishibashi v. Sasaki, 29 Horitsu shimbun 6 (Tokyo Ct. App. Mar. 22, 1901); Hiraki v. Fuwa, 885 Horitsu shimbun 21 (Tokyo D. Ct. May 14, 1913); [No names given], 2 Horitsu hyoron min 179 (Tokyo D. Ct. Apr. 11, 1913); [No names given], 2 Horitsu hyoron min 113 (Tokyo D. Ct. Mar. 31, 1913).

below for details) from the spouse (and parents-in-law) who rejected them. The gist of the rule was straightforward.

*If*

(a) a man and a woman were duly wed in a public ceremony,
(b) they then cohabited, *and*
(c) one spouse refused to register the marriage without an acceptable reason,

   *then* the rejected spouse,

(i) could not sue for specific performance (i.e., could not force the other spouse to register the marriage), *but*
(ii) could sue for emotional, out-of-pocket, and reputational damages, determined by the respective social and educational backgrounds of the two parties (see below for details).

A famous 1915 case illustrates how the rule worked. The husband in the case argued that a "marriage takes effect only upon the filing with the registry, . . . and whether to register a marriage remains entirely at the discretion of the parties."[35] He chose, he explained, to exercise his discretion not to register it. Soon after their wedding, he had been hospitalized. Despite his suffering, his bride had refused to visit him. Who needs such a wife, he concluded, and opted to end the relationship. The court agreed that she could not force him to marry her, but also held that he owed her damages:

Where one party, without a proper reason, breaches his or her promise and refuses to marry, that party must compensate the other for any tangible or intangible damages that the other incurred by believing the promise.[36]

His bride's cold heart did not constitute sufficient reason, and he owed her compensation.

*The presence of an agreement.* Like any legal rule, the principle had its ambiguities. As noted in parts (a) and (b) of the formula, a spouse owed damages only when the couple both had been publicly wed, and had lived together. Yet the courts had developed the rule to protect voluntary agreements to marry, and many people without weddings or cohabitation still seemed to have agreed to marry. At the same time, the courts hesitated to invite swearing contests over who promised what to whom before jumping into bed. Pillow talk is not something judges referee well, and Japanese judges knew that.

[35]Taninaka v. Nozawa, 21 Daihan minshu 49, 51 (Daishin'in [Supreme Court] Jan. 26, 1915).
[36]Id. at 52.

The result was a line that was less clear than the formula implied. Where the parties had both wed and cohabited, the outcome was straightforward: the party refusing to register the marriage owed the other damages. Sometimes, though, courts also enforced contracts to marry where a couple had lived together but had not had a public wedding.[37] Sometimes they enforced contracts where they had wed but not yet lived together.[38] On rare occasions they enforced contracts where they had neither wed nor cohabited.[39] Yet they also rejected many claims where one party asserted that the other had promised to marry, but could not (having either not wed or not cohabited) produce sufficient verifiable evidence of the promise.[40]

*Exculpatory reasons.* The hardest lines to draw concerned part (c) of the formula: what constituted an acceptable reason for refusing to register a marriage. As scholars like Watanabe and Hendry suggest, the parties often cited family opposition.[41] After all, they usually could not legally register the marriage without their parents' consent (see Section 3). Notwithstanding, the courts overwhelmingly rejected family opposition as a defense.[42] Even when parties recited the traditional Japanese formula that

[37]See, e.g., Nomura v. Isomura, 8 Horitsu hyoron min 853 (Daishin'in [Supreme Court] June 1, 1919) (declaring wedding not necessary); Yoshizawa v. Nohara, 8 Horitsu hyoron min 282 (Tokyo Ct. App. Jan. 30, 1919); Oda v. Matsumoto, 4726 Horitsu shimbun 28 (Saga D. Ct. Aug. 25, 1941); Nakayama v. Ishiwatari, 3704 Horitsu shimbun 10 (Tokyo D. Ct. Apr. 12, 1934); Ono v. Yamanouchi, 8 Horitsu hyoron min 197 (Tokyo D. Ct. Mar. 10, 1919).

[38]See, e.g., Saito v. Ito, 3231 Horitsu shimbun 10, 20 Horitsu hyoron min 210 (Tokyo Ct. App. Dec. 16, 1930) *(muko yoshi* ceremony)

[39]See, e.g., Okabayashi v. Okabayashi, 3240 Horitsu shimbun 4, 20 Horitsu hyoron min 208 (Daishin'in [Supreme Court] Feb. 20, 1931).

[40]See, e.g., Enomoto v. Nakada, 3738 Horitsu shimbun 4 (Tokyo Ct. App. July 20, 1934), *aff'g* 3525 Horitsu shimbun 5, 22 Horitsu hyoron min 479 (Tokyo D. Ct. Feb. 16, 1933); Okumura v. Yumoto, 9 Horitsu hyoron min 1142 (Tokyo Ct. App. June 11, 1920); Okawa v. Matsuda, 4298 Horitsu shimbun 5 (Tokyo Minji D. Ct. July 4, 1938); Ishibashi v. Ishii, 4139 Horitsu shimbun 3 (Tokyo Minji D. Ct. May 25, 1937) (where one spouse is already married); Fukazawa v. Ota, 3549 Horitsu shimbun 7, 22 Horitsu hyoron min 481 (Tokyo D. Ct. Feb. 24, 1933); Takano v. Kobayashi, 3304 Horitsu shimbun 9, 20 Horitsu hyoron min 989 (Mito D. Ct. July 30, 1931); Takaishi v. Akizuki, 4371 Horitsu shimbun 13 (Nagasaki Ward Ct. Dec. 23, 1938).

[41]"[I]t is routinely noted that one of the major tasks confronting the new bride is learning 'the ways of the house' *(kafu)* of her husband," reports Robert Smith (1983: 93). "In the past, her failure to do so served as the rationale for sending her back to her natal house."

[42]In addition to the cases cited in note 43, see Arakawa v. Ohashi, 13 Horitsu hyoron min 497 (Daishin'in [Supreme Court] Apr. 14, 1924); Chin v. Nakayama, 3734 Horitsu shimbun 11 (Tokyo Ct. App. June 25, 1934), *modifying sub nom.* Nakashima v. Chinza, 3570 Horitsu shimbun 5 (Tokyo D. Ct. June 17, 1933); Takahashi v. Iwata, 3702 Horitsu shimbun 17 (Tokyo Ct. App. Mar. 8, 1934); Yamada v.

the other spouse "did not fit the ways of the house" (*kafu ni tekisezu*), the courts routinely held them liable.[43] Complained one mother-in-law:

> She never bothers to put away valuables. She hasn't balanced the accounts for even a month. In caring for the house, she's worse than a ten-year old. Housework's a real problem because she's never gotten a single piece of clothing clean. I remind her of these things regularly, but she's got this habit of lying to us. Apparently, she's never done a kind thing for any of our neighbors either.[44]

To the court, none of this mattered. In refusing to register the marriage, her son and family breached their contract to marry and owed the bride damages.

Over the pre-War decades, litigants unsuccessfully plied the courts with a stream of other reasons. In general, the cases suggest that courts more readily excused prospective wives than prospective husbands. Consider the reasons prospective husbands gave but courts rejected: her family demands that I loan them large amounts of money;[45] her family did not pay the dowry they promised;[46] she has chronic tuberculosis;[47] her father has a criminal record;[48] she is feeble and sleeps during the day;[49] and she

Fujiyama, 3697 Horitsu shimbun 7 (Tokyo Ct. App. Feb. 28, 1934); Okubo v. Yoshida, 3369 Horitsu shimbun 12 (Tokyo Ct. App. Dec. 12, 1931); Fujimoto v. Matsumoto, 6 Horitsu hyoron min 904 (Osaka Ct. App. Oct. 6, 1917); Nishijima v. Tanaka, 1178 Horitsu shimbun 24 (Nagoya Ct. App. Oct. 3, 1916); Ueide v. Hashimoto, 29 Horitsu hyoron min 826 (Tokyo Minji D. Ct. May 6, 1940); Senba v. Higashi, 3506 Horitsu shimbun 17 (Hakodate D. Ct. Nov. 25, 1932); Kimura v. Hatsuyama, 3205 Horitsu shimbun 4 (Tokyo D. Ct. Nov. 26, 1930); Maeda v. Handa, 3724 Horitsu shimbun 5 (Odawara Ward Ct. June 30, 1934); Matsuyama v. Sato, 3710 Horitsu shimbun 16 (Yamagata Ward Ct. May 19, 1934); Oshino v. Ota, 3577 Horitsu shimbun 5 (Tsuchiura Ward Ct. No date, journal issue of July 23, 1933); Akiyama v. Komoike, 4201 Horitsu shimbun 9 (Osaka Ward Ct. Sept. 8, 1937); Suzuki v. Yabusaki, 2371 Horitsu shimbun 17, 14 Horitsu hyoron min 145 (Matsudo Ward Ct. Dec. 27, 1924).

[43]See, e.g., Tanizaki v. Kurihara, 25 Daihan minroku 492, 8 Horitsu hyoron min 455 (Daishin'in [Supreme Court] Mar. 21, 1919); Fukuda v. Iida, 1939 Horitsu shimbun 17 (Tokyo Ct. App. Dec. 6 1921); Makiuchi v. Tsukada, 1237 Horitsu shimbun 21, 6 Horitsu hyoron min 214 (Tokyo Ct. App. Feb. 5, 1917); Fujiwara v. Kimoto, 1182 Horitsu shimbun 24 (Osaka Ct. App. Oct. 13, 1916); Shimojima v. Sekiguchi, 3190 Horitsu shimbun 15 (Tokyo D. Ct. Oct. 8, 1930); Komori v. Tsuji, 3074 Horitsu shimbun 12 (Tokyo D. Ct. Nov. 29, 1929); Minami v. Inoue, 2334 Horitsu shimbun 18 (Osaka D. Ct. Oct. 8, 1924).

[44]Fujimoto v. Matsumoto, 6 Horitsu hyoron min 904, 905 (Osaka Ct. App. Oct. 6, 1917).

[45]Kamiya v. Suzuki, 3540 Horitsu shimbun 6 (Tokyo D. Ct. Mar. 6, 1933).

[46]Ichimura v. Iizuka, 13 Horitsu hyoron min 291 (Tokyo Ct. App. June 18, 1923).

[47]Goto v. Oyama, 3965 Horitsu shimbun 4 (Daishin'in [Supreme Court] Mar. 12, 1936).

[48]Sekiguchi v. Iwasaki, 3038 Horitsu shimbun 9, 18 Horitsu hyoron min 1137 (Tokyo Ct. App. Mar. 22, 1929).

[49]Mori v. Sugiyama, 9 Horitsu hyoron min 538 (Tokyo D. Ct. June 11, 1920).

refuses to live in my city.[50] To be sure, some of the other reasons were less compelling. Predictably, the courts rejected them too: we don't love each other;[51] we're sexually incompatible;[52] her family is poorer than I thought;[53] numerological considerations are inauspicious;[54] she ran home when she became pregnant;[55] she had someone else lecture me after a fight;[56] she is fifteen years older than I;[57] and – apparently there being no shame in litigation – she has venereal disease (which I gave her).[58]

Only for grave problems did most courts let men escape an agreement to marry without compensating their fiancée. There were exceptions. On rare occasions, a court did accept reasons like laziness or disrespect for the husband's family.[59] In general, though, they accepted only very serious problems in the relationship: she has a child from an earlier liaison;[60] she is pregnant with someone else's child;[61] or she left me when she found I was too poor.[62]

[50]Sakai v. Nagano, 3076 Horitsu shimbun 12 (Chiba D. Ct. Dec. 23, 1929). This excuse was unsuccessful despite the fact that the wife had a legal duty (and right) to live with her husband. Civil Code, § 789; see *In re* Sorano, 9 Daihan minshu 926 (Daishin'in [Supreme Court] Sept. 30, 1930); Akatsuka v. Akatsuka, 1632 Horitsu shimbun 12 (Tokyo D. Ct. Oct. 6, 1919); Kawai v. Kawai, 496 Horitsu shimbun 20 (Tokyo D. Ct. Mar. 25, 1908);

[51]See, e.g., Wakabayashi v. Suda, 3162 Horitsu shimbun 7 (Tokyo Ct. App. July 3, 1930); Makiuchi v. Tsukada, 1237 Horitsu shimbun 21, 6 Horitsu hyoron min 214 (Tokyo Ct. App. Feb. 5, 1917); Ikeda v. Ono, 3161 Horitsu shimbun 6 (Aug. 4, 1930).

[52]See, e.g., Makiuchi v. Tsukada, 1237 Horitsu shimbun 21, 6 Horitsu hyoron min 214 (Tokyo Ct. App. Feb. 5, 1917).

[53]Kikuchi v. Arakawa, 4295 Horitsu shimbun 12 (Tokyo Minji D. Ct. Apr. 28, 1938); Takemoto v. Ishikawa, 14 Horitsu hyoron min 754 (Tokyo D. Ct. Jan. 26, 1925). Lest this seem a totally unsympathetic complaint, note that the defendant in *Kikuchi* was a young physician at a university hospital. He had married his wife (as a *muko yoshi*) thinking that her family's resources would give him the time he needed for research, and possibly even to study abroad. Upon marriage, however, he found not only that he could not quit his hospital job and undertake full-time research, but also that his mother-in-law expected him to see patients privately at night as well.

[54]Mihashi v. Yanagida, 3168 Horitsu shimbun 5 (Yokohama D. Ct. Aug. 27, 1930).

[55]Senba v. Higashi, 3506 Horitsu shimbun 17 (Hakodate D. Ct. Nov. 25, 1932).

[56]Okuma v. Okuma, 3078 Horitsu shimbun 16 (Tokyo Ct. App. Dec. 23, 1929).

[57]Wakabayashi v. Suda, 3162 Horitsu shimbun 7 (Tokyo Ct. App. July 3, 1930).

[58]Yanagikawa v. Iwata, 1648 Horitsu shimbun 13 (Osaka Ct. App. Dec. 15, 1919); Yamada v. Kawanobe, 3712 Horitsu shimbun 17 (Tokyo D. Ct. June 30, 1934).

[59]Uchida v. Iijima, 3247 Horitsu shimbun 15 (Tokyo Ct. App. Feb. 17, 1931); [No names given], 5 Horitsu hyoron min 148 (Kobe D. Ct. No date, journal issue of 1916); Nakayama v. Fujimoto, 3300 Horitsu shimbun 9, 20 Horitsu hyoron min 992 (Myoji Ward Ct. Aug. 8, 1931); Iijima v. Hasegawa, 1589 Horitsu shimbun 19 (Tsuchiura Ward Ct. June 23, 1919).

[60]Masukawa v. Yamabe, 3657 Horitsu shimbun 5 (Osaka D. Ct. Dec. 26, 1933).

[61]Iwasaki v. Tabuse, 1846 Horitsu shimbun 18 (Tokyo Ct. App. Mar. 5, 1921).

[62]Ito v. Mihashi, 1164 Horitsu shimbun 22 (Tokyo Ward Ct. May 3, 1916); see also Suzuki v. Kuroda, 2703 Horitsu shiimbun 7 (Osaka D. Ct. May 13, 1927) (she publicly and falsely accused me of sexual relations with my foster mother).

There being far fewer cases holding women liable under these contracts, there are fewer examples of reasons women gave that courts would not accept as valid reasons for refusing to register the marriage. At least one court did hold that a woman could not simply claim that her in-laws treated her badly.[63] Generally, though, courts accepted from women a wide variety of excuses. Most clearly, women could properly refuse to register the marriage if their prospective husbands beat them (indeed, the beating was a tort for which they could collect compensation as well).[64] But courts also let women escape their marriage contract for the sort of reasons they would seldom accept from men: he demands money before he will register the marriage;[65] he wants sex too often;[66] or his family criticizes me too much.[67]

As an example of how far some courts would go to protect women, consider one Tokyo District Court case from 1919.[68] After their wedding, the husband-to-be had cooled on his wife and visited brothels. Angry, she left him. He begged her to return, and promised to register the marriage if she did. Instead, she sued him for breach of contract to marry. Never mind that visiting brothels was legal, that she had left him (not vice versa), and that he wanted to register the marriage if she would only agree. The court awarded her damages. In patronizing prostitutes, it explained, he implicitly breached the marriage contract and could not now rectify matters by offering to register it. Once he had gone to the brothels, she could sue him for contract damages.

*Damages.* Although the rules for determining damages were vague, the cases suggest a few generalizations. First, spurned spouses-to-be could not sue for specific performance. Regardless of the terms of the contract, courts would not force reluctant spouses to register a marriage.[69] Second, spurned spouses-to-be collected damages whose amounts var-

---

[63]Suzuki v. Sugita, 22 Horitsu hyoron min 483 (Tokyo D. Ct. Mar. 17, 1933).

[64]See, e.g., Kaneko v. Inoue, 3194 Horitsu shimbun 9, 20 Horitsu hyoron min 33 (Tokyo Ct. App. Sept. 29, 1930); Yamazaki v. Onagawa, 3833 Horitsu shimbun 4 (Tokyo D. Ct. Apr. 6, 1935); Yamanaka v. Akasaka, 3700 Horitsu shimbun 5 (Osaka D. Ct. May 30, 1934); Seien v. Seien, 2754 Horitsu shimbun 8 (Takase Ward Ct. July 5, 1927).

[65]Hirano v. Miyanouchi, 1404 Horitsu shimbun 21 (Tokyo D. Ct. Apr. 24, 1918).

[66]Seien v. Seien, 2754 Horitsu shimbun 8 (Takase Ward Ct. July 5, 1927).

[67]Tsurui v. Shibata, 3210 Horitsu shimbun 12 (Daishin'in [Supreme Court] Nov. 29, 1930).

[68]Abe v. Ono, 8 Horitsu hyoron min 1086 (Tokyo D. Ct. Sept. 8, 1919).

[69]See, e.g., Kiyama v. Sadaishi, 8 Horitsu hyoron min 541 (Daishin'in [Supreme Court] Apr. 23, 1919); Sugina v. Ono, 10 Horitsu hyoron min 94 (Tokyo Ct. App. Dec. 14, 1920); Makiuchi v. Tsukada, 1237 Horitsu shimbun 21 (Tokyo Ct. App. Feb. 5, 1917); Sakamoto v. Harada, 1160 Horitsu shimbun 28 (Sapporo D. Ct. June 27, 1916).

Table 5.2. *Awards granted women for physical and psychological harm in contract-to-marry cases, where reported decision provides detail about the defendant's assets or income*

| Date | Award | Defendant's status, assets, or income |
|------|-------|----------------------------------------|
| 1920 | ¥500 | Shop with revenues of ¥5 to ¥7/day. |
| 1923 | 150 | 5 to 7.5 acres of agricultural land |
| 1925 | 700 | Income of ¥70/month |
| 1929 | 500 | House and 2.2 acres of agricultural land |
| 1929 | 700 | Salary of ¥42/month and pension of ¥416/year |
| 1929 | 1,000 | "Middle-class" farm family with house and 1.2 to 1.5 acres of agricultural land |
| 1930 | 800 | "Middle-class" farm family with 44 acres of agricultural land |
| 1932 | 7,000 | Member of the peerage |
| 1934 | 700 | 2.5 acres of agricultural land |
| 1934 | 300 | Assets of ¥20,000, and ¥400 to ¥500/year pension |
| 1938 | 1,000 | Physician with ¥200/month income |
| 1941 | 2,500 | Assets of ¥30,000 |

*Note:* Awards are given in nominal amounts, unadjusted for changes in price levels. *Sources:* Chin v. Nakayama, 3734 Horitsu shimbun 11 (Tokyo Ct. App. June 25, 1934), aff'g sub nom. Chin v. Nakayama, 3570 Horitsu shimbun 5 (Tokyo D. Ct. June 17, 1933); Takahashi v. Iwata, 3702 Horitsu shimbun 17 (Tokyo Ct. App. Mar. 8, 1934); Kaneko v. Inoue, 3194 Horitsu shimbun 9 (Tokyo Ct. App. Sept. 29, 1930); Okuma v. Okuma, 19 Horitsu hyoron min 419 (Tokyo Ct. App. Dec. 23, 1929); Sekiguchi v. Iwasaki, 3038 Horitsu shimbun 9 (Tokyo Ct. App. Mar. 22, 1929); Ishizuka v. Shibuya, 13 Horitsu hyoron min 293 (Tokyo Ct. App. Aug. 3, 1923); Oda v. Matsumoto, 4726 Horitsu shimbun 28 (Saga D. Ct. Aug. 1, 1941); Kikuchi v. Arakawa, 4295 Horitsu shimbun 12 (Tokyo Minji D. Ct. Apr. 28, 1938); Harada v. Mizuno, 21 Horitsu hyoron min 1142 (Tokyo D. Ct. Nov. 17, 1932); Sakai v. Nagano, 3076 Horitsu shimbun 12 (Chiba D. Ct. Dec. 23, 1929); Takemoto v. Ishikawa, 14 Horitsu hyoron min 754 (Tokyo D. Ct. Jan. 26, 1925); Yoshida v. Ito, 9 Horitsu hyoron min 264 (Tokyo D. Ct. Mar. 30, 1920).

ied widely, would not support a family comfortably, but were generally substantial nonetheless. Like modern divorce courts in the West, the pre-War Japanese courts determined the compensation by the parties' social, economic, and educational backgrounds. Because they seldom published the wealth or income of the parties, the cases do not disclose the algorithm they used. In most of the cases they reported, however, they awarded damages in the ¥200 to ¥500 range. Table 5.2 reports the closest thing to an algorithm I could construct – the contract damages for physical and emotional distress that courts awarded women in those rare cases I was able to locate where the reported decision gave significant details about the defendant's financial status.

Third, if a spouse-to-be from a rich family seemed to have taken advantage of one from a poor family, the courts awarded particularly large amounts. Although they never said so explicitly, they seem implicitly to have been bound by a sense of noblesse oblige. One of the largest amounts they awarded, for example, was a 1932 award of ¥7,000. The plaintiff was a young servant woman – and her prospective husband was her former employer and a member of the peerage.[70]

Last, spurned women collected more than spurned men.[71] About this, the courts were explicit: They used the "rule of experience that men usually suffer less psychological damage from breach of a contract-to-marry than women."[72] At times, their partiality toward women was almost bizarre. In part, for example, they justified their awards to women as compensation for loss of their virginity. Yet they awarded these amounts even to brides who obviously had not been virgins at the time of the marriage contract. They awarded sizeable loss-of-virginity damages, for example, to divorcées and former geisha.[73]

### 5.2 Asymmetries in divorce

Modern scholars routinely criticize the sexual asymmetries in pre-War divorce law. The "provisions for divorce were weighted heavily in favor of the husband," argues B. J. George Jr. (1965: 511). Susan Pharr (1981:50) concludes, "The Civil Code consistently favored the husband in provisions relating to divorce, marriage, property rights, and other questions coming under family law. Adultery constituted legal grounds for divorce only if committed by the wife."[74] Husbands could sue for divorce if their "wife has committed adultery" (Civil Code, § 813), in other words, but wives could not divorce their husbands for their infidelity. Wives who had

[70]Harada v. Mizuno, 21 Horitsu hyoron min 1142 (Tokyo D. Ct. Nov. 17, 1932). Another unusually high recovery case (¥2,500) involved a factory owner who had agreed to marry one of the workers in his factory. See Oda v. Matsumoto, 4726 Horitsu shimbun 28 (Saga D. Ct. Aug. 1, 1941).

[71]For example, in Suzuki v. Sugita, 22 Horitsu hyoron min 483 (Tokyo D. Ct. Mar. 17, 1933), the court held that the wife had breached the marriage contract in leaving her husband on the grounds that his family treated her badly – but then held her liable for only ¥200 when their out-of-pocket expenses for the wedding alone were ¥1,050.

[72]Ikeda v. Tsuchii, 13 Horitsu hyoron min 495, 496 (Okayama D. Ct. Mar. 30, 1924).

[73]Okaku v. Ushiyama, 3257 Horitsu shimbun 13 (Tokyo Ct. App. Mar. 23, 1931) (divorcée); Ishida v. Morimoto, 20 Horitsu hyoron min 552 (Tokyo D. Ct. Mar. 6, 1931), aff'd sub nom. Fujimoto v. Ishida, 21 Horitsu hyoron min 560 (Tokyo Ct. App. Apr. 7, 1932) (geisha).

[74]See also Garon (1993: 720) ("a husband could sue for divorce if his wife committed adultery, whereas adulterous actions by the husband did not constitute grounds for divorce"); Bernstein (1991a: 8) ("A wife's adultery [but not her husband's] constituted grounds for legal divorce and criminal prosecution").

sexual relations with men other than their husbands (whether married or unmarried) committed a crime (Criminal Code, § 183),[75] but husbands who had sexual relations with unmarried women did not.

*Tort rules.* Such is a simple summary of the statute – but if it seems asymmetrical, in crucial ways the courts vitiated those asymmetries. Most prominently, they did *not* turn a blind eye to a philandering husband. Although a husband who had sex with an unmarried woman did not commit a crime, he commited a tort against his wife. Accordingly, she could sue him for damages. As the Supreme Court explained in 1926:

> For a home to be peaceful, safe, and prosperous, the husband and wife must both remain moral. Accordingly, each spouse owes a duty under the marriage contract to act morally. Should one spouse act immorally and damage the peace, safety, or prosperity of the family, he or she violates the terms of the marriage contract and the rights of the other spouse. Just as a wife owes a duty of chastity to her husband, therefore, a husband owes the same duty of chastity to his wife.
>
> Granted, Civil Code § 813 (c) does not make a husband's adultery grounds for divorce, and Criminal Code § 183 does not make adultery by a man a crime. This, however, was simply a peculiar legislative strategy based on ancient traditions. In no way does it prevent a wife from demanding chastity of her husband under the Civil Code.[76]

Nor was this just high-court theory. Women could – and did – collect damages from their husbands for their adultery.[77] The suits were simply part of a broader legal framework allowing wives to sue their husbands for their torts. Generally, the women collected the money as part of their divorce suits, but they could also sue separately.[78] Where one husband brought in another woman while his wife was away, for example, the court awarded his wife damages for mental distress.[79] Where another maintained a mistress, his wife became incensed, and they divorced by mutual agreement.[80] After divorce, she sued him in tort for the damage to her honor. In granting her the money, the Osaka District Court explained:

[75]*Keiho [Criminal Code]*, Law No. 45 of 1907.

[76]Japan v. [Unnamed], 5 Daihan keishu 318, 325–6 (Daishin'in [Supreme Court] July 20, 1926).

[77]Although married women generally could not sue without their husband's consent, Civil Code, § 12 (d), that restriction did not apply where her husband had interests adverse to hers, id., at § 17(f).

[78]See Hagihara v. Sho, 14 Daihan minroku 340 (Daishin'in [Supreme Court] Mar. 26, 1908).

[79]Ueno v. Ueno, 892 Horitsu shimbun 21 (Tokyo D. Ct. July 14, 1913).

[80]On divorce by mutual agreement, see Bryant (1984).

Both husbands and wives must make honesty the basis of their relationship, and cooperatively promote the peace and prosperity of their life together. If during the course of a marriage a husband makes someone not his wife his mistress, has sexual relations with her, and ignores his wife, he violates customary norms of morality. Not only that, he flagrantly insults his wife and sullies her honor.[81]

Obviously, he must compensate her for the damages she suffers from such a tort. Indeed, suggested the Supreme Court, if a husband mistreated his wife and then refused to agree to an out-of-court divorce, his wrongful refusal itself justified tort damages.[82]

*Divorce rules.* Neither did courts enforce the asymmetries in the Code's divorce rules.[83] Rather, they routinely let women divorce their husbands for adultery.[84] The rule was clearest where a husband lived with another woman. Consistently and repeatedly, the courts held that his wife could

[81]Tsujimoto v. Hirai, 2889 Horitsu shimbun 13, 15 (Osaka D. Ct. July 25, 1928).

[82]Hagihara v. Sho, 14 Daihan minroku 340 (Daishin'in [Supreme Court] Mar. 26, 1908) (where husband commits a "grievous insult").

[83]Moreover, part of the asymmetry disappears in a closer reading of § 813 itself. According to § 813 (c), a wife can sue for divorce if her husband is sentenced for "illicit sexual intercourse." Because sex with a married woman was a crime, even by the terms of the Civil Code itself a husband could safely have had sexual relations without risking divorce only if he had sex with an *un*married woman. See de Becker (1921: 526 n.*).

[84]Adultery was not the sole, or even the principal, misconduct for which women could divorce their husbands. For example, courts routinely held that a wife could divorce a husband who beat her (even if he beat her only once). See, e.g., Hisata v. Hisata, 1849 Horitsu shimbun 17 (Tokyo Ct. App. Apr. 11, 1921); [No names given], 627 Horitsu shimbun 17 (Daishin'in [Supreme Court] Feb. 2, 1910); [No names given], 533 Horitsu shimbun 18 (Daishin'in [Supreme Court] Oct. 10, 1908); Shichida v. Shichida, 13 Daihan minroku 580 (Daishin'in [Supreme Court] May 24, 1907); Murooka v. Murooka, 287 Horitsu shimbun 17 (Daishin'in [Supreme Court] No date, journal issue of June 25, 1905); Haneda v. Haneda, 2049 Horitsu shimbun 20 (Tokyo Ct. App. June 13, 1921); Hanetomi v. Hanetomi, 1144 Horitsu shimbun 20 (Tokyo Ct. App. May 19, 1916); Ohashi v. Ohashi, 1605 Horitsu shimbun 17 (Tokyo D. Ct. June 25, 1919); Sekine v. Sekine, 981 Horitsu shimbun 18 (Tokyo D. Ct. Oct. 30, 1914).

Courts also recognized many other grounds for divorce. For example, if an irate husband falsely reported to the police that his wife had committed adultery, the wife could divorce him. See, e.g., Hayashi v. Hayashi, 666 Horitsu shimbun 13 (Tokyo Ct. App. No date, journal issue of Sept. 20, 1910) (public accusation of adultery); Saito v. Saito, 659 Horitsu shimbun 12 (Osaka D. Ct. No date, journal issue of Aug. 15, 1910) (same); Yano v. Yano, 564 Horitsu shimbun 18 (Osaka Ct. App. Mar. 23, 1909) (same); Nonoyama v. Nonoyama, 321 Horitsu shimbun 11 (Tokyo Ct App. Nov. 20, 1905) (initiation of burglary investigation to frame wife); Makita v. Makita, 516 Horitsu shimbun 23 (Tokyo D. Ct. No date, journal issue of Aug. 20, 1908) (public accusation of adultery). Likewise, if he wrote sufficiently insulting letters to her relatives, she could divorce him. See, e.g., Sugimura v. Sugimura, 1285 Horitsu shimbun 23 (Tokyo Ct. App. Apr. 26, 1917); Shiokawa v. Shiokawa, 1211 Horitsu shimbun 23 (Tokyo Ct. App. Dec. 14, 1916).

properly sue for divorce. Under § 813 (e) of the Code, she could divorce her husband if she "received from the other spouse either abuse making cohabitation intolerable or a grievous insult." According to the courts, a husband who lived with another woman committed just that insult.[85]

Often, however, the courts let a wife divorce her husband for adultery even if he did not live with his lover. Granted, they did not recognize all one-night stands as grievous insults. Rather, they demanded sexual relations with "something more" before they would grant a divorce for the husband's adultery. That "something," though, could range from an illegitimate child to the wife's own sensitivity about adultery.

For example, in 1908 a court granted a wife a divorce on the grounds that her husband had fathered two children by their adoptive daughter (in Japan, parents often adopt sons and daughters as adults).[86] In 1922 a court let a wife divorce her husband on the grounds that the husband had fathered children by two of their housemaids.[87] And in 1930, a court granted a divorce on the grounds simply that the husband had kept a mistress. Although he had been married to his wife for several years, they still had no children. He needed an heir, he explained. The Tokyo Court of Appeals (the most prestigious court after the Supreme Court) rejected the explanation:

> The appellant [husband] notes that although he has been married to the appellee [wife] for over eight years, they do not have a child. Although he began to keep a mistress and have sexual relations with her, he argues that his conduct should be judged by those traditional norms that recognize the importance of continuing the male line of family heads. In modern society, however, such norms have been transmitted merely as historical artifacts.
>
> Marriage is a union of one man and one woman for the purpose of living

---

[85]See, e.g., Iida v. Iida, 2976 Horitsu shimbun 14 (Daishin'in [Supreme Court] Mar. 1, 1929) (holding, moreover, that wife could bring such suit even where she was already cohabiting with someone else herself); Tanshi v. Tanshi, 24 Daihan minroku 2365 (Daishin'in [Supreme Court] Dec. 19, 1918); Hayashida v. Hayashida, 2042 Horitsu shimbun 26 (Tokyo Ct. App. July 3, 1922); Shinozuka v. Shinozuka, 1550 Horitsu shimbun 20 (Tokyo Ct. App. Apr. 2, 1919); Okamoto v. Okamoto, 774 Horitsu shimbun 22 (Osaka Ct. App. Feb. 9, 1912); Fukumori v. Fukumori, 687 Horitsu shimbun 24 (Osaka Ct. App. Oct. 19, 1910); Moriyama v. Moriyama, 2651 Horitsu shimbun 9 (Oita D. Ct. Nov. 29, 1926); Ueno v. Ueno, 892 Horitsu shimbun 21 (Tokyo D. Ct. July 14, 1913); Saito v. Saito, 659 Horitsu shimbun 12 (Osaka D. Ct. No date, journal issue of Aug. 15, 1910); Matsuo v. Matsuo, 623 Horitsu shimbun 21 (Kobe D. Ct. No date, journal issue of Feb. 15, 1910); Yoshihama v. Yoshihama, 566 Horitsu shimbun 13 (Yokohama D. Ct. No date, journal issue of Apr. 30, 1909); Kashiwagi v. Kashiwagi, 557 Horitsu shimbun 9 (Osaka D. Ct. No date, journal issue of Mar. 15, 1909).

[86]Kogane v. Kogane, 492 Horitsu shimbun 16 (Tokyo D. Ct. No date, journal issue of Apr. 20, 1908). On the adoption of adults, see Bryant (1990).

[87]Iijima v. Iijima, 2330 Horitsu shimbun 17 (Tokyo Ct. App. July 3, 1922).

together as a couple. It does not necessarily have as its purpose the raising of children. Accordingly, one spouse may not violate his or her duty of truth and fidelity in order to have sexual relations with another merely because his or her marriage is childless. This rule follows from both legal principles and general social norms.[88]

Apparently, moreover, adultery mattered most when the wife cared most. In 1924, the Supreme Court permitted a wife to divorce her husband where all he did was have sexual relations with another woman after he knew his wife was sensitive about the issue. The court explained:

The appellee wife had become indignant and mentally unstable after the appellant [husband] had sexual relations with another woman. As a result, the appellant had special reason to exercize sexual prudence with respect to his wife. He refused to change his ways, however, had sexual relations with his servant, and treated his wife coldly. Given his behavior, she had no choice but to return to her parents' home. Ultimately, his behavior constitutes both a grievous insult and abuse making cohabitation intolerable.[89]

Furthermore, the courts did not necessarily give divorcing fathers custody of the children. Again, scholars do argue the contrary. "In cases of divorce," historian Gail Lee Bernstein (1991a: 8) unambiguously declares, "the husband took custody of the children." Pharr (1981: 50) flatly concludes that "[w]hen there was a dispute over the custody of a child, the wishes of the husband prevailed." In fact, however, the Code mandated two basic rules. First, if the parties negotiated custody in their divorce agreement, the courts were to enforce that agreement (§ 812). Second, if the parties could not agree on the issue, the courts were to look to the best interests of the child (§ 819). Under the latter test, they could – and did – sometimes give custody to the mother.[90]

## 6   CONCLUSION

In several fundamental ways, imperial Japanese family law did not create the hierarchical world that observers usually describe. First, the family head could not force other members to live where he pleased. Instead, if they refused to obey him, all he could do was to try to expel them from the family registry, and to refuse to support them economically. Crucially,

---

[88]Tanaka v. Tanaka, 3087 Horitsu shimbun 9, 11 (Tokyo Ct. App. Dec. 20, 1929).

[89]Kajita v. Kajita, 2254 Horitsu shimbun 15, 16 (Daishin'in [Supreme Court] Mar. 19, 1924).

[90]See, e.g., Ichikawa v. Ota, 4726 Horitsu shimbun 19 (Daishin'in [Supreme Court] Sept. 9, 1941); Araki v. Takahashi, 17 Daihan minshu 378 (Daishin'in [Supreme Court] Mar. 9, 1938); Morishita v. Morinaga, 2 Daihan minshu 642 (Daishin'in [Supreme Court] Nov. 29, 1923); Suzuki v. Suzuki, 3540 Horitsu shimbun 6, 20 (Tokyo D. Ct. Mar. 6, 1933). On custody generally, see Suginohara (1940: 138–46).

though, he could expel them only when he could prove that his initial order that they move was "necessary" for the good of the house; his duty to support them was minimal; and most family members planned eventually to leave the family anyway.

Second, the family head could not veto a member's marriage choice. Instead, the rule tracked the residence rules. If a member married against the head's wishes, the head could remove him or her from the family registry – and no more. Upon marriage, however, virtually all children but the oldest son left the family anyway.

Third, the family head did not need to pass all his property to his oldest son. Should he want to divide his estate among all his children, he was free to pass up to half his estate to those other than the next family head. And a man or woman who was not a family head (if he or she had more than one child) could not pass all the property to the oldest son even if he or she wished.

Last, a husband and his family had far less power over a bride than usually noted. If the family found the bride unsatisfactory, even if the marriage was not yet legal they could not freely send her home. If they tried, she could sue them for damages to her psyche. If a husband misbehaved, he did not face divorce rules heavily biased in his favor. Instead, just as he could divorce his wife if she committed adultery, she could often divorce him for adultery as well. Again, she could sue him for damages to her psyche or honor.

Imperial Japan was not a world where hierarchical families would have facilitated household production, and the law the courts enforced was not one that imposed hierarchical families. Imperial Japan was not a world where rules that let husbands exploit their wives would have facilitated household production either, and the law did not let husbands exploit wives. Rather, the Civil Code let Japanese choose the family structure they wanted, and let wives rely on the law to protect them. That individual autonomy which the labor market gave individuals in practice, the Civil Code largely guaranteed them by law.

# 6

## Promissory credibility: Sex

### INTRODUCTION

Few industries tug as strongly at the heartstrings as the sexual services industry. Take the tales social historian Mikiso Hane tells. A "growing chasm" separated rich and poor in pre-War Japan (1982, 34), he writes. "[T]he condition of the peasants remained pathetic in contrast with the growing well-being of bourgeois capitalists," and peasants found themselves waging "a bitter struggle for survival" (id., at 31, 27). Within this impoverished world, some of "the most pitiful victims . . . were the young farm girls who were sold to brothels" (id., at 207).

Unfortunately, the poignancy masks the ingenuity with which prostitutes and brothel owners overcame the chronic informational asymmetries in the contracting process. In most industries, prospective employees know their own productivity better than employers; employers know their own operations better than employees; both have an incentive to lie; and both would do best if both could communicate honestly. Given that most employers and employees care what others say about them, reputational effects mitigate some of these problems. Often, however, employers and employees can – and do – draft labor contracts to reduce any remaining informational problems. In the sexual services industry, they drafted those contracts with a remarkable resourcefulness.

In the following two chapters, I consider two issues central to the thesis in this book: narrowly – how did workers and employers respond to such informational asymmetries in the labor market; and more broadly – how independently and selfishly did they behave? To explore these questions, I study two very different industries. In Chapter 7, I explore how workers and employers dealt with informational problems in one of the largest labor markets in imperial Japan: the market for workers in the cotton-spinning factories. In this chapter, I trace the way they dealt with them in the legal sexual services market: a smaller market, perhaps an odder market and a market said to be plagued by the market failures that so many scholars so readily conclude characterized imperial Japan.[1]

Consider the basic informational problem in the legal sexual services industry. The brothel owner knew the market for prostitutes, and could estimate with reasonable accuracy how well any woman would do. The would-be prostitute knew her own proclivity to exert effort, but did not know the market. She knew that the brothel owner (and his recruiter) had an incentive to exaggerate her future earnings. And she knew she could not cheaply test the market to verify his promises. If she could have tested it these problems would not have much mattered. Yet because a woman suffered a large one-time reputational loss by becoming a prostitute, she could not cheaply do so. Necessarily, she had to make her job choice without verifiable information.

To address these problems, the legal brothels and prostitutes negotiated long-term indentured servitude contracts. Under these deals, the prostitutes received a large payment up-front – payment sufficient to compensate them for a large portion of their one-time reputational loss. The brothel, in turn, used the contracts to make its promises of future high wages credible. And to mitigate the obvious incentive problems that up-front payments created, the parties gave the prostitutes the right to quit early if they worked hard. I begin this chapter by outlining the pre-War prostitution industry (Section 1) and tracing the evolution of its regulatory scheme (Section 2). I then reconstruct the contractual arrangements themselves (Section 3).

## I  SCHOLARS AND PROSTITUTES

Most scholars explain pre-War Japanese prostitution through what they consider "exploitative" economic growth. Hane's account (quoted at the start of the chapter) is typical. Anthropologist Liza Dalby tells a similar story about the licensed entertainer-prostitutes known as geisha. The geisha, she writes, lived decent lives only compared with the lives ordinary licensed prostitutes (*shogi*) lived: "Dreadful as life was for [the geisha,] they were yet better off than the girls who were sent not to geisha houses but to brothels" (1985: 222).

In part, argues Dalby, that dreadfulness resulted from the way the geisha house used indenture contracts to tie the women to it. Like so many scholars of prostitution in different societies and in different peri-

---

[1] I have largely omitted any discussion of the illegal sector for two reasons: the data are less complete, and the contracts – being criminal – do not raise the contractual issues that are the focus of this chapter.

ods,[2] she claims that the Japanese house owners manipulated the contracts to turn prostitution into debt peonage – and keep the women working beyond the original term. Trapped by "unscrupulous owners who charged the inmates exorbitant rates for room and board, intentionally keeping them in a state of dependence," the geisha worked in "virtual captivity."[3]

Just as in the late twentieth century, such stories sold newspapers and magazines in the early twentieth century. Reporters made the most of them, and routinely wrote of naive women tricked by usurious brothel owners into a life of vice, and tied there by a debt that increased by the month. It was thinly disguised slavery, they argued, and the government should ban it. Such stories apparently also win professorial fame, for prominent scholars have routinely repeated them as well. According to Takeyoshi Kawashima again, the prostitutes were caught in "slavery" through "the power of the patriarchal family system" (1950a: 89; 1955).

The facts were less dramatic. Many families were poor in pre-War Japan. The international depression hit the country early and hard; it hit parts of the countryside especially hard.[4] Given the alternatives, some peasant women chose to become prostitutes. Those who did so earned (what were for them) very high wages. Often, they contracted to stay at a brothel for several years, and collected much of those wages in advance.

The family (*not* a "patriarchal family system," as Chapter 5 shows) had little noticeable effect on this sexual services market. Fathers did not have the legal power to rent their daughters to brothels. Indeed, according to the courts, those who tried necessarily "abused their parental right." Poverty and family destitution were no defense, and they could lose custody over their daughters on that ground alone.[5] Nor did most fathers have the power to rent their daughters extra-legally. As Chapter 3 shows, the large urban market for nonseasonal labor had created a market predominantly for one's *own* labor. By the early Meiji period, most parents could *not* have controlled the labor of their children even had they tried. Instead, children controlled their own labor.

---

[2]E.g., Corbin (1990: 78) (France); Harsin (1985: 293) (France); O'Callaghan (1968: 13) (China); Rosen (1982: 130) (United States).

[3]Dalby (1985: 221). Contrary to Dalby, most women received room and board free. See Sec. 3, *infra*.

[4]See the trend in farm household income in Table 6.2, *infra*. Scholars have often exaggerated this poverty, however, as Smethurst (1986) rightly points out.

[5]Yoshida v. Hamashima, 1954 Horitsu shimbun 9 (Nagasaki Ct. App. Feb. 6, 1922); see also Matsumoto v. Matsumoto, 287 Horitsu shimbun 16 (Tokyo Ct. App. June 16, 1905) (attempt by adoptive parents to force adopted daughter into geisha work is grounds for severing adoption).

Largely (obviously not always), they worked where they wanted and kept what they earned.[6]

By 1924, Japan had 550 licensed red-light districts, 50,100 licensed prostitutes, and 11,500 licensed brothels. These brothels were substantial businesses, not street-corner pimps. Most typically, they served food and drink besides sex, and were large fifteen- to sixteen-room establishments that carried four to seven prostitutes and six to ten additional employees on staff. In addition, Japan had 77,100 licensed geisha. The number of unlicensed (and hence illegal) prostitutes is less clear, but one otherwise reliable observer placed the figure at about 50,000. With a population of 59.7 million, Japan apparently had one prostitute for every 350 people. In the city of Kyoto, the figure was one for every 150.[7] By contrast, in the modern United States, scholars estimate the figure at one for every 650 to 900 (Symanski, 1981: 10).

The women who became prostitutes were not women with access to good jobs. Most licensed prostitutes were badly educated. Notwithstanding that all were at least age eighteen, half had fewer than five years' education and 16 percent had not been to school at all[8] – this at a time when 99 percent of all Japanese primary-school-age children (grades one to six) were in school (Minami, 1986: 19). Such unskilled and unedu-

---

[6]In addition, note the following. First, even though prostitutes could legally quit whenever they pleased (Section 2.2, *infra*), most worked until they had either repaid their debt or served their full term. From 1927 to 1929, for example, only about 1% of all licensed prostitutes quit their work without the brothel owner's consent (Ito, 1931: 213–14). Yet because their parents had signed the indenture contract, the only real cost to quitting was that they and their parents became liable on the note. And if their parents had forced them into prostitution, their parents would have taken the advance, and the prostitutes themselves would have been left judgment-proof.

Effectively, then, the prostitutes' only real risk to quitting was that the brothel owner would seize their parents' assets. As a result, women forced into prostitution by abusive parents could have walked away from their jobs, left their parents to repay the debt, and faded into the anonymity of metropolitan Tokyo. If large numbers of parents coerced their daughters into prostitution against their will, one would expect a significant number of women to do so regularly – to abandon the job and opt for that anonymity over the job they had learned to despise and their parents who had sold them into it. Almost none, however, ever did so.

Second, one would also expect the reformist organizations to assert that the women were being coerced into the jobs. Yet even according to the Salvation Army, only 31% of the women it "rescued" from industry in 1930 (necessarily among the most dissatisfied of all the prostitutes) reported that they had been induced to take the jobs by their parents (Seikaku, 1931b).

[7]The figures are from Fukumi (1928: 26–8, 32, 50–6, 178). Fukumi estimates the total number of licensed and unlicensed prostitutes at 174,000 in the mid-1920s. Nakamura (1954: 222–3) places the total at 276,000. See also Kusama (1930: 14–26).

[8]Fukumi (1928: 66–8) (Tokyo data); Ito (1931: 204); Kusama (1930: 100–3). Licensed prostitutes were required by law to be at least eighteen years old. Naimu sho rei No. 44 of Oct. 2, 1900, § 1.

cated workers generally faced jobs with long hours and low pay. Consider one survey of twelve- to eighteen-year-old night-school students. That they found time for school suggests they worked shorter hours than most. Nonetheless, among those with factory jobs, the modal student worked ten hours a day. Among those with commercial jobs, the modal student worked twelve hours. Of all students, only 13 percent worked fewer than twenty-eight days per month.[9] As Table 6.1 shows, prostitutes on average had 2.54 customers per night in 1924,[10] and likewise worked about twenty-eight nights per month.[11] Prostitution was harsh work. But the alternatives were not easy.

And prostitution paid well. Consider Table 6.2: from 1926 to 1932, prostitute earnings averaged 179 percent of the mean female factory worker's wage[12] and 53 percent of the total mean income of farm households (an average of both landlords and tenants).[13] Oliver Williamson (1985: 35–8) and Price Fishback (1992) recently discussed how American miners demanded higher wages when coal companies provided un-

---

[9]I.e., only 13% had more than two days off per month (Shakai, 1936: 23–5). This is roughly consistent with Ohsato's data for the country as a whole: in 1926, workers in manufacturing industries worked 10.32 hours per day, 27.1 days per month. Ohsato (1966: 58–61); see also Naikaku tokei (1930: 109, 122) (similar figures).

[10]Other estimates roughly confirm these figures. See Maeda v. Yanadani, 841 Horitsu shimbun 21, 22 (Tokyo Ct. App. Nov. 14, 1912) (70–100 customers per month); Uemura (1929: 492–501) (similar figures for urban prostitutes); Kusama (1930: 220–1) (2.54 customers per night in Tokyo, 1924). On the other hand, the figures for the city of Osaka for 1913–15 range from 0.72 customers per night to 0.78. See Uemura (1918: 33–4). By contrast, Corbin (1990: 81) cites studies of the French licensed quarters indicating 4–8 or more clients per night; see Harsin (1985: 283) (even higher figure for France).

[11]In 1924, customers made 4.20 million visits to 4,989 licensed prostitutes in Tokyo. At 2.54 customers per prostitute per working night in 1924, that leads to 331 working days per prostitute. See Table 6.1.

[12]During this period, mean annual wages for all factory workers were: 1926 – ¥554, 1927 – ¥632, 1928 – ¥657, 1929 – ¥666, 1930 – ¥650, 1931 – ¥605, and 1932 – ¥580. See Ohsato (1966: 60, 69). Female factory workers made 30% to 40% of the male wage, though observers argued that much of that difference disappeared when adjustments were made for age, work experience, and tenure on the job; see Rodosho (1952: 14–17). On the wages of women in cotton-spinning factories, see Table 7.8, *infra*.

The Table 6.1 and 6.2 figures on prostitute income are based on data the government required brothel owners to submit, and reliability is an obvious issue. Nonetheless, although the data were widely reported in the pre-War studies of the industry, I know of no abolitionists who complained that the figures were inaccurate. To the contrary, abolitionists themselves used income figures that were quite close. See, e.g., Ito (1931: 229–30). Their quarrel was not with the amount of income, but with whether, given that income, prostitutes could live within it. See Section 3.4, *infra*.

[13]Most prostitutes, of course, came from households with below-average incomes. Note that in 1926–7, farm households had a mean monthly income of ¥96.2. Landowning households had income of ¥112.5, and tenant families had an income of ¥79.2. See Naikaku tokei (1930: 352).

Table 6.1. *Licensed prostitutes in Tokyo – workload and income*

| | A<br>Total<br>customer<br>visits | B<br>Total<br>licensed<br>prostitutes | C<br>Per visit<br>customer<br>expenditure | D<br>Mean<br>daily<br>customers | E<br>Mean<br>annual<br>income |
|---|---|---|---|---|---|
| 1922 | 4,481,000 | 5,995 | ¥4.79 | 2.05 | ¥492 |
| 1923* | 1,096,000 | 3,363 | 4.11 | 3.04 | 263 |
| 1924 | 4,199,000 | 4,989 | 4.68 | 2.54 | 878 |
| 1925 | 3,744,000 | 5,159 | 4.27 | 1.99 | 656 |
| 1926 | 3,944,000 | 5,291 | 3.75 | 2.09 | 641 |
| 1927 | 4,222,000 | 5,732 | 3.77 | 2.14 | 658 |
| 1928 | 4,698,000 | 6,132 | 3.74 | 2.12 | 660 |
| 1929 | 4,183,000 | 6,417 | 3.62 | 1.86 | 554 |
| 1930 | 4,014,000 | 6,794 | 3.08 | 1.71 | 430 |
| 1931 | 4,615,000 | 7,156 | 2.59 | 1.77 | 406 |

*Notes:* (A) Total visits by customers to a licensed prostitute in Tokyo. (B) Licensed prostitutes in Tokyo. (C) Mean amount spent by customer per visit for all expenses, including sex, food, drink, and other entertainment. (D) Mean number of customer visits per prostitute per working night. (E) Mean income of prostitutes in licensed brothels, before repayment of indenture principal, stated at current prices unadjusted for changes in price levels.
*1923 data are unreliable because of the disruption and loss of records caused by the catastrophic earthquake of that year.
*Source:* Keishi cho sokan kanbo bunsho ka, *Showa nana nen keishi cho tokei ichi ippan [An Outline of Police Agency Statistics for 1932]* (Tokyo: Keishi cho sokan kanbo bunsho ka, 1933), pp. 93–8.

sanitary or unsafe conditions; Clark Nardinelli (1982) showed how British children earned higher wages when a factory used corporal punishment. Much the same logic applied in Japan. Japanese peasant women faced an array of options, among which a job as a prostitute was one of the most unpleasant and stigmatizing. In exchange for taking the job, they demanded – and received – high pay. According to one 1934 sample of female workers from a northern prefecture, young women who left home to work earned room and board plus a mean ¥884 per year as a licensed prostitute, ¥575 as a geisha, ¥518 as a bar maid (a job that often involved prostitution), ¥210 as a waitress (also often involving some sex), and ¥130 in other jobs.[14] Ultimately, many more women

[14]Akita prefecture. The figures for Miyagi prefecture were ¥315 for a licensed prostitute, ¥337 for a geisha, ¥187 for a bar maid, ¥132 for a waitress, ¥107 for a factory worker, and ¥78 for work as a maid or child-care worker. Most of these employers probably provided room and board in addition to these wages. Shakai (1935: 160–1). As the sampling techniques are not clear from the these documents, these data should be treated with more caution than the aggregate amounts reported in

Table 6.2. *Mean annual income of female factory workers, farm households, and licensed Tokyo prostitutes*

| | A Factory workers[a] | B Farm households[b] | C Licensed prostitutes[c] | C/A | C/B |
|---|---|---|---|---|---|
| 1926 | ¥312 | ¥1,433 | ¥641 | 2.05 | 0.447 |
| 1927 | 320 | 1,183 | 658 | 2.06 | 0.556 |
| 1928 | 322 | 1,361 | 660 | 2.05 | 0.484 |
| 1929 | 320 | 1,201 | 554 | 1.73 | 0.461 |
| 1930 | 289 | 810 | 430 | 1.49 | 0.531 |
| 1931 | 260 | 552 | 406 | 1.56 | 0.736 |
| 1932 | 245 | 644 | 388 | 1.58 | 0.602 |

*Notes:* Prostitutes also received free room and board; many factory workers did not. Prostitute incomes are incomes *before* any repayment of the indenture principal.
[a]Calculated from daily wage rages. The daily wages are stated at current prices unadjusted for changes in price levels, and are from Rodosho fujin shonen kyoku, *Fujin rodo no jitsujo [The Reality of Female Labor]* (Tokyo: Rodosho, 1952), p. 14. The number of workdays per month are taken from Katsuma Ohsato, *Meiji iko honpo shuyo keizai tokei [Principal Economic Statistics for our Nation since the Meiji Period]* (Tokyo: Bank of Japan, 1966), p. 60.
[b]Somu cho tokei kyoku, *Nihon choki tokei soran [General Long-term Statistics for Japan]*, vol. 4 (Tokyo: Somu cho, 1987), table 18–5-a.
[c]Taken from Table 6.1.

looked for a position as a licensed prostitute than found one: from 1920 to 1927, only 62 percent of the women applying for work as licensed prostitutes in Tokyo found jobs (Chuo shokugyo, 1926: 381–2; Kusama, 1930: 27–30, 36).

Through its licensing scheme, the government effectively created three overlapping hierarchical tiers in the industry: licensed geisha, licensed prostitutes, and unlicensed prostitutes. The geisha were licensed as entertainers, and could not legally market their sexual services. They entered the industry with better educational backgrounds than the licensed prostitutes, and (in theory) took extensive training in singing, dancing, and witty repartee.[15] Although they sang, danced, and chatted for money, most (by one 1930 study, about 80 percent) also traded sexual services for money (Kusama, 1930: 5, 20; Fukumi, 1928: 234).

Tables 6.1 and 6.2 – a point confirmed by the divergence between the figures for Akita and Miyagi prefectures. For evidence of high prostitute incomes in the West, see Rosen (1982: 147–8); Mustang (1989).
[15]Dalby (1985). By one study, 92% of the geisha had completed at least primary school. Of the licensed prostitutes, only 42% had completed at least five of the six primary school years, and 16% had had no schooling at all. Fukumi (1928: 66–8; 216–17).

115

Much below the highest-grade geisha came the licensed and unlicensed prostitutes, women without the geisha's pretense to art. For several reasons, customers preferred the licensed prostitutes to the unlicensed. First, the licensed women probably invested in a reputation for providing high-quality service. They could sell sex legally, and worked for a firm that could market their services legally. As a result, they could safely make such investments. By contrast, unlicensed prostitutes worked under the constant threat that the police would interrupt their careers and close their employer.[16]

Second, the licensed prostitutes were healthier. Licensed brothels at least screened their recruits for contagious diseases, had weekly medical inspections, and maintained special arrangements with designated clinics. Although the medical records are problematic, contemporary studies consistently showed a much lower incidence of venereal disease among the licensed prostitutes than among the unlicensed.[17] Even the abolitionists reported in 1931 that less than 2 percent of the licensed prostitutes had venereal disease (Seikaku, 1931a).

Finally, customers apparently considered the licensed prostitutes physically more attractive. First, many of the unlicensed prostitutes were women no licensed brothel would hire (Kusama, 1930: 37). Second, many unlicensed prostitutes were older. Although customers seem to have preferred women in their late teens and early twenties (by law, licensed prostitutes were at least eighteen, *Naimu sho rei* No. 44 of Oct. 2, 1900, §1), the unlicensed sector included a larger portion of women in their late twenties and early thirties than did the licensed sector (Fukumi, 1928: 59, 144).

Whatever the reasons, prices reflected this consumer preference for the licensed prostitutes over the unlicensed. In the late 1920s, the "special" (highest) grade licensed prostitute in the Yoshiwara district of Tokyo charged ¥14–17 for a full night's assignation, and the fifth (lowest)

---

[16]See Klein & Leffler (1981). On the prohibition of unlicensed prostitution, see *Gyosei shikko ho [Administrative Enforcement Act]*, Law No. 84 of June 1, 1900, §3; *Naimu sho rei* No. 16 of Sept. 29, 1908, §1.

[17]See Keishi cho (1933: 143); Uemura (1918: 47). In 1932, these inspections of licensed prostitutes in Tokyo resulted in findings of disease in 3.22% of the cases. Keishi cho (1933: 143). Of the positive diagnoses, 41.7% were of gonorrhea, 26.2% of chancroid, and 7.6% of syphilis. Id. at 144. Inspections of unlicensed prostitutes resulted in findings of disease in 9.7% of the cases. Id.

Other statistics confirm this difference between licensed and unlicensed infection rates. In a 1927 government study, for example, 32% of the unlicensed prostitutes had venereal disease, but only 2.1% of the licensed prostitutes. Kusama (1930: 288, 291). A third study found an even larger difference: 2.8% of the licensed prostitutes (in 1924), compared to over 40% of the unlicensed prostitutes (in 1925–6). Fukumi (1928: 93, 168–9) (any communicable diseases). See also Chuo shokugyo (1926: 433–5) (similar statistics).

grade licensed prostitute charged ¥6 for a full night. By contrast, the unlicensed prostitutes in the Tamanoi and Kameido areas charged ¥3–5 for a night (Kusama, 1930: 230–1, 242).

## 2 THE REGULATION OF SEX

### 2.1 *The decrees*

Prostitutes used indenture arrangements that were subject to a nineteenth-century regulatory scheme. As explained in the Introduction, American gunboats had forced open Japanese ports in 1853, and the Western nations had imposed on the Japanese oligarchs various "un-equal" treaties. Determined to eliminate these agreements, the government leaders set out to adopt the trappings of Western "sophistication."

In 1872, their chance arrived. A Peruvian ship named the *Maria Luz* sailed into Yokohama harbor for repairs with 231 Chinese coolies hired under eight-year indenture contracts.[18] One jumped overboard and swam to a nearby English gunship. Unsure what to do, the English captain sent him to the local English consulate. The consulate in turn contacted the Japanese Foreign Ministry, and the Ministry called a local judge.

The time seemed perfect to prove Japanese sophistication. The judge did his best, and declared that international trafficking in human beings violated public international law. When Peru objected, the imperial Russian court intervened as arbitrator and backed the Japanese. But the ploy backfired. In the middle of the proceedings, the lawyer for the Peruvian ship declared that Japanese kept their own slaves. Japanese brothels were full, he insisted, of indentured women who were no freer than the coolies.

Embarrassed, the Japanese government immediately liberated all indentured prostitutes. The women could return home, and courts would entertain no suits on their debt.[19] To implement the decree, the Ministry of Justice issued its own regulation:

Indenture contracts rob people of their rights and reduce them to horses and cattle. As one cannot demand that horses and cattle repay their debts, neither can one demand that prostitutes and geisha repay their indenture amounts.[20]

The regulation became infamous for its metaphor, but the point at least was clear: women could leave the brothels and keep the money the broth-

---

[18]For more elaborate accounts, as well as complete versions of the court and arbitration decisions, see Ito (1931: 107–32); see also Stewart (1951: chs. 7–8); Gardiner (1975: ch. 1).

[19]Dajokan fukoku No. 295, § 4, Oct. 2, 1872. The principal national decrees and regulations relating to prostitution are reproduced as a legal appendix in Yamamoto (1983: 747–67).

[20]Shiho sho tatsu No. 22, § 2, Oct. 9, 1872.

el owners had advanced them. Newspapers reported prostitutes loading their effects on to carts and rickshaws, and leaving the brothels in droves (Nakamura, 1954: 174). They may not have abandoned prostitution, but they had every reason to abandon the particular establishment from which they had already received their wages in advance.

Nonetheless, the 1872 decree did not ban prostitution. It merely voided the indenture contracts. By the end of the year, the city of Osaka had adopted a "room rental" licensing scheme to make clear that prostitution was still legal, and other cities soon followed suit. The prostitute was a licensed "independent contractor" under this system, and the brothel was a "room rental service." By 1875, the national government had decided to permit indentures again. Sales of human beings were illegal, it explained, and mortgages of humans were no better. Yet it followed those bans with a cryptic distinction – arrangements where a debtor repaid a debt through a fixed-period labor contract were legal.[21] Once again, indenture contracts were valid.

## 2.2   The courts

For all this earlier confusion, by the turn of the century the courts made clear the legal status of the indenture contracts.[22] In 1896, the Supreme Court announced part of that legal status – the personal service contract itself was necessarily void. Iki Kushi had apparently agreed to work as a prostitute for several years, but now wanted to quit. The Court let her do so. No matter what the financial relations between the parties might be, it held, the personal service contract was an independent agreement. It cited the 1872 decree banning indentures (but not the 1875 decree allowing them) and held:

We see no evidence that the promisor [prostitute] intended to abandon her personal freedom. Even had she so intended, she had no capacity to make such a binding agreement. Hence, the promisee [brothel] can enforce this contract only in ways it can enforce any other contract – in ways that do not bind the person of the promisor.[23]

Four years later, the Supreme Court explained how a disgruntled prostitute could quit. Although she could not leave the brothel unless the

[21]Dajokan fukoku No. 128, Aug. 14, 1875; see Nakamura (1954: 171–8); Yamamoto (1983). In 1900, the government adopted the "room rental" licensing scheme on a national scale. See Naimu sho rei No. 44, Oct. 2, 1900; Keishi cho rei No. 37, Sept. 6, 1900, discussed in Yamamoto (1983: 372–80).

[22]On the case law governing the indentures, see generally Nishimura (1938); Nomi (1980); Kawashima (1955); Wagatsuma (1923, 1955); Yonekura (1985).

[23]Musashino v. Kushi, 2–3 Daihan minroku 50, 52 (Daishin'in [Supreme Court] Mar. 11, 1896).

owner added his seal to her petition to deregister herself as a licensed prostitute, she could force him to do so.[24] Futa Itai had agreed to work for thirty months, but wanted to quit early. The court cited the 1872 law, and noted its 1896 opinion. It had already held such long-term service contracts unenforceable, it declared. If the woman needed the brothel owner's seal to quit, she could compel him to affix it.[25]

In refusing to enforce the personal service agreement, the Supreme Court distinguished the accompanying loan agreement. Never mind that it voided the personal service agreement by citing the 1872 decree – which explicitly declared the loan unenforceable. The Court effectively transformed the indenture contract into two severable contracts: an employment contract and a loan contract. The former it held void, and the latter valid.

For example, on an advance of ¥600, Kei Takahashi became a geisha but quit before the end of her three-year term. Where the lower court ruled the loan as well as the indenture term void as against the public order and good morals, the Supreme Court held the loan enforceable:

When a contract prescribing the method of repaying a loan is held to be void either as against the public order and good morals or for other reasons, the creditor will not receive repayment by the specified method. It does not follow, however, that the loan agreement is void and that the obligor has no duty to repay the debt.[26]

Courts occasionally held to the contrary. On the one hand, some courts enforced the personal service contract. Where one sixteen-year-old enlisted at a geisha house for six years, for example, a district court refused to let her quit. "For a sixteen-year-old who must learn the arts of the geisha," it wrote, "six years is not necessarily long." As the length and other terms were reasonable, the house could enforce the contract.[27]

On the other hand, some courts held even the loan contract void. Although they generally held the loan and service agreements severable, they did not always do so. At root, severability was a question of fact. For example, Yoshie Murakami entered a geisha house on a ten-year contract. Part way through her term she quit, apparently because the house would not train her. When the house sued her on the note, the court sided with her. Her loan and personal service agreements were inseparable, it explained. As this service agreement (like all long-term personal service agreements in the industry) was void, so was the loan: she could quit and

[24]Itai v. Yamada, 6–2 Daihan minroku 81 (Daishin'in [Supreme Court] Feb. 23, 1900); accord Fujiwara v. Kondo, translated and reprinted in Murphy (1909: 140) (Nagoya D. Ct. May 21, 1900); Ohashi v. Suzuki, translated and reprinted in Murphy (1909: 143) (Nagoya D. Ct. June 11, 1900).

[25]Itai v. Yamada, 6–2 Daihan minroku at 83–4.

[26]Mori v. Oshita, 1808 Horitsu shimbun 11, 11 (Daishin'in [Supreme Court] Oct. 30, 1920).

[27]Ito v. Yoshida, 2115 Horitsu shimbun 5, 6 (Yokohama D. Ct. Feb. 7, 1923).

Odd markets in Japanese history

keep the money.[28] And when a lower court held (as it did here) that the two agreements were not severable, the Supreme Court often deferred.[29]

Nonetheless, the drafters of the time apparently knew which loan agreements courts would enforce and which agreements they would not, for most indenture contracts seem to have contained loan agreements that the courts did enforce. Consider the case of Osumi Umezu.[30] She had contracted to work as a licensed prostitute and received a ¥650 advance. Before repaying the advance, she decided to leave. The court let her go. Long-term personal service contracts were void, and if Umezu wanted to quit, she could quit. Her loan, though, remained valid. If she quit, she and her guarantors still owed the amount she had borrowed.

Similarly, Haru Kiyomizu had agreed to work as a geisha and received ¥2,300 in advance, but she had died partway through the contract. When the house sued her father as guarantor, the court held for the house: "When Haru Kiyomizu dies, the debt is no longer repayable through her earnings. Nonetheless, the contractual liability continues." The agreements were severable, and even if she was gone, the note and guarantee were still valid.[31]

3 THE INDENTURE CONTRACTS

In large part, modern scholars misunderstand pre-War Japanese prostitution because they misunderstand the pre-War indenture contracts.[32] Most scholars characterize the contracts as debt peonage: Under the indenture

[28]Murakami v. Izumi, 1986 Horitsu shimbun 7 (Miyagi Ct. App. Apr. 22, 1922). Loan contracts were also held void in Ito v. Ito, 21 Daihan minroku 1718, 1726 (Daishin'in [Supreme Court] Oct. 18, 1915); Sanjo v. Oki, 852 Horitsu shimbun 19 (Tokyo Ct. App. Oct. 11, 1912); Yamashita v. Roka, 947 Horitsu shimbun 26, 27 (Osaka D. Ct. No date, journal issue of June 30, 1914); Ono v. Ueda, 408 Horitsu shimbun 7, 8 (Osaka D. Ct. Oct. 20, 1906).

[29]Yamashita v. Roka, 21 Daihan minroku 905 (Daishin'in [Supreme Court] June 7, 1915); Murakami v. Izumi, 27 Daihan minroku 1774 (Daishin'in [Supreme Court] Sept. 29, 1921).

[30]Umezu v. Abe, 2884 Horitsu shimbun 5, 6 (Daishin'in [Supreme Court] May 12, 1928). Other cases reaching the same result include Shibuya v. Yokoyama, 4355 Horitsu shimbun 7, 9 (Daishin'in [Supreme Court] Nov. 22, 1938); Haneda v. Matsumoto, 2272 Horitsu shimbun 19 (Daishin'in [Supreme Court] Apr. 1, 1924); Mori v. oshita, 1808 Horitsu shimbun 11 (Daishin'in [Supreme Court] Oct. 30, 1920); Watamaki v. Haneda, 10 Daihan minroku 1687, 1691 (Daishin'in [Supreme Court] Dec. 26, 1904); Maeda v. Yanadani, 841 Horitsu shimbun 21 (Tokyo Ct. App. Nov. 14, 1912). Note that the result of holding the personal service contract unenforceable was that brothels were not willing to hire women from the poorest families (women who would effectively be judgment proof). See Murphy (1909: 119, 132).

[31]Kiyomizu v. Takeuchi, 3336 Horitsu shimbun 10, 10 (Daishin'in [Supreme Court] Oct. 23, 1931)

[32]For examples of actual contracts, see Ito (1931: 221–8); Saito (1930); Kusama (1930: 170–204); Chuo shokugyo (1926: 392–400).

agreements, argue scholars, prostitutes worked at a brothel until they repaid their loans. Brothel owners and recruiters enticed them into the industry by claiming that repayment would be fast. In fact, according to the standard academic accounts, they lied. Once a woman enlisted, they charged her usurious rates on the loan and exorbitant prices for necessities. Through the scam, they kept her perpetually in debt, and trapped at the brothel for as long as she would sell. Effectively, as one historian put it, "the licensed prostitute ended her life as a sexual slave."[33]

No doubt some brothel owners did manipulate contractual terms, and no doubt some did tie prostitutes to the brothel for as long as customers would buy their services.[34] Yet the industry-wide records instead show that cases where the brothel owner kept the prostitute tied to the brothel were the rare exception. Consider first the geisha indentures, then the licensed prostitutes.

### 3.1 Geisha indentures

Indentured geisha generally contracted to work only for a set number of years — the mode being three.[35] Routinely, they demanded and received their net expected earnings at the outset — a mean amount in 1925 of ¥959.[36] In exchange, the house trained the women to sing and dance, paid their expenses, gave them a small allowance (generally 10 to 20 percent of their earnings), but kept all other revenues they generated.

As a result, the economics of geisha indentures were simple: if a woman raised less than her advance payment plus room and board and any pocket money over the indenture term, the house bore the loss; if she raised more, the house kept the extra. In effect, the contract ensured: (1) that no one (including the geisha house) would defraud the woman of her

---

[33]Murakami (1971: 50); similar accounts appear in, e.g., Yamamoto (1983: 391–2); Yonekura (1985: 59: 41); Yoshimi (1984: 31–6). To "prove" this account, abolitionists relied on surveys of those prostitutes who quit in violation of their contracts — not a random sample. See, e.g., Ito (1931: 301–7).

[34]For examples of contracts where the women did work until they had fully repaid the loan, see Ito (1931: 227); Kusama (1930: 170–8). See also, e.g., Okuma v. Watanabe, 8-2 Daihan minroku 18, 20 (Daishin'in [Supreme Court] Feb. 6, 1902); Ito (1931: 230–1) (earnings and expenses of one insolvent prostitute over a four-month period); id., at 301–7 (abolitionist data finding that various samples of prostitutes had increase in debt); Chuo shokugyo (1926: 428–32) (high expenses). Note, however, that the contractual interest charge in most cases was zero.

[35]Of 6,603 indentured geisha studied in 1925, 1.5% had one-year contracts, 4.6% had two-year contracts, 29.0% had three-year contracts, 28.5% had four-year contracts, 13.9% had five-year contracts, and 22.5% had contracts of six years or more. Chuo shokugyo (1926: 414); Kusama (1930: 214–15).

[36]Chuo shokugyo (1926: 412–13) (note too that a second study found a mean of ¥955); see also Kusama (1930: 205–6). The mode was ¥1,000 to ¥1,200. Id., at 215.

contractually negotiated earnings, (2) that she would receive food and shelter, however modest, and (3) that she would be free to leave when the initial term expired.[37]

### 3.2 Prostitute indentures

Licensed prostitutes negotiated different contracts. They agreed to work for a maximum number of years, but kept track of their earnings and retained the right to quit early if they were successful. In the mid-1920s, the maximum time for which they agreed to work was usually six years.[38] In exchange, they too received an advance of their net earnings – with the women who signed the longer-term contracts receiving the larger advances (Kusama, 1930: 208–9). In the mid-1920s, the mean advance was ¥1,194.[39]

In calculating the prostitute's earnings, the brothel first deducted its own fee. Generally, that fee varied from 67 to 75 percent of the prostitute's gross billings. The prostitute received the remaining 25 to 33 percent of the gross. She usually applied 60 percent of this amount toward the principal on her loan, and kept the rest for current expenses. In most cases, she did not explicitly pay interest, for most contracts did not contain an interest charge. Instead, the brothels applied an implicit interest rate to her advance in calculating her share of the gross earnings.

Under the standard contract for licensed prostitutes, the prostitute could fulfill her part of the bargain either by repaying the principal or by serving the maximum contractual term. If (through the 60% she applied

---

[37]This contract was known as *marukakae*, and was the contract most common among geisha who sold sex (Kusama, 1930: 5). Approximately 60% of all Tokyo geisha used this type of contract. Id. For descriptions of these and other types of geisha contracts, see Fukumi (1928: 237–43); Higuchi (1921: 45–50); Kusama (1930: 2–5).

Occasionally, a girl was "adopted" into the geisha house in exchange for a payment to the parents. Courts routinely declared such adoptions void. See, e.g., Takayama v. Takayama, 907 Horitsu shimbun 24 (Tokyo Ct. App. Oct. 9, 1913); Kato v. Kato, 514 Horitsu shimbun 11 (Tokyo Ct. App. July 7, 1908); Ito v. Ito, 802 Horitsu shimbun 17 (Tokyo D.C. July 5, 1912).

[38]Chuo shokugyo (1926: 414–15) (79.4% of licensed prostitutes had six-year indentures); Kusama (1930: 211) (73.0% of licensed prostitutes had six-year indentures). This was apparently the longest contract allowed them. See Ito (1931: 220).

[39]Fukumi (1928: 70). The median was ¥1,000–1,200. See also Chuo shokugyo (1926: 412–15) (citing two studies, one with a mean of ¥1,222 for 1925, one with a mean of ¥1,018); Kusama (1930: 206) (same). Where it had been customary to deduct ¥200–300 for clothing, bedding, miscellaneous household effects, and the placement fee, the industry eventually shifted to a system in which the parent or prostitute received the entire indenture amount, but then borrowed an additional amount to cover those expenses (Kusama, 1930: 213). On typical charges for these materials, see id., at 260–3. The mean charge by placement agencies in 1926 was 8.5% of the advance. Chuo shokugyo (1926: 400).

toward the loan) she repaid the loan principal before the end of her term, she could quit. If at the end of her term she had not yet repaid the amount, she could still quit. In the meantime, most brothels gave her room and board.[40]

### 3.3 Contractual enforcement

Such was not just the way most parties drafted the contracts; it was also the way they implemented them. Modern scholars routinely assert that brothel owners used violence and coercion and ignored contractual niceties. Granted, some abolitionists did recount anecdotes of hooligans and corrupt owners.[41] Yet the industry-wide data instead suggest the contrary: that the owners regularly kept their part of the bargains.

Consider first some simple finances (Table 6.1; Kusama, 1930: 227–8). In 1925, consumers made 3.74 million visits to the 5,159 licensed prostitutes in Tokyo. Aside from charges for food and drink, they spent ¥11.1 million. Of this amount, the prostitutes kept 31 percent, or ¥3.4 million – ¥656 per prostitute. Under the usual arrangement, each prostitute would have paid 60 percent of this amount (¥394) toward the loan principal and kept the rest (¥262) for personal expenses. With an initial loan of ¥1,194, the average prostitute should have repaid her principal in about three years.

Note that a prostitute should not have found it hard to live on ¥262 – 21.8 per month. After all, she received room and board free. Young industrial workers earned modal monthly wages of less than ¥2 if they also received room and board, and ¥15–16 per month if not.[42] Adult factory workers (generally not receiving room and board) received a mean monthly wage in 1925 of ¥47.[43]

[40]Keishi cho (1933: 96) (aggregate earnings data); Fukumi (1928: 97–9, 220) (contractual terms); Okubo (1906: 246–7) (same); Kusama (1930: 283) (same); Ito (1931: 229) (allocation of earnings); Fukumi (1928: 115–16) (expenses).

[41]E.g., Murphy (1909); see also de Becker (1899: 186–8) (fraudulent bookkeeping). Note, however, that by 1928 even some abolitionists were writing that it had become quite simple for licensed prostitutes to quit with both unserved time and unpaid debts. They noted the risk of hooligans only in the case of unlicensed brothels. See Ishijima (1928).

[42]Shakai (1936: 53). The figures are for twelve- to eighteen-year-olds, and date from 1935. For purposes of comparison, note that the average daily factory wage (adults, both sexes) in 1925 was ¥1.75, and in 1935 was ¥1.88. See Ohsato (1966: 68).

[43]Ohsato (1966: 60, 68) (twenty-seven days at ¥1.746 per day; 1925). In 1926–7, working-class Japanese families spent 40% of their expenses on food, and 16% on housing. Naikaku tokei (1930: 353); See also Seiji keizai (1951: 7) (similar data for mid-1930s). In 1926, men earned ¥2.35 per day at factory work, while women earned ¥0.96 per day. Rodosho (1952: 14); see Naikaku tokei (1930: 130) (¥2.10 for men, ¥0.88 for women; 1924).

Moreover, not only do these back-of-the-envelope calculations suggest that prostitutes (by the terms of their contracts) should have quit after a mean of slightly more than three years, industry-wide data corroborate the estimates. In the early 1920s, of 42,400 licensed prostitutes studied, 11,400 (27%) had worked less than one year, 16,200 (38%) were in their second or third years, 10,400 (25%) were in their fourth or fifth years, 3,100 (7%) were in their sixth or seventh years, and 1,300 (3%) had worked more than seven. The mean number of prostitutes in each of their fourth or fifth years (5,200), in other words, was less than half those in their first (11,400).[44] Similarly, consider the entry and exit from the industry. During 1922, 18,800 women registered as prostitutes, and 18,300 women deregistered. Of the work force of some 50,000, about one-third turned over each year.[45]

Second, consider the incidence of after-acquired debt among prostitutes.[46] Modern scholars routinely claim that brothel owners kept their prostitutes tied to the brothel by increasing their debts. And as of 1925, 92 percent of the 5,000-odd Tokyo licensed prostitutes did have some outstanding debt to the brothel besides their initial advance.[47] Yet 37 percent had less than ¥200 outstanding, and an additional 19 percent had only ¥200–400 outstanding. Recall that the prostitutes had initially borrowed about ¥1,200. Only half of them had outstanding additional debts of at least one-third that amount, and only 5 percent had outstanding debts of at least an additional ¥1,000.

---

[44]Ito (1931: 208-11). In another study of 5,734 licensed prostitutes, 29% were in their first year, 36% were in their second or third year, 26% were in their fourth or fifth year, 8% were in their sixth or seventh year, and 2% had been there longer than seven years. Kusama (1930: 281).

[45]Yamamoto (1983: 388). Ito (1931: 211–13) uses data primarily from 1923, but the data are less reliable because of the way he haphazardly includes some data from other years. He finds that 13,500 registered in one year and 11,000 deregistered. Uemura (1918: 62, 184–7) finds that, in Osaka, one-third of the new registrations were not genuinely new recruits but rather, inter alia, prostitutes moving from one city to another or reenlisting with a new indenture contract. If, following Uemura, one assumes that one-third of Yamamoto's 18,800 registrants were not genuinely new registrants, then the annual industry turnover rate would be about one-fourth. In general, only about 1 percent of the licensed prostitutes quit their jobs with outstanding debt (Ito, 1931: 213–14).

[46]The data are from Fukumi (1928: 122–3); see also Chuo shokugyo (1926: 433); Kusama (1930: 280). Much the same is true of the geisha. According to one 1926 study of 2,554 Tokyo geisha with after-acquired debt, 63% had borrowed less than ¥200, and an additional 22% had borrowed ¥200–400. Only 7% had borrowed at least an additional ¥1,000. See Kusama (1930: 258–9).

[47]On the reasons for this extra debt, see note 39, *supra*. The existence of the extra debt at the outset suggests, of course, that prostitutes probably pooled their income with their families. That itself, however, is no evidence of any "exploitation," as rational family members often decide to pool incomes to diversify risks.

Table 6.3. *Licensed prostitutes in Tokyo,*
*1925 – age*

| Age | Number | Age | Number |
|-----|--------|-----|--------|
| 18–20 | 1,104 | 26 | 330 |
| 21 | 737 | 27 | 254 |
| 22 | 632 | 28–9 | 306 |
| 23 | 631 | 30–4 | 185 |
| 24 | 515 | 35–9 | 29 |
| 25 | 423 | 40 and older | 6 |

*Source:* Takao Fukumi, *Teito ni okeru bai'in no kenkyu [A*
*Study of Prostitution in the Capital]* (Tokyo: Hakubunkan,
1928), pp. 58–9.

More to the point, the longer a prostitute had worked at a brothel, the
smaller the chance she had after-acquired debt outstanding. Consider
again the 5,000-odd Tokyo licensed prostitutes. Among those in the first
year of their contract, 1,484 had some after-acquired debt. Among those
in their third year, only 703 had such debt, and among those in their
sixth, only eighty-four. Once they had adjusted to their new job, in other
words, they learned to save and repaid their debts. Most did borrow
money beyond their original advance, but they borrowed it early in their
career and repaid it fast.

Third, consider Table 6.3, the age distribution of licensed prostitutes in
Tokyo. By law, a woman could not become a licensed prostitute until age
eighteen, and most (though not all) prostitutes began work at a brothel
between ages eighteen and twenty-one.[48] Yet beyond age twenty-one, the
number of prostitutes working falls steadily. Were brothels manipulating
debts to keep their prostitutes employed beyond their initial six-year
terms, the number of licensed prostitutes working in each age bracket
should have held constant into the late twenties. Instead, Table 6.3 shows
a steady decline.[49] The table does show different age cohorts of women in

[48]See Naimu sho rei No. 44 of Oct. 2, 1900, § 1 (minimum age). Fukumi (1928), the
source for Table 6.3, does not break out the age distribution of the eighteen- to twenty-
year-olds. During one ten-month period in 1925–6, however, 494 women registered as
licensed prostitutes in the Shin-Yoshiwara district of Tokyo. Of these women, 24%
were 18-years-old, 17% were 19, 13% were 20, 14% were 21, 7% were 22, 6% were
23, 5% were 24, 5% were 25, and 10% were over 25. Uemura (1929: 545–56); see
Kusama (1930: 122–3). Using these enlistment rates and assuming no retirements
before age 20, we can (very roughly) estimate the composition of the 1,104 women of
ages 18–20 in Table 6.3 as: age 18 – 223, age 19 – 380, and age 20 – 501.

[49]Other sources confirm these data. See Kusama (1930: 136–8). That prostitution
was a transitional job women took only for few years in their early twenties is consis-

1925, rather than a history of one cohort. Because the number of licensed prostitutes in Tokyo stayed relatively stable, however, these figures should approximate the attrition in a given age cohort over time (Fukumi, 1928: 45).

The basic point, therefore, is that the brothel owners did not, on any wide scale, manipulate the indenture contracts to keep prostitutes tied to the brothel far beyond the term of the initial contract.[50] Women enlisted for a limited number of years with the understanding that they could quit early if they worked hard. Many did. Most of the rest apparently quit when their term expired.[51]

To be sure, because prostitutes incurred a fixed cost (a reputational loss) in entering the industry, one might have expected many to reenlist. Once they had worked as a prostitute, their fixed cost was sunk. If their earnings stayed constant, many thus should have found it profitable to stay in the industry. Prostitute earnings, however, did not stay constant. Instead, they fell with age (Kusama, 1930: 207). Apparently, only those few who earned the most money and found the job least offensive considered it worthwhile to reenlist or to work more independently in the unlicensed sector.[52] Most of the rest seem to have considered the work not worth the new lower wages – for most seem to have quit.

### 3.4 Control and credit

In addition to debt peonage, modern scholars raise two hypotheses to explain why brothel owners and prostitutes used multiyear indenture contracts: that the contracts enabled the brothels to control the prostitutes, and that they enabled peasants without credit to borrow. Nonetheless, although the contracts did provide credit and may sometimes have constrained the prostitutes, neither thesis explains why licensed brothels and prostitutes used them so pervasively.

tent with studies of prostitution in other societies. See Walkowitz (1980: 19); Hobson (1987: 86–7).

[50]Nor should we be entirely surprised that the brothels appear to have exploited prostitutes less than generally alleged. After all, brothels were repeat players in a competitive market. They could more cheaply recruit if they developed a reputation for treating their prostitutes relatively fairly. Some even worked to reassure their recruits by using standard form contracts approved by the local police station. See Shibatani v. Yokoyama, 4355 Horitsu shimbun 7, 8 (Daishin'in [Supreme Court] Nov. 22, 1938).

[51]In a study of licensed Osaka prostitutes, Uemura (1918: 62, 184–7) finds that less than one-third of the 18,800 annual registrants were reenlistments – but how much less than one-third is unclear from his data.

[52]Fukumi (1928: 147) suggests that a very few licensed prostitutes did work as unlicensed prostitutes when they had fulfilled their contractual terms.

*Control.* If brothel owners used the indenture contracts to control prostitutes (e.g., Kawashima, 1951), they did not choose a very straightforward way of doing so – or even the most effective. Suppose A deposits a large sum of money with B. B can now constrain A, for B has A's cash. By paying the bond, A makes itself vulnerable to B; A does not thereby gain control over B. Consider banks. Banks concurrently lend money to borrowers and exercise control over the borrower's business. They bargain for the control, though, because they have lent the money and become vulnerable. They do not lend the money because they thereby gain control. Likewise, when a brothel owner paid a prostitute several years' wages in advance, he made himself vulnerable to her – not vice versa.[53]

More basically, if the brothel owners had wanted to control the prostitutes, they had other far more straightforward and powerful ways of doing so. Most obviously, they could have forced the prostitute to deposit money (e.g., part of her earnings) with the brothel (payable to her when she quit). Instead, they effectively deposited their own money with the prostitute. In demanding that the prostitute post a bond, the brothels would have had plenty of precedents. For example, some textile factories routinely withheld a portion of their employees' wages. If and when the employee fulfilled the terms of her contract, she received the withheld amount. If she reneged, she forfeited it (see Chapter 7, Section 3.2). Similarly, American indentured servants often received a large lump-sum payment called "freedom dues" at the end of their indenture term (Engerman, 1986: 268–9). By paying the servant those dues only if he or she satisfactorily completed the contract, the employer gave the servant an incentive not to shirk. Were Japanese brothel owners determined to control their employees, they could easily have used such a system. In fact, they did not.

*Credit.* That prostitutes would use the indenture contracts to obtain credit makes more sense. Because of the international depression, the bad harvests, or the vicissitudes of the textile market, perhaps pre-War Japanese peasants had little to eat. With no assets to transfer, they had nothing to sell. With no assets to pledge, they had no way to borrow. Unable to raise cash otherwise, women sold themselves. Perhaps peasants used the indenture contracts, in other words, to overcome failures in the credit market. On its face, the hypothesis works. If true, moreover, it would

[53]Some contracts provided penalties that applied when the prostitute quit early, but courts often refused to enforce the penalty clauses. In some cases, the courts even considered the clauses reason to invalidate the entire debt contract. See, e.g., Murakami v. Izumi, 28 Daihan minroku 1774, 1780–1 (Daishin'in [Supreme Court] Sept. 29, 1921).

explain the contracts in a way consistent with many Western indenture contracts.[54]

Although the brothels no doubt did give credit to many peasants who wanted it,[55] failures in the credit market cannot explain why brothels and prostitutes used multiyear indenture contracts so pervasively. First, as noted above, courts refused to enforce long-term personal service agreements. As a result, the indenture contract could not substitute for other ways (e.g., collateral, guarantees) of enforcing loans, and thus could not have alleviated any basic credit-market failure. Suppose a brothel owner recruited a woman through a ¥1,200 indenture, and two months later found that she wanted to quit. Although he could sue on the note, he could not legally force her to work. Because of the judicial refusal to enforce personal service contracts, in other words, prostitute indentures were little safer than unsecured loans. Consequently, brothel owners tried to recruit only women from families with assets they could seize (Murphy, 1909: 119, 132). When in 1896 the Supreme Court voided the personal service contracts, it effectively stopped the poorest women from using the indentures to raise cash.[56]

---

[54]See, e.g., Cloud & Galenson (1987); Emer (1986); Feeny (1989); Galenson (1984); Grubb (1985, 1988); Popkin (1979: 54). Note, however, that the need for credible commitments (Section 3.5, *infra*) could also help explain the use of indenture contracts in international migration. The worker incurred a high fixed cost in relocating to a new country, and the recruiter had much better information (and an incentive to lie) about the opportunities available there. As a result, the recruiter could have been paying the worker a large part of his or her wages in advance in order to make the promises about the benefits of emigration credible.

[55]When registering as prostitutes at the local police office, women were required to give their reasons for doing so, and almost all wrote "poverty." The point is meaningless, however, for if they wrote anything else, the police refused their application to register. See Chuo shokugyo (1926: 390); Kusama (1930: 32–3). Nonetheless, most prostitutes apparently did come from lower-class backgrounds. See Kusama (1930: 47–75).

[56]To be sure, abolitionist writers occasionally claimed that hooligans and corrupt police used violence to prevent women from quitting in violation of their contracts. See, e.g., Ito (1931: 308). Yet note several points. First, the evidence suggests that brothel owners did not manipulate the indenture contracts to keep women at the brothel for the full six years, but instead let many women quit after two or three years. At least when women had repaid their initial debt, the brothel owners seem to have followed the letter of the law. See Section 3.3, *supra*.

Second, if brothel owners could successfully enforce indenture contracts through these illegal means, then unlicensed brothels (with dubious access to the judicial system) should have been offering them as well. In fact, however, unlicensed brothels often did not offer indentures, and offered only small amounts when they offered any at all. See Chuo shokugyo (1926: 413); Keishi cho (1935: 509–10); Kusama (1930: 216–7).

Third, other abolitionists reported that by the 1920s it had become quite simple for licensed prostitutes to quit in violation of their contractual terms. These abolitionists noted the risk of hooligans only in the case of unlicensed (and hence illegal) prostitutes. See Ishijima (1928).

Second, were peasants demanding the long-term contracts because they needed large loans, they would have demanded them of other employers besides the licensed brothels and geisha houses. Notwithstanding this, the multiyear indentures were rare outside of the brothels and houses. Take, for example, some of the largest employers of women in pre-War Japan: the textile companies. Textile firms employed a total of 751,000 women in 1925, and each factory employed a mean sixty-nine workers (Fukuoka, 1928: 55). By contrast, the modal brothel had only six prostitutes on staff, and the modal geisha house had only one geisha.[57] As a result, a textile firm should have been able to diversify credit risks more effectively than a brothel or geisha house. In turn, peasants interested in exchanging several years' worth of labor for credit should have found textile factories more receptive than brothels. Yet such was not the case. Instead, to the extent the factories offered indentures, they apparently offered only very short contractual terms and very small advances – enough money to pay the workers' travel and readjustment costs, perhaps, but not much more.[58]

True, a woman indentured at a brothel should have received a larger advance than a woman indentured elsewhere for the same length of time, if only because sex paid better than most other manual labor. Yet that fact alone does not explain why the multiyear indentures were so common at the brothels and so rare elsewhere. High wages in the sex industry did not induce most poor women to become prostitutes. Neither, therefore, should large loans have induced most credit-short women to become prostitutes. If credit had been driving the multiyear indentures, in other words, a broad range of employers should have offered them. Some credit-short women would then have chosen prostitution because of the large advances. But many others would have opted for smaller loans from employers with less unpleasant jobs, just as most poor women avoided prostitution despite the high wages. Notwithstanding all this, multiyear indenture contracts were nearly universal among licensed prostitutes and common among geisha. Among factory workers, they were rare.[59]

[57]Fukumi (1928: 50–1, 203–4) (Tokyo data). Four Tokyo brothels had one prostitute; the two largest had twenty-one each; 66% of the brothels had from four to eight prostitutes. Id., at 50–1. Only two Tokyo geisha houses had more than ten geisha. Id., at 203–4.

[58]See note 5, *infra*.

[59]Hane (1982: 175), Nishimura (1938: 1026), and Sievers (1983: 63) suggest that some factories did use some indentures. Yet other empirical data suggest that multiyear indenture contracts were uncommon among industrial workers. First, of 1,077 twelve- to eighteen-year-old workers (in a cross section of industries) surveyed in 1935, only 59 were aware of any indentures, and only one (the highest) had an indenture of ¥400–500. The male indentures were all for under ¥100. Shakai (1936: 45, 49); see Fukuoka (1928: 40); Suehiro (1931: 4).

Second, Tamura (1956: 38–9) reports that of all workers working under indenture contracts in 1951–2, 63% went into "pure" prostitution, 8.1% became maids at

## 3.5    Credible commitments

Apparently, neither the hypothesis that brothels wanted power over prostitutes, nor the hypothesis that many peasants needed credit, satisfactorily explains why brothels and prostitutes so often used multiyear indenture contracts. Consider instead, therefore, the possibility that they negotiated the contracts for reasons relating (1) to the need for "credible commitments" (Williamson, 1983; 1985: chs. 7–8), and (2) to the efficient allocation of legal costs.

*The contracting problem.* A woman entering the sexual services industry faced several problems relevant here. First, in entering the industry, she brought substantial stigma upon herself. Because of this stigma, she would take the job only if she could expect to earn a total amount that at least compensated her for this "reputational loss."

To be sure, one can exaggerate the loss. All else equal, the women for whom the loss was least severe should have chosen the job most often. And one study (of 300 licensed prostitutes who quit in violation of their employment contracts – not a random sample) did suggest that ex-prostitutes were not necessarily social outcastes: 29 percent returned to their parents, 12 percent took factory jobs, 5 percent found office work, and most of the rest took other "respectable" jobs like nurse's aid positions.[60]

Nonetheless, most contemporaneous sources suggest instead that prostitutes skirted the margins of respectability if licensed geisha, and abandoned all claims to it if not. Quoting a Japanese source, one astute (and otherwise relatively nonmoralistic) turn-of-the-century Tokyo observer captures what seems the general consensus: an ex-prostitute "has violated the virtue of chastity, wasted the flower of her youth in vicious living, and as she is unaccustomed to attend to the proper duties of women her future prospects are anything but cheerful and reassuring" (de Becker, 1899: 248).

Second, the would-be prostitute had little reliable information about how much money she would earn in the industry. Given that the stigma attached when she entered the industry, moreover, she had no cheap way to discover her market "price." And given the uncertainty of the aging

hotels, brothels, bars, and geisha houses, 8% went into agriculture, 3.8% became factory workers, 3% became geisha, 3% became waitresses or bar maids, and 2.9% became child-care workers. See also Kanzaki (1953: 99); Rodosho (1953: 74, app. 74). Third, one early 1930s survey of indentured women found that the mean indenture for licensed prostitutes was ¥900, geisha ¥800, bar maids ¥400, and factory workers ¥130. Shakai (1935: 159).

[60]Ito (1931: 494–5). Indeed, Garon (1993: 716) argues that a large percentage of prostitutes married well to boot.

process, even if she knew her current price she had no way of knowing how rapidly it would decline over time. Third, the would-be prostitute could not diversify her human capital. She was her own most valuable asset, yet that asset was not one whose risks she could easily diversify.

The brothel owner faced very different problems. His were not problems of information or diversification. First, he had much better information about the sexual services market than a recruit. In most cases, therefore, he could estimate what a recruit would earn more accurately than the recruit herself could. Second, he could diversify his investments. When he invested in a prostitute's human capital (by buying her services for several years), he could eliminate much of the associated risk by simultaneously contracting with several prostitutes.

Instead, the brothel owner's problem was one of credibility. Although he hoped to recruit young women by promising them money, he could not easily make his promises about future earnings credible. For although he had better information about a potential recruit's earning capacity than the recruit herself, he also had an incentive to lie. He was asking her to suffer a certain and significant reputational loss, in exchange for income that was risky at best and about which he had considerable incentive to exaggerate. To be sure, her investments were not specific to the brothel – but neither does the point matter: once a brothel owner had enticed a recruit into the industry by exaggerating her market earning potential, she could not improve her position by switching to another brothel.

*Piece-rate and flat-rate contracts.* These problems of informational asymmetry and promissory credibility foreclosed a piece-rate (productivity-based) contract between the brothel owner and the recruit. The contract would have solved one basic problem in the industry: how to motivate a recruit to work hard at what was a fundamentally unpleasant job. Unfortunately, it did not give the recruit the assurance she needed. She needed to know – before she entered the industry – that her earnings as a prostitute would exceed her earnings elsewhere by an amount large enough to offset the stigma and disamenities involved. That assurance, however, was something the piece-rate contract could not assure her.

A flat daily wage did little to improve matters.[61] Most obviously, it gave the prostitute an incentive to shirk. But it also gave the brothel owner an incentive to fire workers who generated revenues less than their contractual daily wage, and to discharge even relatively productive workers during low demand periods (or to threaten to discharge them unless they agreed to a wage cut). Given that a prostitute could expect the revenue she

---

[61]The geisha effectively did earn a flat daily wage, but they faced less severe disamenities than the licensed prostitutes.

generated to decline over time (Kusama, 1930: 207), the problem was particularly acute – for she had to worry that the owner might fire her before she had had a chance to recoup her initial reputational loss.

*Fixed-term contracts and sign-on bonuses.* Because the prostitute incurred a high initial fixed cost, a brothel owner could recruit her effectively only if he credibly promised to employ her long enough for her to recoup that fixed cost. He could recruit effectively, in short, only if he promised her not just a minimum daily wage, but also a minimum total wage. To do so, he had to promise her a minimum employment term besides a minimum wage. Even with such a guaranteed term, though, the problem of credibility remained. To promise credibly that he would employ a recruit for a given period of time, the owner had to be able to promise that he would keep her employed even if her revenues fell permanently below her contractual wage. Such a promise is not one most owners would have found easy to make credible.

A sign-on bonus could have alleviated some of the problems of credibility. The brothel owner might, in other words, have paid the prostitute enough money up-front to offset a substantial portion of her reputational loss. That ploy, however, would now have given the prostitute an incentive to pocket the money, quit, and move to a rival brothel.[62] What the brothel and prostitute needed was a contract that credibly promised a minimum total compensation package – but did so without simultaneously giving the prostitute an incentive to quit.

*Indenture contracts.* The indenture contract (described in Section 3.2 above) mitigated many of these problems. Under the contract, the owners gave the prostitute a minimum daily wage: the indenture advance plus room and board, divided by the maximum indenture term. They gave her an incentive to work hard: the chance to quit early. They gave her a minimum total compensation package: the indenture amount plus room and board. And they gave her a disincentive to quit or move elsewhere: the requirement that she repay that part of her advance she had not yet earned.

That much the parties could have accomplished with an unindentured contract that combined a minimum daily wage with a performance-based bonus and a minimum contractual term. Yet the indenture contract differed from such a hypothetical contract in one critical way: under the indenture contract, the brothel owner paid the prostitute a substantial

[62]Note, however, that the geisha houses did organize a central clearing house through which they enforced on each other an agreement not to hire any geisha who reneged on her contract with another geisha house (Chuo shokugyo, 1926: 392).

portion of her earnings up-front, and thereby allocated the burden of invoking the legal system in a dispute to himself.

By agreeing to bear the cost of invoking the legal system in a dispute, the brothel owner helped make his promises credible. For credibility can derive from the assignment of legal costs. If a dispute arose under the hypothetical minimum-wage-bonus-minimum-term contract (e.g., if the brothel owner reneged on the promised wage), the prostitute had to invoke the legal apparatus to recover her promised wages – for the brothel owner had not yet paid her the total promised compensation. By contrast, if a dispute arose under the indenture contract, the brothel owner had to invoke the legal system – for he had already paid her three- to six-years' wages. Effectively, the brothel owner's willingness to advance the prostitute her promised earnings made his promise to pay those earnings credible. Were the legal system free, such a loan would not add credibility. But legal systems are not free. In Japan as here, possession is nine parts of the law. Because most peasants would have found the legal system foreign and intimidating, the most straightforward way to make them a credible promise was to advance them cash on the barrel.

Note that the indenture contract not only helped make the brothel owner's promises credible, it also allocated the cost of invoking the legal system efficiently. Recall that parties generally bargain in the shadow of the law.[63] As a result, if a dispute occurred, either the owner or the prostitute would have invoked (or threatened to invoke) the legal system. Hence, the efficient deal was the one that placed that burden on the party able to invoke the system most cheaply.[64] As a repeat player, most brothel owners could afford to invest in the information and legal talent necessary to manipulate the judicial apparatus. By contrast, most prostitutes and their parents had little education or sophistication, and as one-shot players were less likely to find it cost-effective to learn how to use the legal system.

Given these cost asymmetries, the parties took the efficient route: they placed the transactions costs (here, the cost of marshaling the legal system) on the party that could bear them most cheaply. Under the contracts, if the prostitute tried to renege, the owner had to recover his

[63]See Mnookin & Kornhauser (1979); Ramseyer & Nakazato (1989). Note that prostitutes would have received information about their legal rights not just by word of mouth from other prostitutes, but also from the abolitionists. During most of the period from 1890 to 1940, a wide variety of abolitionists worked hard to encourage prostitutes to quit. One detailed description of the process appears in Murphy (1909); accounts also regularly appeared in such abolitionist journals as *Seikaku*.

[64]Even if litigation rarely ensued, imposing the litigation burden on the party able to invoke the courts most cheaply was still efficient, because it lessened the possible scope of *ex post* opportunism in the negotiations over a dispute.

money. If the owner tried to renege, the prostitute already had the cash.[65]

## 4  CONCLUSION

In twelfth-century Toulouse, the public brothels split their profits with the local university (Shadwell, 1911). Not so in Japan. Japanese brothels never tried to buy academic support, and never had it. Instead, academics have consistently castigated the brothels for "enslaving" peasant women. Indenture contracts were an important part of the tales they told: poor and unsophisticated, peasant women unwittingly accepted indenture contracts that the brothel owners used to reduce them to sexual slaves.

These patronizing tales cheat the prostitutes of their due – for they drastically understate the resourcefulness that they (indeed, that most ordinary human beings) could show, even in dire situations. Although prostitution was harsh work, most brothel owners were not able to manipulate indenture contracts to keep prostitutes at work indefinitely, and most prostitutes did not become slaves. Instead, licensed prostitutes generally enlisted under six-year indenture contracts. They earned (what were for them) very high incomes. Many repaid their debts in three or four years and quit early. Most of the rest quit when their contracts expired.

Within this world, brothels and prostitutes used indentures to help make the employment market itself possible – for severe informational asymmetries plagued the market. Despite the promises of high incomes, a woman entering the industry for the first time could never be sure. She knew she suffered a loss in social status if she took the job, knew some brothel owners had an incentive to lie about the money she would make, and knew most owners would be able to invoke the courts more easily than she. Precisely because she could never be sure of the money, she found the indenture contract advantageous. Through the contract, the brothel owners could promise her total earnings large enough to offset a substantial part of her lost status, could make that promise credible by paying her in advance, and could shoulder the costs of invoking the legal system themselves. Through the contract, both the brothels and the prostitutes could advance their private best interests.

[65]I located only three suits by prostitutes (all geisha) against their houses for nonpayment of earnings. I found seven cases in which parents or guarantors complained about the house's (or brothel's) seizure of their assets (based on claims that the prostitute had quit in violation of her contract), and at least a dozen cases where a house or brothel sued the prostitute or her parents or guardians for nonpayment on her debt. Reported cases are not, of course, a representative sample of all disputes. See Priest & Klein (1984).

# 7

## Cartels: Cotton spinning

### INTRODUCTION

Just once, you should come see a farming or fishing village. You won't find a single girl. All you'll see are shriveled old grannies. The girls are all gone, left the village for work. . . . We guys are left, but we're lonely. Real lonely. Even suppose I can take the loneliness. How am I going to find a wife? I want a wife so bad I'm going crazy. But no girl'll marry a poor farmer anymore. Even when they come back to the village from the factories, they've turned completely high-class. With their hair done up and perfumed and all, they won't even look at us.

It was a letter to the editor of a Tokyo daily newspaper.[1] And it captured at least some of the economic impact of the textile industry. Having made a minor fortune in the textile mills, the women had raised their sights, and raised them high.

To explain why the textile workers were able to obtain these high wages, in this chapter I explore the informational logic to the employment arrangements they used. Because each firm was so large and because so many women regularly quit work to return home and marry, potential employees had access to a steady flow of verifiable information about their potential employers. Owners, however, did not have accurate information about their recruits, could not readily monitor each recruit's performance, and could not precisely verify what their plant managers told them. Absent better information on these matters, they could not always induce their employees and managers to take the steps they wanted them to take.

To mitigate these informational problems, the cotton-spinning firms offered two sets of contracts. First, to induce their employees to work hard, they paid extremely high wages (though lower than the wages

[1]Quoted in Yamamoto (1977: 121). Of course, there may have been other reasons factory women would not give this man the time of day – there usually are. Of the 1,536 women in cotton-spinning factories surveyed in 1927, 801 said they hoped to marry a farmer. See Chuo shokugyo (1929: 22–3).

prostitutes earned). Indeed, during most of the pre-War period, they apparently paid two to three times the market-clearing wage. Second, to induce their managers not to cut these "efficiency wages" during times of slack demand, they joined a cartel. Through it, they bound themselves to reduce the number of machines they operated during slack demand, and removed much of their managers' incentive to slash the efficiency wages.

Within this book, this chapter plays a dual role. On the one hand, it illustrates again the rationality and ingenuity with which participants in pre-War labor markets bargained to their mutual best interests. In doing so, it repeats in a second market the exercise in chapter 6. On the other hand, it also examines the occasional charge that pricefixing cartels were widespread in pre-War Japan and seriously hampered economic performance. Because the cotton-spinning cartel was by most accounts the most prominent of these cartels, I examine the effect it had on Japanese economic performance.

At the outset, I summarize the history of cotton spinning in Japan (Section 1). I outline the nature of the cartel in the industry, and note how it could not have earned the firms monopoly rents (Section 2). This fact, in turn, presents the chapter's puzzle: If the cartel could not have cut production or raised prices, what manner of beast was it? The answer is that the firms formed the cartel not to raise prices but to preserve their efficiency wage labor contracts. Accordingly I both describe the labor contracts (Section 3) and explain the cartel's role (Section 4).

## 1    THE INDUSTRY

By the first decades of this century, Japanese spinners had already outcompeted the English firms. They consumed more raw cotton than the English, and spun more yarn. Domestically, they dominated the economy. They produced over a quarter of all manufactured goods, and employed over 40 percent of all factory workers (Muto, 1927: 5; Seki, 1954: 60, 435).

During the half century before World War II, the Japanese cotton textile firms weathered three major crises: one at the turn of the century, one in the early 1920s, and one in the mid-1930s. The first crisis hit at the end of the 1890s when Japanese economic performance dipped badly. Whereas from 1886 to 1898 manufacturing volume had doubled, during the four years from 1898 to 1902 it fell. When the Boxer Rebellion broke out and Japanese firms could no longer sell to China, bad matters simply turned worse. In the textile industry, output fell 11 percent from 1898 to 1900, and another 8 percent from 1900 to 1904 (Fujino et al., 1979: 244–5; Seisan, 1912: 1).

A second crisis hit the cotton firms in 1920. As it had been to many

firms in many countries, World War I had been good to Japanese spinners. During the War, many Allied competitors had switched to military
production, and even those that had not found the sea lanes precarious
and the Suez Canal closed. In East Asia, all of this dramatically raised
cotton prices. From 1916 to 1919, the price of cotton yarn rose 4.5 times
but that of raw cotton only 2.7 times. Given that raw cotton costs were
four-fifths of the price of cotton yarn, this price differential gave entrepre-
neurial spinners a nice profit (Mihashi, 1934: 37–8; Nippon kangyo,
1928: 43–9).

Although Japanese spinners found themselves well placed for exploiting these high yarn prices, they were badly placed for the bust that followed. From 1915 to 1919, they watched real profits per spindle more
than double. When the War ended and prices fell, they watched their
profits plummet. Granted, they did not do as badly as many observers
claimed. Although cotton yarn prices fell, so did raw cotton prices. Nonetheless, as with the firms elsewhere that had ridden the wartime boom,
the spectacular wartime profits disappeared. From 1920 to 1926, real
profits per spindle fell two-thirds (Table 7.1; Lazonick & Mass, 1984;
Mihashi, 1934: 37–8).

The problems stemmed from two facts. First, not all firms had hedged
themselves against price changes. Those that had agreed to buy raw cotton
at the earlier high prices without agreeing to sell at fixed prices now lost
badly. Second, even firms that had hedged sometimes found the protection
worthless – for their partners could renege. Although those that had
contracted to sell high should have done well, they did well only if their
buyers did not default. Many buyers did. Where the price changes had
eliminated the buyer's assets, even courts could not help (Seki, 1954: 43–6).

A third crisis hit the industry some ten years later. After the general
financial collapse of 1929–31, many governments turned to protectionist
strategies. Some of these strategies they designed explicitly against Japanese products. Japanese firms, for example, particularly threatened British competitors. From 1928 to 1935, Japanese cotton fabric exports rose
from 1.4 to 2.7 billion square yards, while British exports fell from 3.9 to
1.9 (U.S.) billion square yards (Nishikawa, 1987: 190; Seki, 1954: 436–
41). To slow this competitive shift, Commonwealth countries adopted
stringent tariffs, and many added quantity restraints to boot. By mid-
1936, Japanese cotton weavers faced trade barriers in a majority of their
markets: Fifty-six countries had adopted barriers and over half were
quotas. By one estimate, the barriers affected 67 percent of Japanese
cotton fabric exports.[2]

---

[2]Fujino et al. (1979: 244–5); Nishikawa (1987: 192); Robson (1957: 268); Seki
(1954: 55).

Table 7.1. *Profitability in the cotton spinning industry*

| | Profits/firm (¥1,000) | Profits/spindle | Profits/¥1,000 capital |
|---|---|---|---|
| 1907 | 629 | ¥17.14 | 354.3 |
| 1908 | 307 | 6.17 | 136.7 |
| 1909 | 515 | 8.18 | 181.8 |
| 1910 | 203 | 3.49 | 79.7 |
| 1911 | 368 | 5.77 | 139.6 |
| 1912 | 547 | 10.29 | 232.9 |
| 1913 | 646 | 11.77 | 243.7 |
| 1914 | 545 | 8.61 | 193.9 |
| 1915 | 741 | 10.81 | 249.2 |
| 1916 | 1,431 | 19.91 | 415.4 |
| 1917 | 2,201 | 30.93 | 543.2 |
| 1918 | 2,225 | 27.43 | 443.7 |
| 1919 | 1,730 | 26.78 | 330.1 |
| 1920 | 1,756 | 25.78 | 228.5 |
| 1921 | 1.154 | 16.92 | 150.2 |
| 1922 | 1,213 | 17.18 | 152.5 |
| 1923 | 780 | 11.15 | 88.8 |
| 1924 | 956 | 10.99 | 97.2 |
| 1925 | 895 | 9.31 | 85.1 |
| 1926 | 862 | 8.44 | 78.5 |

*Notes:* Total capital is the sum of paid-in capital and accumulated profits. Profits are in constant 1934–6 yen.
*Sources:* Calculated from data found in Ryokichi Watanabe, *Nihon mengyo ron [The Theory of the Japanese Cotton Industry]* (Tokyo: Nippon hyoron sha, 1931), p. 41; Kazushi Ohkawa et al., *Choki keizai tokei: Bukka [Long-term Economic Statistics: Prices]* (Tokyo: Toyo keizai shimpo sha, 1967), pp. 135–6.

## 2   THE COTTON CARTEL

### 2.1   *Organization*

These crises were not lean years the cotton-spinning firms stoically endured for the sake of the years of plenty to come. Instead, the firms sought safety in numbers. By 1882, they had already organized themselves into the "Great Japan Spinning Federation" (Dai-Nippon Boseki Rengo Kai, abbreviated "Boren"). By all accounts, they were the first in the textile industry to cartelize. By several accounts, they were among the first in *any* modern Japanese industry to cartelize (Shinomiya, 1990:

193–4). To the cotton-spinning firms, the Boren became the principal means by which they sought to respond to these crises.

The conventional story is simple enough. Initially, the spinning firms used the Boren to gain monopsonistic power in the labor market: to lower wages by not bidding for each others' workers (Hashimoto, 1935: 26). Soon, they used it to gain monopolistic power in the product market: to raise profits by enforcing quantity restraints. By 1890 they were coordinating reduced operating hours, days, and machines (Table 7.2). Workers and consumers suffered, so the story goes, but with no antitrust statute it was all legal.

Superficially, it was also plausible business strategy. *If* there had been large-scale economies, perhaps new firms would have found it hard to enter the industry without access to substantial capital. *If* capital markets were underdeveloped, perhaps the new firms could not have obtained

Table 7.2. *Quantity restraints in the cotton-spinning industry, 1890–1930*

| Beginning date | Duration (months) | Restraints |
|---|---|---|
| 1890 June | 1 | No work for 8 days and nights per month |
| 1899 Jan. | 1 | No work for 4 days and nights per month |
| 1900 May | 2 | Same |
| 1900 July | 3 | Either no night work or a 40% reduction in machines used |
| 1900 Oct. | 3 | Same |
| 1901 Jan. | 3 | Same |
| 1902 July | 6 | No work for 4 days and nights per month |
| 1908 Jan. | 4 | No work for 5 days and nights per month |
| 1908 May | 6 | Either no night work for 3 months or a 27.5% reduction in machines used for 6 months |
| 1908 Nov. | 18 | 20% reduction in machines used |
| 1910 Oct. | 6 | Either (1) a 27.5% reduction in machines used or (2) no night work for 4 days and nights per month plus 2-hour reduction per day plus a 12.5% reduction in machines used |
| 1911 Apr. | 6 | Same |
| 1911 Oct. | 6 | Either (1) a 10% reduction in machines used or (2) no work for 5 days and nights per month |
| 1912 Apr. | 6 | No work for 4 days and nights per month |
| 1914 Aug. | 4 | No work for 4 days and nights per month and a 10% reduction in machines used |
| 1914 Dec. | 8 | No work for 4 days and nights per month and a 20% reduction in machines used |
| 1915 Aug. | 6 | No work for 4 days and nights per month and a 10% reduction in machines used |

Table 7.2. *(cont'd)*

| Beginning date | Duration (months) | Restraints |
|---|---|---|
| 1918 Jan. | 6 | A 10% reduction either in the machines used or in the days worked |
| 1918 July | 6 | Same |
| 1920 May | 1 | No work for 6 days and nights per month |
| 1920 June | 2 | No work for 4 days and nights per month, a 10% reduction in the machines used, and a reduction of 4 hours/day |
| 1920 Aug. | 13 | Same, but with a 20% machine cut |
| 1921 Sept. | 3 | Same, but 10% machine cut |
| 1927 May | 6 | No work for 4 days and nights per month, a 15% reduction in machines used, and a reduction of 4 hours/day |
| 1927 Nov. | 20 | No work for 4 days and nights per month, a 23% reduction in machines used, and a reduction of 4 hours/day |
| 1930 Feb. | 5 | No work for 2 days and nights per month, and a 10% reduction in machines used |
| 1930 June | 5 | No work for 2 days and nights per month, and a 20% reduction in machines used |
| 1930 Nov. | 2 | Same |

*Sources:* Otokichi Shoji, *Boseki sogyo tanshuku shi [A History of the Spinning Operation Reductions]* (Osaka: Nippon mengyo kurabu, 1930); Seisan chosa kai (ed.), *Shuyo kogyo gairan [Survey of Major Industries]* (Tokyo: Seisan chosa kai, 1912); Shotaro Kojima, *Waga kuni shuyo sangyo ni okeru karuteru teki tosei [Cartel Controls in the Major Industries in Our Country]* (Tokyo: Yufukan shobo, 1932), pp. 407–18.

that access except from one of the large conglomerates (the *zaibatsu*).[3] Given the size of the globe, they arguably could not have entered the industry quickly even with the best financial connections. Domestic firms did not make competitive spinning machines, after all, until the late 1920s (Chokki, 1990: 258). Before then, a firm intent on undercutting the cartel would have had to import its machines from Great Britain or the United States.

During the five decades before the War, the spinning firms coordinated capacity cuts eleven times (Table 7.2). They launched the first in 1890, but disbanded it within a month. They launched the last in 1930, and continued it for eight years (Seki, 1954: 110). All told, they maintained capacity restraints for twenty years. According to Table 7.3, moreover, production per unit of capital equipment declined during the cuts. On

[3]In fact, capital markets *were* well developed. See Ramseyer & Rosenbluth (1995).

Table 7.3. *Quantity restraints and spindle productivity*

|      | Mandated reductions | Bales/spindle |      | Mandated reductions | Bales/spindle |
|------|------|------|------|------|------|
| 1899 | 0%   | 578  | 1916 | 1.9% | 684  |
| 1900 | 9.9  | 475  | 1917 | 0    | 654  |
| 1901 | 3.8  | 499  | 1918 | 0    | 578  |
| 1902 | 7.2  | 570  | 1919 | 0    | 576  |
| 1903 | 0    | 581  | 1920 | 31.5 | 492  |
| 1904 | 0    | 515  | 1921 | 47.0 | 454  |
| 1905 | 0    | 657  | 1922 | 0    | 508  |
| 1906 | 0    | 699  | 1923 | 0    | 465  |
| 1907 | 0    | 663  | 1924 | 0    | 453  |
| 1908 | 16.8 | 545  | 1925 | 0    | 485  |
| 1909 | 20.0 | 556  | 1926 | 0    | 490  |
| 1910 | 12.4 | 566  | 1927 | 28.9 | 453  |
| 1911 | 19.7 | 521  | 1928 | 47.2 | 401  |
| 1912 | 9.7  | 626  | 1929 | 23.6 | 440  |
| 1913 | 0    | 664  | 1930 | 21.8 | 374  |
| 1914 | 7.6  | 646  | 1931 | 25.3 | 358  |
| 1915 | 27.9 | 620  |      |      |      |

Mean bales/spindle, when restrictions in place: 506
Mean bales/spindle, when no restrictions in place: 559
Mean mandated reduction when restrictions in place: 21.2%
Mean actual reduction: 9.5%

*Notes:* Mandated reductions are calculated on the basis of 20-hour workdays (2 shifts), 28-workday months, 7-hour nights. 1916 is treated as an unrestricted year. Bales/spindle gives the number of cotton bales produced, divided by the number of spindles in place.
*Sources:* Calculated from data found in Table 7.2; Keizo Seki, *Nihon mengyo ron [A Theory of the Japanese Cotton Industry]* (Tokyo: Tokyo daigaku shuppan kai, 1954), p. 446.

average, they mandated production cuts of about 20 percent. On average, production per spindle fell about 10 percent.

## 2.2  Leaks

Nevertheless, as a long-term monopoly-pricing strategy this cartel never had a chance. First, the Japanese cotton-spinning firms faced constant pressure from potential entrants. This simply was not an industry with large entry barriers. The most spectacularly successful late entrant was Nisshin boseki. Cotton merchant Hirazaemon Hibiya had launched the

141

firm in 1907. By 1910 it was in the second quintile of firms; by 1930 it ranked sixth in a field of over sixty (Nisshin, 1969; Dai-Nippon, *Geppo,* various years). Smaller firms continued to enter the industry throughout the pre-War period.

Second, the cartel never incorporated all members (much less all potential members) of the industry, or limited investments in new productive capacity.[4] Let us consider each of these issues in turn.

*Incomplete membership.* The Boren never included all members of the industry. Most obviously, it excluded foreign competitors, this at a time when producers often joined cartels across national boundaries (Hara & Kudo, 1992: 2). The Boren began as an organization of Japanese spinning firms, and forever remained that. Nonetheless, those firms sold in what was always a global market. Despite variations in thread quality, many firms in many countries produced interchangeable thread. Granted, foreign spinners could not necessarily compete in the domestic Japanese market. Tariffs on imported cotton products helped ensure that. Notwithstanding, Japanese firms did compete abroad with spinners from several countries – most prominently, Great Britain, United States, France, Germany, and India.

The spinners sold much of their product in this competitive international market. Even when they sold to domestic weavers, those weavers often exported the finished fabric (Mihashi, 1934: 7). Given these international *fabric* markets, Japanese spinners generally could not have charged monopoly *yarn* prices to domestic weavers: as long as a downstream product faces a competitive market, upstream cartels with fewer than all producers (e.g., a spinning cartel that excludes foreign competitors) will seldom be able to raise prices. Indeed, because many of the largest Japanese spinners (like the large American spinners) ran integrated spinning and weaving operations, many Boren members sold fabric on the international market directly (Table 7.4).[5]

Until 1936, the Boren could not even convince all Japanese spinners to join.[6] To be sure, it tried to make membership worthwhile. It never made

[4]In addition, note that the cartel did not take several obvious steps open to it. The firms could have tried to restrict output through their coordinated import scheme involving the N.Y.K. (described below), but did not. Indeed, they could have set prices, but did not.

[5]Although these integrated firms operated fewer than 20% of all looms, they operated the most efficient ones. In 1936, they ran nearly three-fourths of the 46,000 automatic looms in use. With a fifth of the looms, they wove a third of the fabric. See Table 7.4; Shoko (1936: 413) (automatic loom use). On integrated spinning and weaving operations in the West, see Lyons (1985); Temin (1988).

[6]As of September 1927, for instance, eleven spinning companies representing 6% of all cotton spindles were outside the Boren (Nippon kangyo, 1928: 55–8). The remaining eleven firms joined the Boren in May 1936 (Zaisei, 1936: 210).

Table 7.4. *Spinning firms in the weaving industry*

| | A<br>Total<br>looms | B<br>Spinning<br>looms | C = B/A | D<br>Total<br>fabric | E<br>Spinning<br>fabric | F = E/D | G = E/<br>firm<br>revenues |
|---|---|---|---|---|---|---|---|
| 1905 | | 6,077 | | 715 | 154 | 21.5% | 11.9% |
| 1910 | | 17,002 | | 1,222 | 332 | 27.2 | 18.5 |
| 1915 | | 27,931 | | 1,824 | 710 | 38.9 | 27.3 |
| 1920 | | 43,725 | | 6,936 | 2,950 | 42.5 | 27.0 |
| 1925 | 365,369 | 61,918 | 16.9% | 7,719 | 2,732 | 35.4 | 22.5 |
| 1930 | 348,903 | 69,147 | 19.8 | 4,933 | 1,631 | 33.1 | 25.5 |
| 1935 | 385,980 | 83,308 | 21.6 | 8,104 | 2,466 | 30.4 | 21.7 |

*Notes:* (A) Total number of cotton weaving looms in use. (B) Total number of cotton weaving looms used by spinning firms. (C) Percentage of cotton weaving looms used by spinning firms. (D) Value in current prices (× ¥100,000) of total cotton fabric produced. (E) Value in current prices (× ¥100,000) of cotton fabric produced by spinning firms. (F) Percentage of total cotton fabric produced by spinning firms. (G) Percentage of spinning firm revenues attributable to weaving operations.
*Sources:* Calculated from data found in Shozaburo Fujino, Shino Fujino, & Akira Ono, *Choki keizai tokei: Sen'i kogyo [Long-Term Economic Statistics: Textile Industry]* (Tokyo: Toyo keizai shimpo sha, 1979), pp. 74–83, 242–3; Miyohei Shinohara, *Choki keizai tokei: kokogyo [Long-Term Economic Statistics: Mining and Manufacturing]* (Tokyo: Toyo keizai shimpo sha, 1972), pp. 194–5; Shoko daijin kanbo tokei ka (ed.), *Shoko sho tokei hyo [Statistical Tables for the Ministry of Commerce and Industry]* (Tokyo: Tokyo tokei kyokai, various years).

it indispensable. In 1893 it negotiated a favorable shipping contract with the N.Y.K., the Mitsubishi shipping firm (reprinted in Seisan, 1912: 26–9). Under this agreement, the N.Y.K. agreed to pay large rebates to association members who used it for their raw cotton. More specifically, the N.Y.K. charged shippers full price, but at the end of the accounting season rebated to Boren members a large portion of that price.

Unfortunately for the Boren, the bulk shipping market was a competitive market. As one scholar recently put it, "collusion among shippers has never survived" in this industry (Pirrong, 1992: 128). The Japanese shipping firms launched periodic price wars with the Western firms, and were not always the low bidder. Yet the Boren could have made membership advantageous only if the N.Y.K. charged prices below international competitive prices, and if no other international shipping firm were willing to match those prices.[7]

[7]Kojima (1932: 478–511) (shipping cartels); Nihon keiei (1988: 7–74, 123–9) (competition between N.Y.K. and the western firms); Wray (1984: 289–308, 400–8) (same); Wray (1989a: 187) (existence of irregular "tramp shipping"). Indeed, *if* the Boren had been a pricefixing scheme and *if* the N.Y.K. had had a lock on cotton

Table 7.5. *Spinning cartel cheating*

|  | A Mandated reductions | B Spinning factories | C Spindles (× 1,000) |
|---|---|---|---|
| 1920 | 31.5% | (40) | 355 |
| 1921 | 47.0 | 89 | 299 |
| 1922 | 0 | (159) | 394 |
| 1923 | 0 | (1) | 284 |
| 1924 | 0 | 20 | (91) |
| 1925 | 0 | (8) | 451 |
| 1926 | 0 | 37 | 293 |
| 1927 | 28.9 | (22) | 263 |
| 1928 | 47.2 | 6 | 531 |
| 1929 | 23.6 | 38 | 233 |
| 1930 | 21.8 | 18 | 595 |
| 1931 | 25.3 | 15 | 221 |

Mean new spindles while restrictions in place: 328,000
Mean new spindles while no restrictions in place: 266,000
Mean new spinning factories while restrictions in place: 14.8
Mean new spinning factories while no restrictions in place: −22.2

*Notes:* (A) Cartel-mandated reductions. (B) Net increase (or decrease) in number of spinning factories with five or more employees. (C) Net increase (or decrease) in number of operating spindles.
*Sources:* Calculated from data found in Table 7.2; reproduced from J. Mark Ramseyer & Frances M. Rosenbluth, *The Politics of Oligarchy: Institutional Choice in Imperial Japan* (New York: Cambridge University Press, 1995), ch. 10.

Renegade spinners simply did not need the N.Y.K. Although the Boren firms could together obtain bulk discounts, so could most other spinners. Major spinning firms would have qualified for equivalent discounts elsewhere. Whatever clout the Boren had, as the shipping arm of the Mitsubishi empire the N.Y.K. was not the sort of firm on which it likely could have imposed monopsonistic prices. Unless it was indeed extracting monopsonistic rents, though, renegade firms could have competed without joining it.[8]

imports, one would expect the Boren to have enforced its quantity restraints through its control over raw cotton imports. Given that the spinners depended critically on cotton imports, that bottleneck offered the perfect monitoring device. The Boren did not do so – both because it was *not* a pricefixing scheme, and because the N.Y.K. did *not* have a lock on the import trade.

[8]In addition, note two points. First, the Boren convinced the domestic raw-cotton

*Investment limits.* As Table 7.2 details, the Boren never tried to limit the total number of spindles. Instead, it mandated cuts only in either operating hours or the percentage of spindles used. This made for a bizarre cartel, for to earn its members monopoly rents the Boren had to cut the quantity produced. To do that, it could not just cut hours or furlough existing spindles. It needed also to limit the purchase of new spindles. That it never did. In letting firms buy new spindles but not letting them use them fully, it apparently ensured only that its members invested inefficiently.

Even as the Boren mandated production cuts, spinning firms continued to buy new equipment (Table 7.5). Despite the capacity restraints, they aggressively built new factories and installed new spindles. Indeed, they built more factories and installed more spindles while the restraints were in place than while they were not. Were this a production-restriction cartel, it was one that failed.

## 2.3 *Temporary local gains?*

Even if the Boren firms could not have earned monopoly rents long-term, perhaps they hoped to exploit a temporary local monopoly.[9] Expansion in the industry did take time. Because most firms already operated

producers not to sell to non-Boren firms. Because domstic producers raised a small fraction of the cotton consumed, this was not a major barrier. Second, in 1930 the Boren convinced the cotton yarn sellers' association not to buy yarn from non-Boren firms. In return, Boren members agreed to sell only to members of the sellers' association. See Kojima (1932: 413); Nippon kangyo (1928: 54–5); Seki (1954: 114–16). At this point, the only firms safely able to remain outside the Boren would have been those that *both* spun and wove, and those that could market their yarn independently. As Table 7.4 shows, however, the biggest Japanese firms operated integrated spinning and weaving factories.

[9]Consider three additional hypotheses. First, many Japanese historians (e.g., Nishikawa, 1987: 154; Takamura, 1971: 2: 178–91) suggest a very different explanation for the cartel: that the largest spinning firms used the restrictions to gain a competitive advantage over the smaller firms. Recall, however, that membership in the cartel was voluntary, that spinning firms imported raw cotton in a competitive international market, and that they sold yarn and fabric on a competitive international market. As a result, this explanation necessarily fails. The large spinning firms could have induced the small firms to join the Boren (or to remain in the Boren) and suffer the exploitative consequences only if the small firms earned a net gain by doing so. Hence the large firms would have had to compensate the smaller firms for any exploitation the small firms suffered. Because of the competitive market constraints, however, the large Boren firms had no way of using the Boren to generate sufficient monopoly rents to pay that compensation and still earn a profit.

Second, Okazaki (1987) suggests a ingenious alternative: Small spinners were heavily invested in low-count thread, and large spinners were invested in high-count thread. Small spinners wanted to move into high-count thread and used the cartel to give them breathing space to do that. Aside from whether the cartel would have given any breathing space without international market power, and aside from whether large firms would ever have agreed to such a plan, Okazaki's theory does not explain why twenty-five to twenty-eight days a month, twenty to twenty-two hours a day, non-Boren firms could not have dramatically expanded production without buying new machines. Yet until the 1920s, almost all machines came from either Great Britain or the United States. Even with a telegraphed order, expansion would have taken quite a while. Meanwhile, perhaps the Boren firms could have earned monopoly returns.[10]

As an explanation for the Boren, none of this could have worked – short-term monopoly returns cannot explain the measures the Boren took. Most basically, the measures were not short-term. Rather, they lasted for months and years. Nor did the Boren ignore the measures once competition eroded any monopoly price. Instead, month after month, Boren firms regrouped to change the percentage of spindles furloughed, the number of days closed, or the number of hours per day worked. To the firms themselves, the cuts meant more than any short-term advantage.

Second, as noted earlier the Boren firms never tried to limit total production. Absent such an agreement, they could not have raised prices. As Tables 7.2 and 7.5 show, although they required each other to reduce the percentage of their equipment that they operated, they let each other freely expand the total amount of that equipment. Had they wanted to affect prices, they would not have agreed just to cut the stock used. They would also have agreed to idle any new equipment they bought. Because they did not do so, the Boren firms would not likely have raised prices, even temporarily. According to Gary Saxonhouse, the American economist who has spent the most time on the industry, they did not: Boren firms did not "restrict industry output, even on a cyclical basis."[11]

### 3  COTTON LOGIC

The basic puzzle thus remains: If the Boren firms were not trying to earn monopoly rents, what did they think they were doing? The answer, I

small firms would find advantageous a scheme that disabled themselves as much as it disabled their competitors.

Third, participants at one presentation of this chapter offered another intriguing hypothesis: The Boren firms used capacity cuts to preserve their collective reputation for treating workers fairly. Absent a cartel, some firms would have tried to hire workers into their factory during times of peak demand, then fire them during slack demand. Unfortunately, the cartel neither limited expansion during boom times nor limited contraction during the busts.

[10]On the hours and days worked, see the tables at the end of any issue of Dai-Nippon, *Geppo;* on the source of spinning machines, see Tatsuki (1990: 40).

[11]Saxonhouse (1976: 122; 1991). Note that this is consistent with the 9.5 percent fall in productivity during the cartel (Table 7.3). The cartels were in place during slack demand. Even if they had been completely ineffective, production would have fallen somewhat during their tenure – if only because consumers were less willing to buy the yarn.

suggest, is that they were trying to solve two principal-agent problems at once: to pay workers enough to reduce their "shirking," and to enable their managers to commit credibly to keeping wages at levels that would mitigate that shirking.[12] Let us turn first to the wages in the industry (Sections 3.1, 3.2), then to the managerial problems (Section 3.3).

### 3.1 *Efficiency wages*

*Monitoring and shirking.* Picture the problem that the owners of the new mills faced. In a society where almost all manufacturing occurred in small shops, they built massive factories. In a world where machines ran on muscle or water, they introduced steam and later electricity. In the new factories, they installed large, complicated, and expensive British-made machines.

To run these powerful new factories and machines, the owners needed managers and workers they did not have. They needed managers who could organize individual workers into teams suited to factory production. They needed managers who could structure incentives so that the workers individually would not free-ride on each other. They needed managers who could teach people to run the new machines and to avoid breaking them. As of 1891, however, they had only one formally trained engineer for every six factories (Saxonhouse, 1976: 109; Noshomu, *Noshomu tokei,* 1903: 63).

The owners also needed workers who would work obediently, regularly, and carefully. As the new ring spindles were relatively easy to operate, they did not need workers who understood much physics or chemistry, or workers with much physical strength. They did need workers who would not ignore instructions, who would not skip work on a whim, and who would not take breaks that disrupted production at the entire plant. They needed, in short, workers with what we now call "basic work habits." Before the industrial revolution, few people considered such habits basic, for few people needed them in either agrarian or handicraft production. Eventually, school teachers did bring these habits to Japanese peasant children. As of 1891, though, only a quarter of the workers at the spinning plants had attended primary school (Saxonhouse, 1976: 32).

Somehow, the mill owners had to teach their workers to use the new

---

[12]Readers may also ask why the Boren (like many trade associations) did not try to manipulate the political process to form a legally enforceable cartel. The reason, explained in Ramseyer & Rosenbluth (1995: ch. 10), is that the *zaibatsu* firms had the greatest political influence in pre-war Japan, and the *zaibatsu* firms had interests contrary to the Boren.

machines safely and effectively, to convince them to work together as a team, and to induce them not to free-ride on each other. Fundamentally, this was largely a matter of incentives. Unfortunately, to use the optimal incentives the owners had to be able to monitor workers individually and to dispense appropriate penalties and rewards. Yet precisely because it involves joint production, team work is hard to meter. Precisely because cotton spinning involved team work, the owners found it hard to meter their workers – and hard, therefore, to reward and discipline them appropriately.

This is complicated enough where the technology is familiar; it is harder still where everything about the factory is strange.[13] With new machines, an owner often will have no idea how much he (the owners and managers of these factories were generally men) can expect of a recruit. Not knowing what to expect, he cannot set the proper piece rate. Predictably, many of the earliest Japanese factory owners produced nothing so much as chaos. Their workers did not know how to use the machines, their managers did not know how to structure incentives to motivate workers, and absent appropriate incentives the workers had little reason to learn to use the machines.

Contemporary observers chronicled the chaos in Japanese factories. "If a supervisor can see the employees (particularly day laborers), they work attentively," reported one otherwise sympathetic man in 1899 (Yokoyama, 1899: 179). "But as soon as he disappears, they gossip in groups of two or three." "The day after payday," another observer (Noshomu, 1903a: 235) wrote, "employees regularly skip work." According to the oral histories of the workers themselves, they even slept on the job (Yamamoto, 1977: 180).

*Market-clearing wages.* Workers shirked in these early factories for a simple reason: They preferred leisure to work and had no reason not to indulge that preference. Through their work, they earned the going rate – a wage that cleared the market. But when labor markets clear, workers who quit one job can easily find another. And if all firms pay the market-clearing wage, a worker will earn the same wage in her (most textile workers were women) new job as she earned in the old. Workers can safely work when they want, rest when they want. In agricultural and handicraft industries, such work habits seldom disrupt. In a modern factory, they wreak havoc.

---

[13]Given the asymmetric distribution of information between workers and managers regarding worker abilities, and the inability of managers to commit credibly to a given wage structure, piece-rate contracts never entirely solve the incentive problem (Miller, 1992: ch. 5; Holmstrom, 1982).

If the spinning mills could have monitored their workers cheaply, they could have mitigated this problem. If their managers might have noticed and fired them when they shirked, workers would have shirked less profligately. Yet monitoring is not free, and hence the problem. The more monitoring costs, the more cheaply workers can indulge their preference for leisure over work. If losing their job costs them little (if they earn market-clearing wages) and if monitoring is often ineffective (if they can often shirk unnoticed), rational workers may choose to shirk as they please.

*Efficiency wages.* All this generates the well-known paradox of "efficiency wages": the more monitoring costs, the more likely employers can lower labor costs by raising wages.[14] If workers shirk because they can easily earn equivalent wages elsewhere, a firm can sometimes save money by paying them more. For when it does so, workers who lose their job lose income. Rather than lose their well-paying job (a risk they retain if the firm maintains even moderate levels of monitoring), they may now decide to reduce their shirking. Even if all equivalent firms pay the same high wages, workers who lose their job still lose – for wages above market-clearing levels necessarily generate unemployment. Given the higher unemployment levels, fired workers now spend longer finding their next job.

The classic example is Ford. In 1914, Henry Ford paid his workers $2.34 per day. The wage was the going rate and cleared the market. Because everyone else paid it too, jobs were easy to find. Workers could quit Ford in the morning, observers recalled, and find another job by noon. As a result, Henry Ford found himself with an annual turnover rate of 370 percent, and chaos in his assembly line. To solve this problem, he doubled wages. At $5 a day, workers now stood in line for a Ford job. At $5 a day, Ford boasted, "I have a thousand men who if I say 'Be at the northeast corner of the building at four A.M.,' will be there at four A.M." (Miller, 1992: 65–71).

The large Lancashire cotton-spinning mills in the nineteenth century similarly paid efficiency wages (Huberman, 1986, 1991a,b). Because they regularly experimented with new technology, they regularly found it hard to monitor their employees. "In the heyday of industrialization, managerial methods of supervising workers and monitoring how much they could produce were unsophisticated," explains Michael Huberman (1991a: 88). Even though the larger Lancashire firms tried to mitigate these problems with piece-rate wages, they still "had difficulty in linking effort to output and setting piece rates." Accordingly, they chose not to

[14]Rasmusen (1989: 166–7; 1992: 475); Shapiro & Stiglitz (1984); Stiglitz (1987).

Table 7.6. *The Kanebo wage premium*

|      | Boren mean | Kanebo mean | Kanebo premium |
|------|-----------|-------------|----------------|
| 1898 | 14.99     | 19.60       | 30.8%          |
| 1908 | 24.89     | 29.00       | 16.5           |
| 1919 | 80.51     | 84.10       | 4.5            |

*Notes:* Daily wages in current sen (¥ 1/100).
*Source:* Calculated from data found in Dai-Nippon boseki rengo kai (ed.), *Dai-Nippon boseki rengo kai geppo [Great Japan Spinning Federation Monthly Newsletter]* (Osaka: Dai-Nippon boseki rengo kai, various years) (1918 data unavailable).

rely exclusively on monitoring. Instead, they "paid efficiency wages to reduce the loss of productivity associated with shirking."

*The Japanese mills.* Turn-of-the-century Japanese cotton-spinning firms also paid efficiency wages. The giant Kanebo firm did so most extravagantly, advertising not just its wages but also the various other amenities it offered. Modern scholars often doubt whether it improved employee welfare as much as it claimed, but in doubting they miss the point. Kanebo did not adopt its scheme out of charity. Instead, it adopted it as a simple profit-maximizing efficiency wage strategy. Its wage premium was stark. Table 7.6 details (1) the mean daily wage paid by all Boren firms to their female workers as of the middle of each year, (2) the comparable figure for Kanebo, and (3) the resulting premium attributable to Kanebo employment. In the late nineteenth century, Kanebo paid close to a third more than its competitors. Although Kanebo's wage dominance faded, it faded only because other firms soon hiked their wages as well. As Table 7.7 shows, the larger firms did adopt efficiency wages before the smaller firms did; but as Table 7.8 shows, by 1910 the industry as a whole paid textile workers double what they could earn on the farm.

The Japanese story does not parallel early-nineteenth-century Lancashire completely. Where only the larger Lancashire firms paid high wages, by 1915 large and small Japanese firms alike paid similar rates (Table 7.7).[15] Because large and small firms used the same technology in Japan, similar wages and hours are exactly what one would expect. By the turn of the century, almost all Japanese mills used standard steam-powered Platt Brothers machines (Tatsuki, 1990: 37; Saxonhouse, 1991). Whatever monitoring problems large firms experienced, small firms faced them too. After large firms found it advantageous to pay high wages, small firms soon followed suit.

[15] A point confirmed by separate calculations in Odaka (1989: 161).

Table 7.7. *Mean hours and wages in the spinning industry, by firm size*

| A. Daily Hours Quintile | 1900 | 1905 | 1910 | 1915 | 1921 | 1925 |
|---|---|---|---|---|---|---|
| First | 19.4 | 22.7 | 22.9 | 22.3 | 19.8 | 19.7 |
| Second | 19.0 | 21.7 | 22.3 | 21.9 | 19.0 | 21.1 |
| Third | 18.8 | 23.3 | 20.6 | 23.0 | 20.1 | 19.6 |
| Fourth | 16.9 | 22.8 | 22.6 | 23.1 | 20.1 | 19.9 |
| Fifth | 18.1 | 22.4 | 21.4 | 22.8 | 19.5 | 20.2 |
| B. Daily Wages Quintile | 1900 | 1905 | 1910 | 1915 | 1921 | 1925 |
| First | ¥0.193 | ¥0.239 | ¥0.298 | ¥0.319 | ¥1.109 | ¥1.323 |
| Second | 0.195 | 0.224 | 0.268 | 0.302 | 1.073 | 1.096 |
| Third | 0.175 | 0.217 | 0.284 | 0.310 | 1.201 | 1.222 |
| Fourth | 0.164 | 0.190 | 0.246 | 0.344 | 1.079 | 1.225 |
| Fifth | 0.153 | 0.192 | 0.236 | 0.305 | 1.060 | 1.260 |
| *Mandated cuts:* | 9.9% | 0.0% | 12.4% | 27.9% | 31.5% | 0.0% |

*Notes:* The firms are divided into quintiles on the basis of the number of spindles in each firm. Wages are daily wages for female workers in current yen. The data are for the months of July for each year except when July was unavailable (when nearest available month was used instead). Mandated production cuts are taken from Table 7.3. Hours are number of hours of operation of factories operated by firm. Here 1921 is substituted for 1920 because of the unavailability of 1920 data.
*Sources:* Calculated from data found in Dai-Nippon boseki rengo kai (ed.), *Dai-Nippon boseki rengo kai geppo [Great Japan Spinning Federation Monthly Newsletter]* (Osaka: Dai-Nippon boseki rengo kai, various years).

*The quantity of labor.* Given their efficiency wage strategy, Japanese spinners could not respond to demand shocks by cutting wages. Instead, they had to cut the *quantity* of labor they hired. Recall that they paid a premium in order to induce employees not to shirk. If they now cut that premium, they increased shirking. In the long run, they thereby raised their total labor costs.

Because most textile workers came from (and could generally return to) the agricultural sector, whether they found shirking advantageous largely depended on the difference between their spinning wage and their agricultural wage. During much of the pre-War period, about 80 percent of the cotton-spinning workers were women, and about 60 percent of these women came from the farm (Chuo, 1929: 5; Shindo, 1958: 365). If the demand for cotton yarn fell, therefore, spinning firms paying efficiency wages could safely cut wages only if agricultural wages (the sector to which they would most likely have returned) also fell. In fact, agricultural

Table 7.8. *The price and quantity of labor in cotton spinning*

|      | A<br>Daily<br>(current ¥) | B<br>Hourly<br>(constant sen) | C<br>Spin/agri. | D.<br>Quantity<br>(person-days) |
|------|------|-------|------|--------|
| 1890 | 0.08 | 2.22  |      | 2,762  |
| 1892 | 0.09 | 2.71  | 1.37 | 4,984  |
| 1894 | 0.10 | 2.95  | 1.43 | 7,842  |
| 1896 | 0.12 | 2.85  | 1.47 | 9,405  |
| 1898 | 0.16 | 3.27  | 1.17 | 15,413 |
| 1900 | 0.19 | 3.96  | 1.61 | 15,236 |
| 1902 | 0.22 | 4.10  | 1.71 | 16,933 |
| 1904 | 0.22 | 4.07  | 1.75 | 13,952 |
| 1906 | 0.25 | 4.02  | 1.84 | 20,153 |
| 1908 | 0.27 | 4.13  | 1.90 | 17,999 |
| 1910 | 0.29 | 4.68  | 2.14 | 23,263 |
| 1912 | 0.32 | 4.38  | 1.65 | 25,200 |
| 1914 | 0.33 | 4.79  | 2.21 | 29,271 |
| 1916 | 0.33 | 4.74  | 2.08 | 32,616 |
| 1918 | 0.47 | 4.10  | 1.57 | 29,415 |
| 1920 | 1.31 | 8.95  | 2.74 | 34,103 |
| 1922 | 1.30 | 9.49  | 2.38 | 41,885 |
| 1924 | 1.29 | 10.26 | 2.38 | 35,627 |
| 1926 | 1.30 | 10.70 | 2.38 | 45,118 |
| 1928 | 1.35 | 11.76 | 2.83 | 38,720 |
| 1930 | 1.16 | 13.97 | 2.56 | 33,710 |
| 1932 | 0.85 | 11.16 | 2.79 | 33,197 |
| 1934 | 0.77 | 9.62  | 2.43 | 38,830 |
| 1936 | 0.73 | 8.76  | 2.01 | 40,158 |

*Notes:* (A) Mean daily wage in yen for female workers in cotton-spinning sector, current prices. (B) Mean hourly wage in sen (¥1/100) for female workers in cotton-spinning sector, constant 1934–36 prices. (C) Mean annual wage for female workers in cotton spinning sector, divided by mean annual wage for female workers in agricultural industry. (D) 1,000 person-days worked by female laborers in spinning sector.
*Sources:* Calculated on the basis of data from Shozaburo Fujino, Shino Fujino & Akira Ono, *Choki keizai tokei: Sen'i kogyo [Long-Term Economic Statistics: The Textile Industry]* (Tokyo: Toyo keizai shimpo sha, 1979), pp. 27, 256–77; Takahiko Hashimoto, *Nippon menshiseki gyo shi nempo [A Timeline for the Japanese Cotton Yarn Spinning Industry]* (Tokyo: Bunka shi nempyo seisaku kenkyu kai, 1935); Noshomu sho somukyoku tokeika (ed.), *Noshomu tokei hyo [Agricultural and Commercial Statistics]* (Tokyo: Noshomu sho somukyoku tokeika, various years); Kazushi Ohkawa et al., *Choki keizai tokei: Bukka [Long-Term Economic Statistics: Prices]* (Tokyo: Toyo keizai shimpo sha, 1967), pp. 134–6; Takejiro Shindo, *Mengyo rodo sanko tokei [Reference Statistics Regarding Labor in the Cotton Industry]* (Tokyo: Tokyo daigaku shuppan kai, 1958), pp. 500–3; Matsuji Umemura et al., *Choki keizai tokei: Norin gyo [Long-Term Economic Statistics: Agriculture and Forestry]* (Tokyo: Toyo keizai shimpo sha, 1966), pp. 220–1.

wages often did not move in tandem with the demand for cotton yarn. Hence, if a spinning firm sought to pay double or triple the agricultural wage, it could not necessarily respond to demand shocks by lowering wages. Instead, it often had to lower production.[16] Japanese firms did just that – when demand fell, they cut the quantity of labor they hired (Table 7.8).

Note a complication: If spinning firms cut output by firing workers, they potentially vitiated their efficiency wage scheme, for workers would discount their higher wages by their higher probability of being fired. Rather than lay off existing workers, however, Japanese spinning firms apparently cut production by delaying new hires. In most years, one-fourth to one-third of their workers quit voluntarily anyway. They quit because they had never planned to work a long time. They had come to the factory to work a few years and save. Having done exactly as they planned, they returned to their farm to marry. Because so many women quit each year, the spinning firms could adjust output to demand shocks simply by delaying new hires (Hosei, 1936: 187–91; Uno, 1915a,b).

### 3.2 The evidence of efficiency wages

Several aspects of the Japanese cotton-spinning industry suggest (even if they do not prove) that the firms paid efficiency wages. Consider the price of labor, the stability of the wage premium, oral evidence from the women involved, and the use of performance bonds.

*The price of labor.* Few facts about the spinning firms are more prominent than the high wages they paid their workers (Table 7.8). Most of these workers were young women off the farm with few marketable abilities other than agricultural skills. By 1910, the cotton-spinning firms paid them double the agricultural wage. They continued to pay at least double for most of the next three decades.[17]

---

[16]That cutting production would generally lower per-unit production costs is straightforward: On a short-term basis, cutting production quantity lowers marginal (and short-term average variable) production costs because the marginal cost curve cuts average cost curves from below, and because the short-term average variable cost curve lies below the average total cost curve. In a long-term equilibrium, of course, firms will sell at a price equal to long-term total average costs.

[17]Shindo (1958: 396) finds similar ratios for the early post-War years. I use mean *annual* wage rates for female agricultural workers rather than mean *daily* wage rates (as, e.g., Takamura (1971: 1: 302) does) for two reasons. First, agricultural work was highly seasonal where textile work was steadier. Thus, daily textile and agricultural rates do not give an accurate picture of the relative expected earnings of women in the two sectors. Second, spinning firms generally provided housing (or at least provided heavily subsidized housing) in addition to wages; yearly agricultural contracts probably did as well, though daily work did not.

Note that most spinning firms did charge for board. According to one 1927 survey

Other data indirectly confirm these high wages. Take one 1927 survey of 3,966 workers at twelve cotton-spinning factories. These women sent home each month mean amounts ranging from 5.2 percent of their wages at one factory to 60.5 percent at another. Unfortunately, the report does not give the number of respondents within each plant. Averaging the twelve factory means, however, gives a mean of 36.0 percent. *In addition,* these women every month saved another 7.0 to 52.1 percent of their pay. Averaging the factory means gives 24.3 percent. All told, the women apparently saved or sent home nearly 60 percent of their wages: amounts ranging from a mean of 43.2 percent at the lowest factory to 67.5 percent at the highest.[18]

*The stable premium.* If the shadow wage for many workers was their wage in agricultural employment, the cotton-spinning firms paid them a premium over that wage that held relatively steady (Table 7.8).[19] In general, textile workers earned double or triple the agricultural wage. Again, the point suggests (certainly it does not prove it, for agricultural and textile wages might sometimes have moved in tandem even absent efficiency wages) that the firms considered it important to offer their workers a wage that stayed much higher than the wage those workers could have earned elsewhere. The firms paid these high wages even when they themselves faced dramatic cuts in demand; even when corporate profits fell, employee wages held firm.

*Oral accounts.* According to the workers themselves, not only did the firms pay high wages, they supplied reasonable working conditions. High wages in themselves would not, of course, prove that the firms paid efficiency wages. Instead, the firms might have paid market-clearing wages that compensated for unusually harsh disamenities. According to the women themselves, however, they generally suffered few such disamenities.

of twelve cotton-spinning factories, the women paid the factory a mean food charge ranging from 10.8 percent of salary at one factory to 22.8 percent at another. The mean of the twelve factory means was 16.9 percent. Chuo Shokugyo (1929: 69–70); see Hosei (1936: 168). According to Uno (1917), factories charged an average of 9.31 sen/day for board, and subsidized these meals with another 4.57 sen/day.

[18]Chuo (1929: 69–70); Hosei (1936: 140, 184) (corroborating data). Firms sometimes offered the woman (or her family) a sign-on loan of part of her future earnings. Unlike the cash advances in the sex industry (Chapter 6) these loans were relatively small. Of a sample of 8,926 workers hired by large Tokyo-area spinning factories in 1926, workers (or their families) received a mean sign-on loan of only ¥22.23 – about sixteen days' wages. See Chuo (1929: 33); corroborated by data in Hosei (1936: 99, 140).

[19]Obviously, given the different nature of the work, the agricultural wage would not likely have been the exact market-clearing wage in the cotton-spinning industry. I use it nonetheless because of its convenience as a benchmark.

Many historians continue to argue the contrary. Gail Lee Bernstein, for example, describes the lives that the silk-reeling workers (a job with some technical differences from cotton spinning) lived as "deplorable." Workers sang, she adds, songs with titles like the "Song of the Living Corpses."[20] Patricia Tsurumi describes the spinning mill dormitories as "prisons," the wash rooms as "appalling," and the food as "shoddy" and inadequate. Winter days in the factories were cold, and "the hot humid days of summer were hell."[21] Andrew Gordon assigns textile workers "the worst objective situation of any group of workers."[22] And Mikiso Hane concludes that "what frequently came to prevail was unrestrained exploitation."[23]

Such scholars rely too heavily on what journalists and social reformers wrote, for the women themselves told a radically different story. Not only did they earn high wages, they reported almost downright pleasant conditions. That journalists and social reformers on the one hand, and the women on the other, reacted differently to factory conditions should not surprise us. The journalists were urban, educated white-collar professionals. The workers were daughters of poor tenant farmers. That the journalists would have thought the conditions harsh tells us little about what tenant farmers would have thought. That social reformers thought them harsh tells us even less. What else, one might ask, would one expect a reformer to say?

Consider oral historian Shigemi Yamamoto's (1977: 332) experience. Yamamoto interviewed 580 former textile workers for what he planned as their "tragic history." To his surprise, none of the women regretted having taken her factory job, none complained of the food she ate in the factory dormitories, none thought she had been underpaid, and only 3 percent of the women thought their work had been harsh. By contrast, 90 percent thought the food had been good, 70 percent thought their pay had been high, and most found the work "more fun than the work at home."

[20]Bernstein (1988: 63). She rightly notes that the women "may have been better off" than they had been at home. Id., at 67. An English translation of the song appears in Tsurumi (1990: 157–9)

[21]Tsurumi (1990: 132–5, 141). Elsewhere, she properly notes that the wages were higher than other employment opportunities for women, and that the "poorly prepared and spoiled food" that the women supposedly received "would have seemed a splendid feast" to starving peasants. Id., at 132–5, 141, 148–9, 162.

[22]Gordon (1991: 75). The fact that some workers sometimes struck for higher pay or better working conditions is no evidence that pay was low or conditions bad. All else equal, even university professors prefer higher pay to lower, and better working conditions to worse. As a result, it would be curious if workers did *not* sometimes strike. Note that even in the contemporary United States, the workers who strike are not disproportionately concentrated in the lowest paying or most unpleasant jobs.

[23]Hane (1986: 144); see also Malony (1991: 232) ("Girls' salaries were extremely low").

155

"At least I got to eat rice," one former textile worker told Yamamoto. "It was better than staying home." If some women sang Bernstein's "Song of the Living Corpses," others sang very different songs – songs that echo more the notion that time flies when you're having fun (Yamamoto, 1977: 50, 72):

> Shall I fall in love with the boss,
>     or shall I ignore the boss?
> Think about it,
>     and before you know it you've finished the thread.
> Rather than fall for the boss and be hated,
>     I think I'll head for the sunshine,
>     I think I'll head for the young ones.
> I may have left home saying I'd reel thread,
>     but now I'm reeling in guys instead.

"It was harder work at first than I had done before," recalled one old woman. As a young girl, she had left her hometown for a silk-reeling factory. "But since there were lots of us and we all worked together, it was kind of fun. And besides, it paid better" (Yamamoto, 1977: 336). This, one suspects, is hardly what a worker earning market-clearing wages for brutal work would likely recall.

*Performance bonds.* The textile firms offered labor contracts that in other ways corroborated how hard they tried to create incentives for their employees not to shirk. Most dramatically, many firms withheld part of their workers' wages as performance bonds. As it had been for many indentured servants in the Americas (Engerman, 1986: 268–9), part of a textile worker's pay at such firms was contingent on her satisfactorily completing her contract (Chuo, 1929: 67–8; Murakami, 1971: 135). If she shirked, the firm fired her and kept the bond; if she worked well and completed her contract, it paid her the bond when she quit. As one might expect, workers hated these contractual provisions (Noshomu, 1903b: 99). And as a result, only firms that found it unusually hard to monitor their workers (i.e., those firms with the most to gain from paying efficiency wages) would have demanded contracts that placed them in as disadvantageous a position as did these.

## 3.3    Cartels as a corporate governance mechanism

Return, then, to the basic question: If the Boren firms could not earn monopoly rents, why did they coordinate production cuts? The answer, I suggest, derives from the principal-agent slack in corporate governance: absent a cartel, managers would have found it difficult credibly to commit to keeping the firm's efficiency wage regime. In turn, that difficulty de-

Table 7.9. *Scale economies in cotton spinning*

A. *Relative costs*

| Spindles/ factory | Materials | Wages (labor) | Amenities (labor) | Operating Costs | Total |
|---|---|---|---|---|---|
| 5,000 | 21.77 | 104.14 | 16.92 | 22.37 | 165.20 |
| 10,000 | 21.77 | 73.59 | 11.95 | 19.34 | 126.65 |
| 20,000 | 21.77 | 57.66 | 9.35 | 18.84 | 107.64 |
| 30,000 | 21.77 | 51.53 | 8.37 | 18.33 | 100.00 |
| 40,000 | 21.77 | 49.25 | 8.00 | 18.09 | 97.11 |
| 50,000 | 21.77 | 47.97 | 7.79 | 17.93 | 95.46 |
| 60,000 | 21.77 | 47.14 | 7.66 | 17.83 | 94.40 |

B. *Firm size:*

| Number of spindles | Number of firms | Percent | Total spindles | Percent |
|---|---|---|---|---|
| Under 10,000 | 10 | 12.5 | 51,268 | 0.4 |
| 10,000–49,999 | 25 | 31.3 | 614,820 | 5.0 |
| 50,000–99,999 | 14 | 17.5 | 932,828 | 7.5 |
| 100,000–299,999 | 20 | 25.0 | 3,040,996 | 24.6 |
| 300,000–499,999 | 3 | 3.7 | 1,050,604 | 8.5 |
| 500,000 and over | 8 | 10.0 | 6,668,248 | 54.0 |

*Note:* In A, costs are indexed by expenses for 30,000-spindle factories, and are for No. 20 yarn. In B, firm size is as of 1937.
*Source:* Keizo Seki, *Nihon mengyo ron [A Theory of the Japanese Cotton Industry]* (Tokyo: Tokyo daigaku shuppan kai, 1954), pp. 204, 473.

rived from four constraints to the contractual structure of the pre-War cotton-spinning firms:

1 The firm's managers often needed to raise funds from a broad range of investors;
2 The firm needed to respond to demand shocks primarily by cutting production rather than wages;
3 Investors could obtain only noisy information (a) about the wages that their managers paid laborers, and (b) about the demand curve that the industry faced; and
4 Managers hesitated to run the plant at less than full capacity.

Take each of these constraints in turn.

*Dispersed ownership.* Because cotton spinning firms faced significant economies of scale (Table 7.9), many could raise the large amounts of capital they needed only by issuing stock to a wide spectrum of investors.

Together, these firms accounted for a major part of the trades on the Tokyo and the Osaka stock exchanges (Osaka, 1928; Tokyo, 1916). Had they been able to attract money from the large conglomerates (the *zaibatsu*), perhaps they could have avoided widely dispersed stock holdings. Whatever the reason, however, those conglomerates chose not to invest heavily in cotton spinning (Ramseyer & Rosenbluth, 1995: ch. 10). Cotton-spinning entrepreneurs thus often had little choice but to form publicly held firms.

*Demand shock responses.* For reasons explained above, spinning firms could minimize their long-term labor costs only if they responded to demand shocks by cutting production rather than wages. Because of the monitoring and metering problems in the industry, they minimized their wage bill by paying efficiency wages; because most workers came from the farm, they paid efficiency wages only by paying a steady premium above the agricultural wage; because the demand for agricultural and textile labor moved independently, they often could not cut wages without cutting their efficiency wage premium.

*Noisy information.* (1) *Wages.* Public investors in the spinning firms had only noisy information about their firm's wage scales. Had the firm paid its workers a straight daily wage, a straight seniority-based wage, or a straight piece-rate contract, the investors would have had clean information. Their managers could have reported the scale they paid, and they could then have hired an independent auditor to verify the report.

Most cotton-spinning firms, however, blended seniority wages *with* piece-rate wages.[24] A pure fixed or seniority-based contract created incentive problems: workers had less reason to work hard, and more reason to shirk. A pure piece-rate contract created metering and quality problems: cotton spinning involved too much team production to permit a manager to meter individual output cleanly and readily, and piece-rate contracts induced workers to lower the quality of the output they produced. To mitigate these problems, most cotton-spinning firms blended the two contractual forms: They paid a worker by her team's output, but on an individualized per-unit scale that depended on how the manager generally appraised the pace and quality of her work. As a result, a manager periodically rated each worker's skill and diligence, and then adjusted her pay scale as warranted. In turn, the worker could increase her pay both by inducing her team to increase its production (thereby

[24]Uno (1913); Hosei (1936: 160–89). Tsurumi (1990: 148) claims that firms generally used pure piece-rate contracts for women, but this claim is belied by her own account of the many discretionary adjustments made.

increasing her own units of output), and by impressing her supervisor (thereby increasing her per-unit wage).

Investors received only noisy information about all this because the factory hired new workers regularly, but the investors could not readily gauge whether a manager promoted the workers on the per-unit scale at the optimal pace. To create the right incentives for their workers, the investors had to delegate discretion to their manager. In the process, they necessarily left themselves vulnerable. If a manager wanted to cheat on the firm's efficiency wages, he could promote his workers too slowly; if he wanted to waste firm resources, he could promote them too quickly. In either case, investors would learn that fact only much later, if they learned it all. Eventually, they might discover that they were paying higher wages than they needed to pay, or that they were incurring higher monitoring costs because their spartan wages had raised employee shirking. Alternatively, they might never know. Firms fail for a myriad of reasons, and many investors never learn why; *ex post,* investors often have trouble disentangling why a firm did so poorly. The managers responsible may have long since left anyway.

*Demand curve.* If investors lacked clean information about their own wage scales, they also lacked clean information about the industry's demand curve. They knew their own firm's sales, granted. Yet with only that information they could not distinguish between a fall in industry-wide demand and a fall in demand specific to their firm. These two problems, however, dictated radically different responses: The former dictated production cuts, while the latter required a product change to meet consumer tastes. Absent industry-wide information, investors could not distinguish the two.[25]

*Managerial reluctance to cut production.* Even where investors would have wanted their manager to cut production, a manager sometimes had an incentive not to do so. To see why, suppose first that he had short-term horizons. Many probably did, for the shortage in well-trained managers enabled people who wanted to switch jobs to switch easily. For them, pre-War Japan was not the Japan of "lifetime employment." Suppose too that a manager discovered that industry-wide demand had fallen. If he either operated the plant at a loss or idled part of it, investors would notice. If he kept the plant at full capacity and kept it in the black by cutting wages, investors would not notice – at least for some time. To cut the short-term wage bill, he needed only to slow the rate at which he promoted his workers. In the long run, by lowering the efficiency wage premium the firm paid, he would increase shirking and raise the firm's wage bill. In the

[25]Price information on yarns would not yield this information because of the broad fluctuations in prices during these years. See Ohkawa et al. (1967: 134–6).

short run, he could avoid an investigation of his managerial activities — and the short run can often last a long time.

This problem stemmed from the noisy information and collective action problems the firm's investors faced. Assume (counterfactually) that a single investor with perfect information owned each cotton-spinning firm. If industry-wide demand fell, the investor could order his manager to cut capacity. If the manager instead cut wages, he could fire him. Now assume (more realistically) that investors had noisy and incomplete information, and that each owned only a small share of the firm. Two problems ensued. First, because of their coarse information sets, investors could not distinguish industry-wide slumps from firm-specific declines. Second, because of their collective-action problems, they had little incentive to intervene in their firm unless they received strong signals that their managers might have misbehaved.[26]

To protect his tenure at a firm, a manager had somehow to ensure that investors received no strong signals that he may have mismanaged it. Should he either run the plant in the red or idle part of it, he sent just such a signal. Investors would then sometimes find it cost-effective to intervene and investigate. If he had idled the plant, he could have done so either because of an industry-wide slump, or because of his own poor performance. If the investors could obtain perfect information, he would not worry. The investors would absolve him and leave. If investors could obtain only noisy and incomplete information, however, then even an honest and able manager faced a nontrivial risk of discharge or demotion. In such a world, he often did better if he sent *no* strong signals that investors might interpret unfavorably.

*The solution.* Firms in the Japanese cotton-spinning industry solved these problems through the Boren. They did so in two steps. First, they pooled information about industry-wide demand. By contributing information about their own firms, they together generated the data that let them gauge the extent they suffered from industry-wide demand shocks. They could then have forwarded that information to their investors, and — if their investors faced no collective-action problems — those investors could have determined whether the firm should cut capacity. Absent collective-action problems, the firms needed the Boren for information pooling, and for nothing more.

Yet the investors in many cotton-spinning firms *did* face collective action problems, and it was to mitigate those problems that the Boren not

[26]True, because the stock was listed on the national exchanges, they could easily sell their interests even if they received only weak signals that their managers had misbehaved. Given that their sale price would have incorporated those signals, though, they would have found the sale small consolation.

only pooled information but also ordered capacity cuts. Just as privately held firms could trust their owner to decide whether to cut production, publicly traded firms could replicate that result by delegating the decision about production cuts to a third party, the Boren. In giving Boren officers the authority over production cuts during demand shocks, managers committed themselves credibly to reducing output during slack times. In the process, they lowered their firm's marginal costs, increased the odds that the firm would stay in the black, and thereby reduced their own incentive to cut the firm's wage scale.[27] In the process, they helped commit themselves to the firm's efficiency wage strategy, and reduced their investors' cost of verifying that they had maintained that strategy. In effect, managers and owners assigned the Boren the task not just of pooling information, but of interpreting it, of enforcing that interpretation, and of (indirectly) protecting wage levels.[28]

The Boren membership patterns loosely corroborate this hypothesis. During the early decades of the century, not all cotton-spinning firms joined the Boren. Of those that listed their shares on either the Tokyo or Osaka stock exchange, though, nearly all did. All such firms faced the principal-agent and collective-action problems described above, and most mitigated them through the Boren. Only privately held firms faced less of a problem, and primarily only they avoided the Boren.[29]

That managers needed to tie their hands also explains some of the more bizarre aspects of the agreements. Recall the details: the Boren often required firms to idle specified percentages of their capacity, but never banned them from augmenting that capacity (Table 7.2). If Boren members hoped to raise prices, this made no sense. Without a way to limit new capacity, they could not have cut production and could not have raised prices.

---

[27]Obviously, managers still had an incentive to cut wages in order to keep the firm in the black if the firm was losing money for other reasons. The Boren did not solve the problem of credible commitments for all purposes – it mitigated it for one of the most common situations in which managers would have had an incentive to cheat on the efficiency wage.

[28]Note that this was a low-risk strategy. In a world without antitrust laws, firms did not incur legal risks in agreeing to cut production. Moreover, in an internationally competitive industry with many spinners from many countries, the firms did not incur many technological risks by sharing information (Saxonhouse, 1991a).

[29]Of the eleven non-Boren cotton-spinning firms listed in Zaisei (1936: 210), none had stock listed on the major exchanges. Although Nippon kangyo (1928: 58), lists two muslin firms outside the Boren and both had publicly traded stock, Kano (1933: 125) lists these firms as not being cotton-spinning firms. It is difficult to differentiate cotton-spinning firms on the basis of name alone. If we eliminate firms that seem to have specialized in flax and wool, however, as of 1925 the only non-Boren cotton-spinning firm on either the Tokyo Stock Exchange or the Osaka Stock Exchange was one Naniwa boshoku. On Boren membership, see Dai-Nippon *Geppo;* on the stock listings, see Osaka (1928); Tokyo (1916); Kano (1933).

By contrast, suppose that the Boren firms negotiated their agreement only to mitigate the agency slack between investors and their managers. The firms now did not use the Boren to ban investments in new capacity because most of the firms had already removed that decision from the prerogative of the managers and assigned it to the investors directly. They did so by regularly draining the firm of cash.[30] Through high dividend policies, they ensured that they often could build new plants only by raising new capital – only by subjecting their new project to the discipline of the capital market (Easterbrook, 1984). The Boren's cartel was a way for managers better to align their incentives with those of their shareholders on those matters entrusted to the managers; decisions about new investments were decisions that shareholders never entrusted to the managers.

### 4   CONCLUSION

Peasants may be poor, Donald McCloskey reminds us, but they are not fools. They respond to market incentives, and they respond rationally. To induce them to work in the new spinning factories, the owners had to make it worth their while. To induce them to work *hard* in the new mills, they had to make it lucrative. The firms did so by paying peasant women double or triple what they could earn on the farm. Largely, their scheme worked. Rather than lose such a well-paying job, the young women worked hard.

Within the firm, that which promoted the welfare of its managers did not always promote the welfare of its investors. In particular, given the noisy information and the diversified ownership patterns in the industry, managers sometimes had an incentive to respond to demand shocks suboptimally – to cheat on the firm's high-wage strategy rather than to cut plant capacity. To commit credibly to cutting capacity rather than wages, the managers placed the firm in the Boren. In the process, they tied their hands: They assigned the decision about wage and production cuts to a third party.

Given all this, the tale of the Boren suggests two relevant lessons. The first is the same as the lesson to Chapter 6: Despite informational asymmetries in the market, firms and employees mitigated the problems through shrewd contractual planning. The second goes to the industrial organization of pre-War Japan: Whatever the case elsewhere in the economy, the cartel in the cotton-spinning industry – the largest, most prominent, and most durable of them all – had nothing to do with fixing prices or earning anyone monopoly rents. If pre-War Japan was plagued by inefficient cartels, no evidence of it appears in the textile industry.

[30]For evidence of high dividend rates in the spinning industry, see Dai-Nippon, *Menshi* (various years).

# 8

## Conclusions

In significant part, the history of law in imperial Japan is a history of the way courts enforced claims to scarce resources. More simply, it is a history of property rights. As one court (somewhat sanctimoniously) put it in 1918, "the inviolability of the right to property is one of the fundamental principles of the Imperial Constitution."[1] Throughout the period, Japanese courts enforced private claims to property, and labor remained an asset controlled by the laborer himself or herself.

Over the past several decades, scholars have detailed the close (though obviously imperfect) relation between institutions that enforce private rights to scarce resources and the dynamics of economic growth. Those institutions, as Douglass North (1994: 359) put it in his Nobel Prize address, "form the incentive structure of a society, and . . . in consequence, are the underlying determinants of economic performance." Through its courts, the Japanese government maintained those institutions scrupulously. The relatively efficient Japanese economic growth in the pre-War years was no surprise. It was the predictable result of the legal rules the government enacted and the courts enforced.

Land and labor are critical ingredients in almost all industries. By the turn of the century, Japanese courts systematically enforced the rights to use land, to exclude others from it, and to transfer it. Most land has value only when improved, and for most of Japanese history improvement has meant irrigation. Over irrigation rights, too, courts enforced such rights. They never did so neatly, for the right to water is not a right easy to partition and meter. Necessarily, therefore, neither is it a right easy to transfer. During most of the Tokugawa period, though, communities did what they could to partition water rights and protect the investments people made in irrigation projects. During the imperial period that followed, the courts rephrased that community custom as law and did the same.

[1]Kikawa v. Hiroshima shi, 1479 Horitsu shimbun 24, 25 (Hiroshima Ct. App. Oct. 19, 1918).

## Odd markets in Japanese history

Although the imperial courts enforced an individual's right to property, they limited acceptable use to that which would not inefficiently harm one's neighbors. If an owner used property in a way that earned modest gains but imposed larger harms on a neighbor, it held the owner liable. If people could cheaply have negotiated and bargained with each other, the courts would not have needed such rules to promote efficient use. Because people could not always negotiate and bargain cheaply, these rules became crucial. Through the rules, the imperial Japanese courts forced owners to internalize the harm they caused.

By the eighteenth century, people also held effective rights to their own labor. They held the rights by virtue of the labor market. By the mid–eighteenth century, most people worked within absconding distance of a nonseasonal urban labor market. By moving to such a market, they could find work under an informal at-will contract. Effectively, this meant that if anyone – whether owner, landlord, or parent – tried to control them, they could profitably abscond. Effectively, this practical ability to abscond gave laborers the right to dispose of their labor on their own.

The imperial Japanese courts confirmed explicitly what the Tokugawa labor market conferred implicitly. Despite the usual accounts of how imperial Japanese law bound people (particularly women) to grossly subordinate and dependent family status, the law did no such thing. Instead, it gave a family head little power over other adults. Generally, it did not let him force others to live where he specified. It did not let him (in his capacity as head) veto whom they married. It did not force him to bequeath all his property to his oldest son. And since most children other than the oldest son left the house in their twenties, he would have had few adults to control anyway. Indeed, the law did not even give husbands the control over their wives that most accounts detail: It did not let husbands freely test their wives by waiting to register a marriage, and it did not let them freely have sexual relations outside of marriage without risking divorce. Given both the presence of relatively efficient labor markets in imperial Japan and the absence of much large-scale household production, autocratic family law would not have promoted efficient growth. Crucially, Japanese courts did not impose autocratic family law.

The market made people autonomous; the law eventually confirmed that autonomy; and suriviving contracts suggest people used their autonomy shrewdly. Workers – whether female or male, poor or rich – routinely rented their labor in ways that promoted their own best interests. Take the group most often thought ruthlessly exploited: prostitutes. The women who considered taking this job (1) knew that they suffered large reputational penalties upon becoming prostitutes, (2) knew that they could not accurately guage their potential income, but (3) knew too that prostitution generated large cash flows. Accordingly, they demanded what were then very high wages, and demanded a large portion of those future wages upfront. In exchange, they agreed to work for a maximum number of years (usually six). They demanded the right to quit early if they proved profitable hires. And many did quit early.

The women who became factory workers obtained similarly advantageous deals. Because work at the cotton-spinning factories involved team production, factory owners could not readily meter each worker's output. Hence, to induce each worker to work hard, they could not use ordinary piece-rate contracts. Instead, they used "efficiency wages": they paid each worker wages that significantly exceeded the market-clearing wage. Because workers now suffered a large financial penalty if fired, they generally redoubled their effort. And to prevent their factory managers from cheating on this high-wage strategy, owners negotiated an elaborate agreement with other factories collectively to idle machines during industry-wide demand slumps.

There are some morals here about writing history: that markets matter in counterintuitive ways; that peasants and women sometimes act more selfishly and resourcefully than bourgeois scholars like to admit; that secondary sources can be wrong. There is a more basic moral too: that writing history without rational-choice theory carries large risks. Most scholars realize that one cannot understand the Tokyo Stock Exchange without that theory. But the importance of the theory goes deeper. Across a wide variety of institutions, across a wide realm of behavior, across a wide expanse of time, across a wide range of relationships — across all of this, people scheme, exchange, calculate, and think. Rational-choice theory is about some of the things that happen when they do.

# References

Note: *Materials preceded by an asterisk contain contracts or records of contracts used for the data set in Chapter 4.*

Abe, Takeshi. 1990. "Men kogyo [The Cotton Industry]." In Abe & Nishikawa (1990: 163).
Abe, Takeshi, & Nishikawa, Shunsaku (eds.). 1990. *Sangyoka no jidai [The Age of Industrialization]*. Tokyo: Iwanami shoten.
Arrow, Kenneth J. 1951. *Social Choice and Individual Values*. New Haven: Yale University Press.
Axelrod, Robert. 1981. "The Emergence of Co-operation among Egoists." 75 *American Political Science Review* 306.
Bai, Koichi. 1992. *Naien naishi kon'in yoyaku no hanrei ho kenkyu [A Study of the Common Law of Contracts to Marry and Common Law Marriages]*. Tokyo: Nihon hyoron sha.
Bardhan, Pranab K. 1984. *Land, Labor, and Rural Poverty: Essays on Development Economics*. New York: Columbia University Press.
Barro, Robert J. 1994. "Democracy and Growth." NBER Working Paper No. 4909 (Oct. 1994).
Barzel, Yoram. 1989. *Economic Analysis of Property Rights*. Cambridge: Cambridge University Press.
Beardsley, Richard K., John W. Hall, & Robert W. Ward. 1959. *Village Japan*. Chicago: University of Chicago Press.
Beason, Richard, & David E. Weinstein. 1993. "Growth, Economies of Scale, and Targeting in Japan (1955–1990)." Harvard Institute of Economic Research Discussion Paper No. 1644 (June 1993).
Becker, Gary S. 1991. *A Treatise on the Family*. Enlarged Edition. Cambridge, Mass.: Harvard University Press.
Becker, Gary S., & George Stigler. 1977. "*De gustibus, not est disputandum.*" 67 *American Economic Review* 76.
Bernstein, Gail Lee. 1988. "Women in the Silk-Reeling Industry in Nineteenth-Century Japan." In Bernstein & Fukui (1988: 63).
——. 1991a. "Introduction." In Bernstein (1991b: 1).
—— (ed.). 1991b. *Recreating Japanese Women, 1600–1945*. Berkeley: University of California Press.
Bernstein, Gail Lee, & Haruhiro Fukui (eds.). 1988. *Japan and the World: Essays*

*on Japanese History and Politics in Honour of Ishida Takeshi*. London: Macmillan.

Berry, Mary Elizabeth. 1982. *Hideyoshi*. Cambridge, Mass.: Harvard University Press.

Bittlingmayer, George. 1982. "Decreasing Average Cost and Competition: A New Look at the Addyston Pipe Case." 25 *Journal of Law & Economics* 201.

Bloch, Marc. 1975. *Slavery and Serfdom in the Middle Ages* (W. Beer, trans.). Berkeley: University of California Press.

Bolgar, Vera. 1975. "Abuse of Rights in France, Germany, and Switzerland: A Survey of a Recent Chapter in Legal Doctrine." 35 *Louisiana Law Review* 1015.

Bolitho, Harold. 1974. *Treasures among Men: The Fudai Daimyo in Tokugawa Japan*. New Haven: Yale University Press.

Bryant, Taimie L. 1984. "Marital Dissolution in Japan: Legal Obstacles and Their Impact." 17 *Law in Japan* 120.

———. 1990. "Sons and Lovers: Adoption in Japan." 38 *American Journal of Comparative Law* 299.

Burness, H. Stuart, & James P. Quirk. 1979. "Appropriative Water Rights and the Efficient Allocation of Resources." 69 *American Economic Review* 25.

Cheung, Steven N. S. 1970. "The Structure of a Contract and the Theory of a Non-exclusive Resource." 13 *Journal of Law & Economics* 49.

Chiba ken chiji kanbo (ed.). 1925. *Chiba ken tokei sho [Chiba Prefectural Statistics]*. Chiba: Chiba ken.

Chokki, Toshiaki. 1990. "Boshoku gyo to koo shita boshokki no hatten [The Development of Spinning and Weaving Machines in Response to the Spinning and Weaving Industry]." In Nakagawa, Morikawa, & Yui (1990: 258).

Chuo shokugyo shokai jimukyoku. 1926. *Geishogi shakufu shokaigyo ni kansuru chosa [An Investigation into the Placement Industry for Geisha, Prostitutes, and Bar Maids]*. Reprinted in Taniguchi (1971).

———. 1929. *Boseki rodo fujin chosa [An Investigation into Women Working in the Spinning Industry]*. Tokyo: Chuo shokugyo shokai jimukyoku.

Cloud, Patricia, & David W. Galenson. 1987. "Chinese Immigration and Contract Labor in the Late Nineteenth Century." 24 *Explorations in Economic History* 22.

Coase, R. H. 1960. "The Problem of Social Cost." 3 *Journal of Law & Economics* 1.

Coleman, Rex. 1956. "Japanese Family Law." 9 *Stanford Law Review* 132.

Corbin, Alain. 1990. *Women for Hire: Prositutes and Sexuality in France after 1850*. Cambridge, Mass.: Harvard University Press.

Crocker, Keith J., & Scott E. Masten. 1988. "Mitigating Contractual Hazards: Unilateral Options and Contract Length." 19 *Rand Journal of Economics* 327.

Cueto-Rua, Julio. 1975. "Abuse of Rights." 35 *Louisiana Law Review* 965.

Dai-Nippon boseki rengo kai (ed.). Various years. *Dai-Nippon boseki rengo kai geppo [Great Japanese Spinning Federation Monthly Newsletter]*. Osaka: Dai-Nippon boseki rengo kai.

———. Various years. *Menshi boseki jijo sanko sho [Reference Regarding Cotton Yarn Spinning Matters]*. Osaka: Dai-Nippon boseki rengo kai.

Dalby, Liza Crihfield. 1985. *Geisha*. New York: Random House.

de Becker, Joseph Ernest. 1899. *The Nightless City, or the "History of the Yoshiwara Yukwaku."* Yokohama: Z. P. Maruya.

———. 1910. *Annotated Civil Code of Japan*. London: Butterworth.

# References

———. 1921. *The Principles and Practice of the Civil Code of Japan*. London: Butterworth.

Demsetz, Harold. 1964. "The Exchange and Enforcement of Property Rights." 3 *Journal of Law & Economics* 1.

Dick, Andrew R. 1992. "The Competitive Consequences of Japan's Export Cartel Associations." 6 *Journal of the Japanese & International Economies* 275.

Easterbrook, Frank H. 1983. "Antitrust and the Economics of Federalism." 26 *Journal of Law & Economics* 23.

———. 1984. "Two Agency-Cost Explanations of Dividends." 74 *American Economic Review* 650.

Elison, George, & Bardwell L. Smith (eds.). 1981. *Warlords, Artists, and Commoners: Japan in the Sixteenth Century*. Honolulu: University of Hawaii Press.

Emer, P. C. (ed.). 1986. *Colonialism and Migration: Indentured Labour before and after Slavery*. Dordrecht: Martinus Nijhoff.

Engerman, Stanley L. 1973. "Some Considerations Relating to Property Rights in Man." 33 *Journal of Economic History* 43.

———. 1986. "Servants to Slaves to Servants: Contract Labour and European Expansion." In Emer (1986: 263).

———. 1994. "Slavery, Serfdom, and Other Forms of Coerced Labor: Similarities and Differences." Unpublished manuscript.

Epstein, Richard A. 1979. "Possession as the Root of Title." 13 *Georgia Law Review* 1221.

———. 1985. *Takings: Private Property and the Power of Eminent Domain*. Cambridge, Mass.: Harvard University Press.

Farris, William Wayne. 1985. *Population, Disease, and Land in Early Japan, 645–900*. Cambridge, Mass.: Council on East Asian Studies Publications.

Feeny, David. 1989. "The Decline of Property Rights in Man in Thailand, 1800–1913." 49 *Journal of Economic History* 285.

Fishback, Price V. 1992. *Soft Coal, Hard Choices: The Economic Welfare of Bituminous Coal Miners, 1890–1930*. New York: Oxford University Press.

Fletcher, William Miles, II. 1989. *The Japanese Business Community and National Trade Policy, 1920–1942*. Chapel Hill: University of North Carolina Press.

Fogel, Robert William. 1983. "'Scientific' History and Traditional History." In Fogel & Elton (1983: 5).

Fogel, Robert William, & G. R. Elton. 1983. *Which Road to the Past: Two Views of History*. New Haven: Yale University Press.

Fogel Robert William, & Stanley L. Engerman. 1974. *Time on the Cross: The Economics of American Negro Slavery*. Boston: Little, Brown.

——— (eds.). 1992a. *Without Consent or Contract: The Rise and Fall of American Slavery – Conditions of Slave Life and the Transition to Freedom: Technical Papers II*. New York: W. W. Norton.

———. 1992b. "The Slave Breeding Thesis." In Fogel & Engerman (1992a: 455).

——— (eds.). 1992c. *Without Consent or Contract: The Rise and Fall of American Slavery – Markets and Production: Technical Papers I*. New York: W. W. Norton.

———. 1992d. "Explaining the Relative Efficiency of Slave Agriculture in the Antebellum South." In Fogel & Engerman (1992c: 241).

Folbre, Nancy. 1994. "Children as Public Goods." 84 *American Economic Review* 86 (papers and proceedings).

Francks, Penelope. 1984. *Technology and Agricultural Development in Pre-War Japan*. New Haven: Yale University Press.

# References

Friedman, David. 1979. "Private Creation and Enforcement of Law: A Historical Case." 8 *Journal of Legal Studies* 399.

———. 1982. "What Is Fair Compensation for Death or Injury?" 2 *International Review of Law & Economics* 81.

Fruin, William Mark. 1973. "Labor Migration in Nineteenth Century Japan: A Study Based on Echizen Han." Ph.D. dissertation, History Department, Stanford University.

———. 1980. "Peasant Migrants in the Economic Development of Nineteenth-Century Japan." 54 *Agricultural History* 261.

Fujino, Shozaburo, Shino Fujino, & Akira Ono. 1979. *Choki keizai tokei: Sen'i kogyo [Long-Term Economic Statistics: The Textile Industry]*. Tokyo: Toyo keizai shimpo sha.

*Fujita, Goro. 1952. *Hoken shakai no tenkai katei [The Development Process of Feudal Society]*. Tokyo: Yuhikaku.

*Fujita, Goro, & Takanari Hattori. 1951. *Kinsei hoken shakai no kozo [The Structure of Early Modern Feudal Society]*. Tokyo: Ochanomizu shobo.

Fukumi, Takao. 1928. *Teito ni okeru bai'in no kenkyu [A Study of Prostitution in the Capital]*. Tokyo: Hakubunkan.

Fukuoka chiho shokugyo shokai jimu kyoku. 1928. *Dekasegi joko ni kansuru chosa [A Survey of Female Industrial Workers Employed Away from Home]*. Fukuoka: Fukuoka chiho shokugyo shokai jimu kyoku.

Fukushima, Shiro. 1962. "Fubo no kon'in doiken to sono ran'yo [The Parental Right to Consent in Marriage and Its Abuse]. "In Kanko iinkai (1962: 12).

Fukutake, Tadashi. 1982. *The Japanese Social Structure: Its Evolution in the Modern Century.* Tokyo: University of Tokyo Press.

*Furushima, Toshio. 1943. *Kinsei Nihon nogyo no kozo [The Structure of Early Modern Japanese Agriculture]*. Tokyo: Nippon hyoron sha.

*———. 1961. "Bakumatsu ki no nogyo hiyo rodosha [Agricultural Laborers during Late Tokugawa]." In Ichikawa, Watanabe, & Furushima (1961: 173).

Fuse, Akiko. 1984. "Japanese Family in Transition, Part I." *The Japan Foundation Newsletter,* Oct. 1984, at 1.

Galenson, David W. 1981. *White Servitude in Colonial America: An Economic Analysis.* Cambridge: Cambridge University Press.

———. 1984. "The Rise and Fall of Indentured Servitude in the Americas: An Economic Analysis." 44 *Journal of Economic History* 1.

———. 1989a. "Labor Market Behavior in Colonial America: Servitude, Slavery, and Free Labor." In Galenson (1989b: 52).

——— (ed.). 1989b. *Markets in History: Economic Studies of the Past.* Cambridge: Cambridge University Press.

Gardiner, C. Harvey. 1975. *The Japanese and Peru, 1873–1973.* Albuquerque: University of New Mexico Press.

Garon, Sheldon. 1903. "The World's Oldest Debate? Prostitution and the State in Imperial Japan, 1900–1945." 98 *American Historical Review* 710.

George, B. James, Jr. 1965. "Law in Modern Japan." In Hall & Beardsley (1965: 484).

Gordon, Andrew. 1991. *Labor and Imperial Democracy in Prewar Japan.* Berkeley: University of California Press.

Grubb, Farley W. 1985. "The Incidence of Servitude in Trans-Atlantic Migration, 1771–1804." 22 *Explorations in Economic History* 316.

———. 1988. "The Auction of Redemptioner Servants, Philadelphia, 1771–1804: An Economic Analysis." 48 *Journal of Economic History* 583.

———. 1992a. "The Long-Run Trend in the Value of European Immigrant Servants, 1654–1831: New Measurements and Interpretations." 14 *Research in Economic History* 167.

———. 1992b. "Does Bound Labor Have to Be Coerced Labor: The Case of Immigrant Servitude in English Colonial America." University of Delaware Working Paper No. 92–08.

———. 1994a. "The Disappearance of Organized Markets for European Immigrant Servants in the United States." 18 *Social Science History* 1.

———. 1994b. "The End of European Immigrant Servitude in the United States: An Economic Analysis of Market Collapse, 1772–1835." 54 *Journal of Economic History* 794.

Haley, John O. 1991. *Authority without Power: Law and the Japanese Paradox.* New York: Oxford University Press.

Hall, John Whitney 1981. "Japan's Sixteenth-Century Revolution." In Elison & Smith (1981: 7).

Hall, John Whitney, & Richard K. Beardsley (eds.). 1965. *Twelve Doors to Japan.* New York: McGraw-Hill.

Hall, John Whitney, & Jeffrey P. Mass (eds.). 1974. *Medieval Japan: Essays in Institutional History.* New Haven: Yale University Press.

Hall, John Whitney, Keiji Nagahara, & Kozo Yamamura (eds.). 1981. *Japan before Tokugawa: Political Consolidation and Economic Growth, 1500–1650.* Princeton: Princeton University Press.

Hall, John Whitney, & Takeshi Toyoda (eds.). 1977. *Japan in the Muromachi Age.* Berkeley: University of California Press.

Hane, Mikiso. 1972. *Japan: A Historical Survey.* New York: Charles Scribner's Sons.

———. 1982. *Peasants, Rebels, and Outcastes: The Underside of Modern Japan.* New York: Pantheon Books.

———. 1986. *Modern Japan: A Historical Survey.* Boulder: Westview Press.

Hanley, Susan B., & Kozo Yamamura. 1977. *Economic and Demographic Change in Preindustrial Japan.* Princeton: Princeton University Press.

Hara, Terushi, & Akira Kudo. 1992. "International Cartels in Business History." In Kudo & Hara (1992: 1).

Hardin, Garrett. 1968. "The Tragedy of the Commons." 162 *Science* 1243.

Hardy, Thomas. 1886. *The Mayor of Casterbridge: The Life and Death of a Man of Character.* London: Smith, Elder.

Harsin, Jill. 1985. *Policing Prostitution in Nineteenth-Century Paris.* Princeton: Princeton University Press.

Hashimoto, Takahiko. 1935. *Nippon menshiseki gyo shi nempo [A Time Line for the Japanese Cotton Yarn Spinning Industry].* Tokyo: Bunka shi nempyo seisaku kenkyu kai.

Hatate, Isao. 1984. "Suiri kaihatsu shi o meguru gijutsu to suishin sha [Technology and Developers Relating to Irrigation History]." In Tamaki, Hatate, & Imamura (1984).

*Hattori, Kiyomichi. 1960. "Shokubai onna hokonin ukejo [Employment Contracts for Prostitutes]." 140 *Nihon rekishi* 98.

Hauser, William B. 1983. "Economic History: Premodern Economy." In 2 *Kodansha Encyclopedia of Japan.* Tokyo: Kodansha.

*Hayami, Akira. 1968. *Nihon keizai shi e no shikaku [Perspectives on Japanese Economic History].* Tokyo: Toyo keizai shimpo sha.

———. 1971. "Tokugawa koki jinko hendo no chiiki teki tokusei [Regional

Characteristics of Population Movement in the Late Tokugawa Period." 64 *Mita gakkai zasshi* 67.

———. 1992. *Kinsei Nobi chiho no jinko, keizai, shakai [Population, Economy, and Society in the Early Modern Nobi Region]*. Tokyo: Sobunsha.

Hayami, Akira, & Matsuo Miyamoto. 1988a. "Gaisetsu [Overview]." In Hayami & Miyamoto (1988b: 1).

——— (eds.). 1988b. *Keizai shakai no seiritsu [The Establishment of an Economic Society]*. Tokyo: Iwanami shoten.

Hayami, Akira, & Nobuko Uchida. 1971. "Kinsei nomin no kodo tsuiseki chosa [An Investigation into the Movement of Early Modern Peasants]." 1971 *Tokugawa rinsei shi kenkyu jo kenkyu kiyo* 217.

Hayami, Yujiro, & Saburo Yamada. 1991. *The Agricultural Development of Japan: A Century's Perspective*. Tokyo: University of Tokyo Press.

Hayashi, Reiko (ed.). 1986. *Ronshu: Kinsei josei shi [Essays on Early Modern Women's History]*. Tokyo: Yoshikawa kobundo.

——— (ed.). 1993. *Nihon no kinsei, 15 [Early Modern Japan, Vol. 15]*. Tokyo: Chuo koro sha.

Henderson, Dan Fenno. 1974. "'Contracts' in Tokugawa Villages." 1 *Journal of Japanese Studies* 51.

*———. 1975. *Village "Contracts" in Tokugawa Japan*. Seattle: University of Washington Press.

Hendry, Joy. 1986. *Marriage in Changing Japan: Community and Society*. Rutland, Vt.: Charles E. Tuttle Co.

Hicks, John. 1969. *A Theory of Economic History*. Oxford: Oxford University Press.

*Hidemura, Senzo. 1950a. "Nansatsu katsuo gyogyo no rodo kankei [Labor Relations in the Bonito Fishing Industry in Southern Satsuma Domain]." 12 *Nihon shi kenkyu* 22.

*———. 1950b. "Tokugawa ki hokubu kyushu ni okeru noson hokonin no shoso [Aspects of Agricultural Village Laborers in Northern Kyushu in the Tokugawa Period]." 16 *Keizaigaku kenkyu* 97.

*———. 1951. "Tokugawa ki noson ni okeru shitsu hokonin no ikkosatsu [An Inquiry into Pledged Servants in Tokugawa Agricultural Villages]." 17 *Keizaigaku kenkyu* 155.

*———. 1955. "Kinsei kita kyushu noson ni okeru shitsu hoko [On Pledged Servants in the Agricultural Villages of Northern Kyushu in the Early Modern Period]." In Miyamoto (1955: 81).

*———. 1961–2. "Kinsei Nihon koyo shi shiryo [Materials on Employment History of Early Modern Japan]." 27 *Keizaigaku kenkyu* 77, 27 *Keizaigaku kenkyu* 121.

Higuchi, Monta. 1921. *Geisha tetsugaku [Geisha Philosophy]*. Tokyo: Jitsugaku kan.

Hobson, Barbara Meil. 1987. *Uneasy Virtue: The Politics of Prostitution and the American Reform Tradition*. New York: Basic Books.

Holmstrom, Bengt. 1982. "Moral Hazard in Teams." 13 *Bell Journal of Economics* 324.

Horei kenkyu kai (ed.). 1925. *Jitsurei hanrei bunrei shinzoku ho soran I [Family Law Overview: Regulations, Cases, Forms]*. Tokyo: Keibun sha.

Hosei daigaku keizai gaku bu (ed.). 1936. *Keihin kogyo chitai o chushin to suru chingin chosa hokoku [Survey Report on Wages Paid Primarily in the Keihin Industrial Area]*. Tokyo: Hosei daigaku keizai gaku bu.

172

# References

Hozumi, Shigeto. 1933. *Shinzoku ho [Family Law]*. Tokyo: Iwanami shoten.

Huberman, Michael. 1986. "Invisible Handshakes in Lancashire: Cotton Spinning in the First Half of the Nineteenth Century." 46 *Journal of Economic History* 987.

————. 1991a. "How Did Labor Markets Work in Lancashire? More Evidence on Prices and Quantities in Cotton Spinning, 1822–1852." 28 *Explorations in Economic History* 87.

————. 1991b. "Industrial Relations and the Industrial Revolution: Evidence from M'Connel and Kennedy, 1810–1840." 65 *Business History Review* 345.

*Ichikawa, Takayoshi. 1961. "Noson kogyo ni okeru koyo rodo [Employment Labor in Agricultural Industry]." In Ichikawa, Watanabe, & Furushima (1961: 107).

Ichikawa, Takayoshi, Nobuo Watanabe, & Toshio Furushima (eds.). 1961. *Hoken shakai kaitai ki no koyo rodo [Employed Labor during the Period of Dissolution of Feudal Society]*. Tokyo: Aoki shoten.

*Igarashi, Tomio. 1981. *Meshimori onna [Prostitutes]*. Tokyo: Shin jinbutsu orai sha.

*————. 1984. *Nihon josei bunka shi [A Cultural History of Japanese Women]*. Tokyo: Azuma shokan.

*Inoue, Sadayoshi. 1958. "Kinseiki noson hokonin no tenkai katei [The Evolutionary Process of Servants in Early Modern Agricultural Villages]." 4 *Rekishi hyoron* 9.

*————. 1960. "Kinsei ni okeru nenki kyujo hokonin no seiritsu katei to kyugin keitai [The Evolution and Wage Structure of Indentured and Wage Laborers in the Early Modern Period]." 142 *Nihon rekishi* 23.

Ishii, Ryosuke. 1948. *Nihon hoseishi gaisetsu [An Outline of Japanese Legal History]*. Tokyo: Kobundo.

*————. 1961. *Zoku Edo jidai manpitsu [More Random Notes on the Edo Period]*. Tokyo: Inoue shobo.

————. 1964. *Hosei shi [Legal History]*. Tokyo: Yamakawa shuppan sha.

*————. 1967. *Yoshiwara*. Tokyo: Chuo koron sha.

*————. 1978. *Nihon dantai ho shi [A History of Japanese Group Law]*. Tokyo: Sobun sha.

*————. 1979. *Shimpen Edo jidai manpitsu, jo [New Edition: Random Notes on the Edo Period, Vol. 1]*. Tokyo: Asahi shimbun sha.

————. 1983. *Nihon hosei shi gaisetsu [Outline of Japanese Legal History]*, Rev. ed. Tokyo: Sobunsha.

Ishijima, Kamejiro. 1928. "Chikagoro no jiyu haigyo [Recent Free Cessation]." *Seikaku*, June 1928, at 24.

*Ishikawa, Matsutaro, & Hiroji Naoe. 1977. *Bushi no ko, shomin no ko, ge [Samurai Children, Commoner Children, Vol. 2]*. Tokyo: Dai-ichi hoki shuppan K.K.

*Ishio, Yoshihisa. 1950. "Kinsei jinshin baibai sairon [Rethinking the Purchase and Sale of Humans in the Early Modern Period]." 27 *Hogaku ronshu* 717.

————. 1975. *Nihon keisei ho no kenkyu [Studies in Early Modern Japanese Law]*. Tokyo: Bokutakusha.

Ito, Hidekichi. 1931. *Kotoka no kanojo no seikatsu [The Lives of Women under the Red Lamps]*. Tokyo: Jitsugyo no nihon sha. Reprinted, Tokyo: Funi shuppan, 1982.

*Ito, Sueshiro. 1929. "Shichi hoko [Pledged Service]." 54 *Rekishi chiri* 613.

*Iwai, Norishige. 1937. "Oiwake yado ni okeru meshimori onna no kenkyu [A

173

Study of Prostitutes at Inns at Forks in the Road]." 3 *Minzokugaku kenkyu* 721.

Iwata, Akira. 1935. *Hanrei kon'in yoyaku ho kaisetsu [Commentary on the Common Law of Contracts to Marry].* Tokyo: Chigura shobo.

Jansen, Marius, & Gilbert Rozman (eds.). 1986. *Japan in Transition.* Princeton: Princeton University Press.

Johnson, Chalmers. 1990. "The People Who Invented the Mechanical Nightingale." *Daedalus,* summer 1990, at 71.

Kalland, Arne, & Jon Pedersen. 1984. "Famine and Population in Fukuoka Domain during the Tokugawa Period," 10 *Journal of Japanese Studies* 31.

*Kanazawa, Harusuke. 1934. "Shirakawa chiho no hokonin seido [The Employment System in the Shirakawa District]." 10 *Shakai keizai shigaku* 1382.

Kaneda, Heiichiro. 1927. "Tokugawa jidai ni okeru koyo ho no kenkyu [A Study of Employment Law in the Tokugawa Period]." 41 *Kokka gakkai zasshi* 1103, 41 *Kokka gakkai zasshi* 1299, 41 *Kokka gakkai zasshi* 1651.

*Kanezashi, Shozo. 1962. "Kinsei ni okeru sen'in no koyo keiyaku ni tsuite [Regarding the Employment Contracts of Sailors in the Early Modern Period]." 13 *Hosei shi kenkyu* 164.

Kanko iinkai (ed.). 1962. *Kenri no ran'yo: ge [Abuse of Rights, 3].* Tokyo: Yuhikaku.

Kano, Shigeru (ed.). 1933. *Tokyo kabushiki torihiki jo [Tokyo Stock Exchange].* Tokyo: Shigeru Kano.

*Kansai daigaku hosei shi gakkai (ed.). 1956. *Osaka shuhen no sonraku shi ryo [Materials on the History of Osaka Area Villages].* Kyoto: Kansai daigaku.

Kantor, Shawn E. 1991. "Razorbacks, Ticky Cows, and the Closing of the Georgia Open Range: The Dynamics of Institutional Change Uncovered." 51 *Journal of Economic History* 861.

———. 1995. "The Political Economy of Coalition-Formation: The Case of Livestock Enclosure in the Postbellum South." 32 *Explorations in Economic History* 82.

Kanzaki, Kiyoshi. 1953. *Musume o uru machi [Towns That Sell Daughters].* Tokyo: Shinko shuppan sha.

Karsten, Peter. 1990. "'Bottomed on Justice': A Reappraisal of Critical Legal Studies Scholarship Concerning Breaches of Labor Contracts by Quitting or Firing in Britain and the U.S., 1630–1880." 34 *American Journal of Legal History* 213.

Kato, Ichiro. 1973. "Nogyo ho [Agricultural Law]." In Ukai et al. (1973: VI-209).

———. 1985. *Nogyo ho [Agricultural Law].*

Kawashima, Takeyoshi. 1950a. "Jinshin baibai no rekishiteki seikaku [The Historical Character of the Purchase and Sale of Humans]." Reprinted in Kawashima (1982: I-80).

———. 1950b. *Nihon shakai no kazokuteki kosei [The Family Structure of Japanese Society].* Tokyo: Nihon hyoron sha.

———. 1951. "Jinshin baibai no horitsu kankei (1) [The Legal Status of the Purchase and Sale of Humans: 1]." 68 *Horitsu kyokai zasshi* 699.

———. 1955. "Jinshin baibai keiyaku no hoteki koryoku [The Legal Effectiveness of Contracts for the Purchase and Sale of Humans]." *Horitsu jiho,* Sept., at 72.

———. 1960. "Kindai ho no taikei to kyokan ni yoru onsen ken [Hot Springs Rights under Custom and the Early Modern Legal Order]." 76 *Hogaku kyokai zasshi* 426.

174

# References

———. 1982. *Kawashima Takeyoshi chosaku shu [The Collected Works of Take-yoshi Kawashima]*. Tokyo: Iwanami shoten.

Kawashima, Takeyoshi, with Michio Nagai & John W. Bennett. 1962. "A Summary and Analysis of 'The Family Structure of Japanese Society.'" In Silberman (1962: 101).

Kawashima, Takeyoshi, Toshitaka Shiomi, & Yozo Watanabe (eds.). 1964. *Onsenken no kenkyu [A Study of Hot Springs Rights]*. Tokyo: Keiso shobo.

Keene, Donald (trans.). 1961. *Four Major Plays of Chikamatsu*. New York: Columbia University Press.

Keishi cho. 1935. *Tamanoi Kameido sekkyakufu honseki narabi zenshakukin shirabe [A Survey of the Indentures and Hometowns of Tamanoi and Kameido Hostesses]*. Reprinted in *Nihon* (1980).

Keishi cho sokan kanbo bunsho ka. 1933. *Showa nana nen keishi cho tokei ichi ippan [An Outline of Police Agency Statistics for 1932]*. Tokyo: Sokan kanbo bunsho ka.

Kitamura, Toshio. 1950. *Nihon kangai suiri kanko no shiteki kenkyu [A Historical Study of Customary Irrigation Rights in Japan]*. Tokyo: Iwanami shoten.

Klein, Benjamin, Robert G. Crawford, & Armen A. Alchian. 1978. "Vertical Integration, Appropriable Rents, and the Competitive Contracting Process." 21 *Journal of Law & Economics* 297.

Klein, Benjamin, & Keith B. Leffler. 1981. "The Role of Market Forces in Assuring Contractual Performance." 89 *Journal of Political Economy* 615.

*Kobayashi, Keiichiro. 1955. "Kinsei sonpo yuri no jittai to jinshin baibai [The Reality of Early Modern Village Prostitution Districts and the Purchase and Sale of Humans]." 89 *Nihon rekishi* 24.

Kobayashi, Mitsue. 1979. "Kanko suiri ken no seikaku to kore o meguru mondai [The Character of Customary Water Rights and Related Issues]." In Ogata (1979: 191).

*Kodera, Tetsunosuke. 1958. *Miyazaki ken kinsei shakai keizai shi [The Early Modern Social and Economic History of Miyazaki Prefecture]*. Miyazaki: Miyazaki ken shiryo hensan kai.

Kojima, Shotaro. 1932. *Waga kuni shuyo sangyo ni okeru karuteru teki tosei [Cartel-Controls in the Major Industries in Our Country]*. Tokyo: Yufukan shobo.

Kokushi daijiten henshu iinkai (eds.). 1988. *Kokushi daijiten [The Great Encyclopedia of National History]*. Tokyo: Yoshikawa kobunkan.

Kotlikoff, Laurence J. 1992. "Quantitative Description of the New Orleans Slave Market." In Fogel & Engerman (1992c: 31).

Kudo, Akira, & Terushi Hara (eds.). 1992. *International Cartels in Business History*. Tokyo: University of Tokyo Press.

Kusama, Yasoo. 1930. *Jokyu to baisho fu [Waitresses and Prostitutes]*. Tokyo: Hanjin sha.

Kussmaul, Ann. 1981. *Servants in Husbandry in Early Modern England*. Cambridge: Cambridge University Press.

*Kyokoka no Tohoku noson (fukkoku ban) [Reprint: The Northeast Farm Villages during the Panic]*. 1984. Tokyo: Funi shuppan.

Landes, Elisabeth M., & Richard A. Posner. 1978. "The Economics of the Baby Shortage." 7 *Journal of Legal Studies* 323.

Landes, William M., & Richard A. Posner. 1987. *The Economic Structure of Tort Law*. Cambridge, Mass.: Harvard University Press.

Lazonick, William, & William Mass. 1984. "The Performance of the British Cotton Industry, 1870–1913." 9 *Research in Economic History* 1.

## References

Leupp, Gary P. 1992. *Servants, Shophands, and Laborers in the Cities of Tokugawa Japan*. Princeton: Princeton University Press.

Levmore, Saul. 1986. "Rethinking Comparative Law: Variety and Uniformity in Ancient and Modern Tort Law." 61 *Tulane Law Review* 235.

———. 1987. "Variety and Uniformity in the Treatment of the Good-Faith Purchaser." 16 *Journal of Legal Studies* 43.

Libecap, Gary D. 1989. *Contracting for Property Rights*. Cambridge: Cambridge University Press.

Liebermann, Yehoshua. 1986. "Economic Efficiency and Making of the Law: The Case of Transaction Costs in Jewish Law." 15 *Journal of Legal Studies* 387.

Lipsey, R., & K. Lancaster. 1956–7, "The General Theory of Second Best." 24 *Review of Economic Studies* 11.

Lyons, John S. 1985. "Vertical Integration in the British Cotton Industry, 1825–1850: A Revision." 45 *Journal of Economic History* 419.

Maine, Henry Sumner. 1906. *Ancient Law*. London: John Murray. Reprinted, Buffalo: William S. Hein, 1983.

*Maki, Hidemasa. 1970. *Kinsei Nihon no jinshin baibai no keifu [The Geneology of the Sale of Humans in Early Modern Japan]*. Tokyo: Sobun sha.

*———. 1971. *Jinshin baibai [The Sale of Humans]*. Tokyo: Iwanami shoten.

*———. 1977. *Koyo no rekishi [A History of Employment]*. Tokyo: Kobundo.

Makino, Kikunosuke. 1908. *Nippon shinzoku ho ron [The Theory of Japanese Family Law]*. Tokyo: Ganshodo.

Malony, Barbara. 1991. "Activism among Women in the Taisho Cotton Textile Industry." In Bernstein (1991b: 217).

Mass, Jeffrey P. 1974. "Jito Land Possession in the Thirteenth Century: The Case of Shitagi Chubun." In Hall & Mass (1974: 157).

Matsumoto, Akio. 1962. "Fuyo seikyuken no genkai [The Limits of the Right to Demand Support]." In Kanko iinkai (1962: 113).

Maynard Smith, John, & G. A. Parker. 1976. "The Logic of Asymmetric Contests." 24 *Animal Behavior* 159.

McChesney, Fred S. 1995. "Be True to Your School: Chicago's Contradictory Views of Antitrust and Regulation." In McChesney & Shughart (1995: 323).

McChesney, Fred S., & William F. Shughart II (eds.). 1995. *The Causes and Consequences of Antitrust: The Public-Choice Perspective*. Chicago: University of Chicago Press.

McKean, Margaret A. 1991. "Defining and Dividing Property Rights in the Commons: Today's Lessons from the Japanese Past." Duke University Program in Political Economy Working Paper No. 150 (Oct. 17, 1991).

Mihashi, Kusuhei (ed.). 1934. *Toyo boseki kabushiki gaisha yoran [A Survey of the Toyo Spinning Corporation]*. Osaka: Toyo boseki K.K.

Miller, Gary J. 1992. *Managerial Dilemmas: The Political Economy of Hierarchy*. Cambridge: Cambridge University Press.

Miller, Geoffrey P. 1993. "Ritual and Regulation: A Legal-Economic Interpretation of Selected Biblical Texts." 22 *Journal of Legal Studies* 477.

*Minami, Kazuo. 1969. *Edo no shakai kozo [The Social Structure of Edo]*. Tokyo: Kaku shobo.

Minami, Ryoshin. 1986. *The Economic Development of Japan: A Quantitative Study*. Houndmills, U.K.: Macmillan.

Miwa, Yoshiro. 1995. *Firms and Industrial Organization in Japan*. London: Macmillan.

# References

Miyake, Yoshiko. 1991. "Doubling Expectations: Motherhood and Women's Factory Work under State Management in Japan in the 1930s and 1940s." In Bernstein (1991b: 267).

*Miyamoto, Mataji. 1948. *Kinsei shogyo keiei no kenkyu [A Study of Commercial Management in the Early Modern Period].* Kyoto: Dai yashima shuppan K.K.

—— (ed.). 1955. *Noson kozo no shiteki bunseki [A Historical Analysis of Agricultural Village Structure].* Tokyo: Nihon hyoron sha.

Mnookin, Robert H., & Lewis Kornhauser. 1979. "Bargaining in the Shadow of the Law: The Case of Divorce." 88 *Yale Law Journal* 950.

*Mori, Kihei. 1950. "Itsubushi shitsu hokonin no kenkyu [A Study of Servants under the Redemptioner Pawn System]." 12 *Nihon shi kenkyu* 336.

Mosk, Carl. 1978. "Fecundity, Infanticide, and Food Consumption in Japan." 15 *Explorations in Economic History* 269.

——. 1979. "The Decline in Marital Fertility in Japan." 33 *Population Studies* 19.

Murakami, Nobuhiko. 1971. *Meiji josei shi [A History of Meiji Women].* Tokyo: Riron sha.

*Murao, Yasuhei. 1977. *Awaguni jinshin baibai shi ko [Thoughts on the Sale of Humans in the Awa Domain].* Tokushima: Kyoiku shuppan sentaa.

Murata, Toshihisa. 1979. "Nihon no nogyo yosui [Agricultural Water in Japan]." In Ogata (1979: 3).

Murphy, U. G. 1909. *The Social Evil in Japan.* 4th ed. Tokyo: Kyobunkan.

Mustang Ranch, Inc. 1989. *Common Stock Prospectus.*

Muto, Sanji. 1927. "Bosekigyo [The Spinning Industry]." In *Shakai keizai taikei [Overview of Social Economics].* No publication information; cataloged in the University of Tokyo Department of Economics library at 12/120P.

Nagahara, Keiji, & Kozo Yamamura. 1977. "Village Communities and Daimyo Power." In Hall & Toyoda (1977: 107).

*Nagano, Hiroko. 1986. "Kinsei koki joshi rodo no hensen to tokushitsu [Special Characteristics and Change in Female Labor during the Late Early Modern Period]." In Hayashi (1986: 103).

Nagasaki ken (ed.). 1913. *Nagasaki ken tokei sho [Nagasaki Prefectural Statistics].* Nagasaki: Nagasaki ken.

Naikaku tokei kyoku. 1930. *Rodo tokei yoran [Outline of Labor Statistics].* Tokyo: Tokyo tokei kyokai.

Nakabe, Yoshiko. 1974. *Kinsei toshi shakai keizai shi kenkyu [Studies in the Social Economic History of Early Modern Cities].* Kyoto: Koyo Shobo.

*Nakada, Kaoru. 1943. *Hosei shi ronshu, dai 3 kan [Essays in Legal History, Vol. 3].* Tokyo: Iwanami shoten.

Nakagawa, Keiichiro, Hidemasa Morikawa, & Tsunehiko Yui (eds.). 1990. *Kindai Nihon keiei shi no kiso chishiki [Basic Information Regarding Early Modern Japanese Management History].* Tokyo: Yuhikaku.

Nakamura, Saburo. 1954. *Nihon baishun torishimari ko [A Treatise on the Regulation of Japanese Prostitution].* Tokyo: Nihon fuzoku kenkyu kai.

Nakamura, Takafusa, & Konosuke Odaka (eds.). 1989. *Niju kozo [Dual Structure].* Tokyo: Iwanami shoten.

Nakane, Chie. 1990. "Tokugawa Society." In Nakane & Oishi (1990: 213).

Nakane, Chie, & Shinzaburo Oishi (eds.). 1990. *The Social and Economic Antecedents of Modern Japan.* Tokyo: University of Tokyo Press.

*Nakayama, Taro. 1927. *Baisho san zen nen shi [A 3000-Year History of Prostitution].* Tokyo: Shun'yodo.

# References

*———. 1931. "Waga kuni jinshin baibai kinshi no hoseishi teki kosatsu [Observations from Legal History on the Ban in Our Country on the Purchase and Sale of Human Beings." *Horitsu jiho,* Sept. 1931, at 843.

Nardinelli, Clark. 1982. "Corporal Punishment and Children's Wages in Nineteenth Century Britain." 19 *Explorations in Economic History* 283.

*Nihon fujin mondai shiryo shusei [Collected Materials on Japanese Women's Issues].* 1980. Tokyo: Domesu shuppan.

Nihon keiei shi kenkyu sho (ed.). 1988. *Nippon yusen kabushiki kaisha 100-nen shi [A 100-Year History of the N.Y.K.].* Tokyo: Nippon yusen kabushiki kaisha.

Nippon kangyo ginko chosaka (ed.). 1928. *Menshi boseki gyo ni kansuru chosa [An Investigation into the Cotton Thread Spinning Industry].* Tokyo: Nihon kangyo ginko chosaka.

Nishikawa, Hiroshi. 1987. *Nippon teikoku shugi to mengyo [Japanese Imperialism and the Cotton Industry].* Kyoto: Minerubwa shobo.

Nishimura, Nobuo. 1938. "Zenshakkin keiyaku ni tsuite [Regarding Indenture Contracts]." 7 *Minsho ho zasshi* 418, 1022.

*Nishiyama, Matsunosuke. 1963. *Kuruwa [Red-Light Districts].* Tokyo: Ikubun kan.

——— (ed.). 1973. *Edo chonin no kenkyu [A Study of Edo Merchants].* Tokyo: Yoshikawa kobun kan.

*———. 1979. *Yujo [Prostitutes].* Tokyo: Kindo shuppan sha.

Nishizaki, Akira. 1927. "Tokugawa jidai ni okeru nogyo suiri no kenri kankei [Water Usage Rights in the Tokugawa Period]." 41 *Kokka gakkai zasshi* 234, 463.

Nisshin Boseki Kabushiki Kaisha (ed.). 1969. *Nisshin Boseki hyakunen shi [A One-Hundred-Year History of Nisshin Boseki].* Tokyo: Nisshin Boseki K.K.

Noda, Yoshiyuki. 1976. *Introduction to Japanese Law.* Tokyo: University of Tokyo Press.

Nomi, Yoshihisa. 1980. Case Comment. 97 *Hogaku kyokai zasshi* 577.

North, Douglass C. 1981. *Structure and Change in Economic History.* New York: W. W. Norton.

———. 1991. "Institutions, Ideology, and Economic Performance." 11 *Cato Journal* 477.

———. 1994. "Economic Performance through Time." 84 *American Economic Review* 359.

North, Douglass C., & Robert Paul Thomas. 1973. *The Rise of the Western World: A New Economic History.* Cambridge: Cambridge University Press.

Noshomu sho. 1903a. *Shokko jijo [Circumstances of Factory Workers].* Reprinted, Tokyo: Koseikan, 1981.

———. 1903b. *Menshi boseki shokko jijo [Conditions of Factory Workers in Cotton Spinning].* Tokyo: Noshomu sho.

———. Various years. *Noshomu tokei hyo [Agricultural and Commercial Statistics].* Tokyo: Noshomu sho somukyoku tokeika.

O'Callaghan, Sean. 1968. *The Yellow Slave Trade: A Survey of the Traffic in Women and Children in the East.* London: Anthony Blond.

Oda, Hiroshi. 1992. *Japanese Law.* London: Butterworth.

Odaka, Konosuke. 1989. "Niju kozo [Dual Structure]." In Nakamura & Odaka (1989: 133).

Ogata, Hiroyuki (ed.). 1979. *Mizu to Nihon nogyo [Water and Japanese Agriculture].*

Ogyu, Sorai. 1722. *Seidan [Political Discourses].* Reprinted in *Ogyu Sorai zenshu*

178

# References

*[The Complete Works of Ogyu Sorai]*, vol. 6 (Tokyo: Kawade shobo shinsha, 1973).

Ohkawa, Kazushi, Tsutomu Noda, Nobuyuki Takamatsu, Saburo Yamada, Minoru Kumazaki, Yuichi Shinoya, & Ryoshin Minami. 1967. *Choki keizai tokei: Bukka [Long-Term Economic Statistics: Prices]*. Tokyo: Toyo keizai shimpo sha.

Ohsato, Katsuma (ed.). 1966. *Meiji iko honpo shuyo keizai tokei [Principal Economic Statistics for Our Nation since the Meiji Period]*. Tokyo: Bank of Japan.

Okazaki, Tetsuji. 1987. "1930-nen dai no Nihon ni okeru keiki junkan [Japanese Business Cycles and Capital Accumulation in the 1930s]." 39–2 *Shakai kagaku kenkyu* 1.

Okubo, Hanayuki. 1906. *Kagai fuzoku shi [A Record of the Customs of the Red-Light District]*. Tokyo: Ryubun kan. Reprinted, Tokyo: Nihon tosho sentaa, 1983.

*Ono, Takeo. 1926. "Tokugawa jidai no noson hokonin [Agricultural Village Laborers in the Tokugawa Period]." 2 *Shakai kagaku* 221.

*———. 1944. *Saitei zoho: Noson shakai shi ron ko [Lectures in Agricultural Village Social History]*. Rev. ed. Tokyo: Ganshodo shoten.

Osaka fu (ed.). 1916. *Osaka fu tokei sho [Osaka Prefectural Statistics]*. Osaka: Osaka fu.

Osaka kabushiki torihiki sho (ed.). 1928. *Okabu 50-nenshi [50-Year History of the OSE]*. Osaka: Osaka kabushiki torihiki sho.

*Otake, Hideo. 1955–6. "Kinseiki no noson hoko [Agricultural Village Labor in the Early Modern Period]." 5 *Kobe hogaku zasshi* 408, 5 *Kobe hogaku zasshi* 544.

*———. 1983. *Kinsei koyo kankei shi ron [The Theory of the History of Early Modern Employment Relations]*. Tokyo: Yuhikaku.

Oyake, Soichi (ed.). 1927. *Shakai mondai koza, dai 12 kan [Lectures on Social Problems, vol. 12]*. Shincho sha.

Parsons, Donald O., & Claudia Goldin. 1989. "Parental Altruism and Self-Interest: Child Labor among Late Nineteenth-Century American Families." 27 *Economic Inquiry* 637.

Patrick, Hugh, & Larry Meisner (eds.). 1976. *Japanese Industrialization and Its Social Consequences*. Berkeley: University of California Press.

Pharr, Susan J. 1981. *Political Women in Japan: The Search for a Place in Political Life*. Berkeley: University of California Press.

Philippi, Donald L. (trans.). 1968. *Kojiki*. Princeton: Princeton University Press.

Pirrong, Stephen Craig. 1992. "An Application of Core Theory to the Analysis of Ocean Shipping Markets." 35 *Journal of Law & Economics* 89.

Polinsky, A. Mitchell. 1983. *An Introduction to Law and Economics*. Boston: Little, Brown.

Popkin, Samuel L. 1979. *The Rational Peasant: The Political Economy of Rural Society in Vietnam*. Berkeley: University of California Press.

Posner, Richard A. 1972. "A Theory of Negligence." 1 *Journal of Legal Studies* 29.

———. 1986. *Economic Analysis of Law*. 3d ed. Boston: Little, Brown.

———. 1993. "What Do Judges and Justices Maximize? (The Same Thing Everyone Else Does)." Chicago Law & Economics Working Paper (2d Series) No. 15 (Mar. 15, 1993).

Priest, George. 1977. "The Common Law Process and the Selection of Efficient Rules." 6 *Journal of Legal Studies* 65 (1977).

# References

Priest, George, & Benjamin Klein. 1984. "The Selection of Disputes for Litigation." 8 *Journal of Legal Studies* 1.

Ramseyer, J. Mark, & Minoru Nakazato. 1989. "The Rational Litigant: Settlement Amounts and Verdict Rates in Japan." 18 *Journal of Legal Studies* 263.

Ramseyer, J. Mark, & Frances M. Rosenbluth. 1995. *The Politics of Oligarchy: Institutional Choice in Imperial Japan.* Cambridge: Cambridge University Press.

Rasmusen, Eric. 1989. *Games and Information.* London: Basil Blackwell.

———. 1992. "An Income-Satiation Model of Efficiency Wages." 80 *Economic Inquiry* 467.

Roback, Jennifer. 1984. "Southern Labor Law in the Jim Crow Era: Exploitative or Competitive." 51 *University of Chicago Law Review* 1161.

Robson, R. 1957. *The Cotton Industry in Britain.* London: Macmillan.

Rodosho fujin shonen kyoku. 1952. *Fujin rodo no jitsujo [The Reality of Female Labor].* Tokyo: Rodosho.

———. 1953. *Nenshosha no tokushu koyo kanko [Special Employment Customs of Minors].* Tokyo: Rodosho.

Root, Hilton L. 1994. *The Foundation of Privilege: Political Foundations of Markets in Old Regime France and England.* Berkeley: University of California Press.

Rosen, Ruth. 1982. *The Lost Sisterhood: Prostitution in America, 1900–1918.* Baltimore: Johns Hopkins University Press.

Rosenthal, Jean-Laurent. 1992. *The Fruits of Revolution: Property Rights, Litigation, and French Agriculture, 1700–1860.* Cambridge: Cambridge University Press.

Rosenzweig, Mark R., & Oded Stark. 1989. "Consumption Smoothing, Migration, and Marriage: Evidence from Rural India." 97 *Journal of Political Economy* 905.

Rothenberg, Winifred Barr. 1992. *From Marketplace to a Market Economy: The Transformation of Rural Massachusetts, 1750–1850.* Chicago: University of Chicago Press.

Rozman, Gilbert. 1973. *Urban Networks in Ch'ing China and Tokugawa Japan.* Princeton: Princeton University Press.

———. 1986. "Castle Towns in Transition." In Jansen & Rozman (1986: 318).

Rubin, Paul H. 1977. "Why Is the Common Law Efficient?" 6 *Journal of Legal Studies* 51.

Saito, Naoshi. 1930. "Yujo yugei jin no uchimaku [The Inside Story of Young Female Entertainers." 135 *Jikei* 67.

Saito, Osamu. 1978. "The Labor Market in Tokugawa Japan: Wage Differentials and the Real Wage Level, 1727–1830." 15 *Explorations in Economic History* 84.

———. 1987. *Shoka no sekai, Uradana no sekai [The World of the Merchant Houses, the World behind the Houses].* Tokyo: Riburopoto.

———. 1992. "Infanticide, Fertility and 'Population Stagnation': The State of Tokugawa Historical Demography." 4 *Japan Forum* 369.

Sakurai, Yuki. 1993. "Mabiki to datai [Infanticide and Abortion]." In Hayashi (1993: 97).

Sato, Elizabeth. 1974. "The Early Development of the Shoen." In Hall & Mass (1974: 94).

*Sato, Seiichiro. 1983. *Akita ken yuri shi [A History of Prostitution Districts in Akita Prefecture].* Akita: Mumeisha shuppan.

# References

Saxonhouse, Gary R. 1976. "Country Girls and Communication among Competitors in the Japanese Cotton-Spinning Industry." In Patrick & Meisner (1976: 97).

———. 1991. "Mechanisms for Technology Transfer in Japanese Economic History." 12 *Managerial and Decision Economics* 83.

Scully, Gerald W. 1992. *Constitutional Environments and Economic Growth.* Princeton: Princeton University Press.

Seiji keizai kenkyu sho. 1951. *Nomin to rodo sha no seikatsu suijun no hendo [Changes in the Living Standards of Farmers and Workers].* [Tokyo]: Seiji keizai kenkyu sho.

Seikaku. 1931a. "Shogi karyubyo cho [A Survey of Venereal Disease among Licensed Prostitutes]." *Seikaku,* March 1931, at 20.

———. 1931b. "Showa gonen kyuseigun no haisho undo [The 1930 Activities of the Salvation Army in Furtherance of the Abolition of Licensed Prostitution]." *Seikaku,* June 1931, at 29.

Seisan chosa kai (ed.). 1912. *Shuyo kogyo gairan [Survey of Major Industries].* Tokyo: Seisan chosa kai.

Seki, Keizo. 1954. *Nihon mengyo ron [A Theory of the Japanese Cotton Industry].* Tokyo: Tokyo daigaku shuppan kai.

Shadwell, Arthur. 1911. "Prostitution." In *Encyclopaedia Britannica.* 11th ed., 22: 457. New York: Encyclopaedia Britannica.

Shakai jigyo kenkyu jo. 1936. *Shuro shonen shojo rodo jijo chosa [Survey of Working Conditions of Working Boys and Girls].* Tokyo: Chuo shakai jigyo kyokai.

Shakai kyoku. 1935. *Tohoku chiho noson hihei jokyo (dai ni hen) [Poverty in the Northeast Region Farm Villages.* 2d ed. Reprinted in *Kyokoka* (1984).

Shapiro, Carl, & Joseph E. Stiglitz. 1984. "Equilibrium Unemployment as a Worker Discipline Device." 74 *American Economic Review* 433.

Shavell, Steven. 1987. *Economic Analysis of Accident Law.* Cambridge, Mass.: Harvard University Press.

Shepsle, Kenneth A., & Barry R. Weingast. 1981. "Structure Induced Equilibrium and Legislative Change." 37 *Public Choice* 503.

Shikitei, Samba. 1809 [1934]. *Kohon ukiyoburo kaichu [Bathhouse of the Floating World: Annotated Manuscript].* Yonekichi Deguchi, ed. Osaka: Genrokudo shoin.

Shindo, Takejiro. 1958. *Mengyo rodo sanko tokei [Reference Statistics Regarding Labor in the Cotton Industry].* Tokyo: Tokyo daigaku shuppan kai.

Shinohara, Miyohei. 1972. *Choki keizai tokei: kokogyo [Long-Term Economic Statistics: The Mining and Manufacturing Industries].* Tokyo: Toyo keizai shimpo sha.

Shinomiya, Toshiyuki. 1990. "Karuteru to sono tokucho [Cartels and Their Characteristics]." In Nakagwa, Morikawa, & Yui (1990: 193).

*Shitanaka, Kunihiko. 1959–60. *Nihon zankoku monogatari [Accounts of Cruelty in Japan],* vols. 1, 3. Tokyo: Heibonsha.

Shizuoka ken chiji kanbo (ed.). 1919. *Shizuoka ken tokei sho [Shizuoka Prefectural Statistics].* Shizuoka: Shizuoka ken.

Shoji, Otokichi. 1930. *Boseki sogyo tanshuku shi [A History of the Spinning Operation Reductions].* Osaka: Nippon mengyo kurabu, 1930.

Shoko daijin kanbo takei ka (ed.). 1936. *Kojo tokei hyo [Census of Manufactures].* Tokyo: Tokyo tokei kyokai.

———. Various years. *Shoko sho tokei hyo [Statistical Tables for the Ministry of Commerce and Industry].* Tokyo: Tokyo tokei kyokai.

# References

Shultz, George P. 1995. "Economics in Action: Ideas, Institutions, Policies." 85 *American Economic Review (Papers & Proceedings)* 1.

Sievers, Sharon L. 1983. *Flowers in Salt: The Beginnings of Feminist Consciousness in Modern Japan.* Stanford: Stanford University Press.

Silberman, Bernard S. (ed.). 1962. *Japanese Character and Culture.* Tucson: University of Arizona Press.

Smethurst, Richard J. 1986. *Agricultural Development and Tenancy Disputes in Japan, 1870–1940.* Princeton: Princeton University Press.

Smith, Robert J. 1963. "Aspects of Mobility in Pre-Industrial Japanese Cities." 4 *Comparative Studies in Society and History* 416.

———. 1983. *Japanese Society: Tradition, Self and the Social Order.* Cambridge: Cambridge University Press.

Smith, Robert J., & Ella Lury Wiswell. 1982. *The Women of Suye Mura.* Chicago: University of Chicago Press.

Smith, Thomas C. 1952. "The Japanese Village in the Seventeenth Century." 12 *Journal of Economic History* 1.

———. 1959. *The Agrarian Origins of Modern Japan.* Stanford: Stanford University Press.

———. 1969. "Farm Family By-Employments in Preindustrial Japan." 29 *Journal of Economic History* 687.

———. 1977. *Nakahara: Family Farming and Population in a Japanese Village, 1717–1830.* Stanford: Stanford University Press.

Somu cho tokei kyoku. 1987. *Nihon choki tokei soran [General Long-Term Statistics for Japan],* vol. 4. Tokyo: Somu cho.

Steenstrup, Carl. 1991. *A History of Law in Japan until 1868.* Leiden: E. J. Brill.

Stewart, Watt. 1951. *Chinese Bondage in Peru: A History of the Chinese Coolie in Peru, 1849–1874.* Durham: Duke University Press.

Stigler, George J. 1964. "A Theory of Oligopoly." 72 *Journal of Political Economy* 44.

Stiglitz, Joseph E. 1987. "The Causes and Consequences of the Dependence of Quality on Price." 25 *Journal of Economic Literature* 1.

Suehiro, Itsutaro. 1931. "Hanrei wo toshite mita jinshin baibai [The Purchase and Sale of Humans, Viewed through Case Law]." *Horitsu jiho,* Sept. 1931.

Sugden, Robert. 1981. *The Economics of Rights, Co-operation & Welfare.* London: Basil Blackwell.

Suginohara, Shun'ichi. 1940. *Hanrei shinzoku ho no kenkyu [The Common Law of Family Law].* Tokyo: Nippon hyoron sha.

Symanski, Richard. 1981. *The Immoral Landscape: Female Prostitution in Western Societies.* Toronto: Butterworth.

Takahashi, Bonsen. 1941. *Nippon jinko shi no kenkyu [A Study of Japanese Population].* 3 vols. Tokyo: San'yu sha.

Takamura, Naosuke. 1971. *Nihon boseki gyo shi josetsu [An Introduction to the History of the Japanese Spinning Industry].* Tokyo: Hanawa shobo.

Takayanagi, Kenzo. 1933. "Sendai han no shichimono hoko [Pledged Service in the Sendai Domain]." 2 *Hogaku* 79, 2 *Hogaku* 206.

*———. 1935. "Koho zakki [Miscellany on Ancient Law]." 4 *Hokagu* 86.

*Takenouchi, Katsu. 1970. *Nihon yujo ko [Thoughts on Japanese Prostitutes].* Tokyo: K. K. Puronzu sha.

*Takeuchi, Toshimi. 1969. *Kazoku kanko to ie seido [The House System and Family Customs].* Tokyo: Koseisha.

# References

*Takikawa, Masajiro. 1927. "Nippon rodo hoseishi kenkyu [Studies in the Japanese Labor Law History]." In Oyake (1927: 125).
*———. 1941. *Nippon hoseishi kenkyu okutsuki [Studies in Japanese Legal History, with Appendix]*. Tokyo: Yuhikaku.
*———. 1948. *Baisho seido no kenkyu [A Study of the Prostitution System]*. Tokyo: Suiko shobo.
Tamaki, Akira. 1984. "Nihon nogyo no kindaika katei ni okeru suiri no yakuwari [The Role of Irrigation in the Modernization of Japanese Agriculture]." In Tamaki, Hatate, & Imamura (1984: 7).
Tamaki, Akira, Isao Hatate, & Naraomi Imamura (eds.). 1984. *Suiri no shakai kozo [The Social Organization of Irrigation]*. Tokyo: Tokyo daigaku shuppan kai.
Tamura, Goro. 1956. "Zenshakkin muko no hanketsu ni tsuite [Regarding the Case Holding Indentures Void]." 63 *Hogaku shimpo* 436.
Taniguchi, Ken'ichi (ed.). 1971. *Kindai minshu no kiroku [A Report of the Modern Populace]*, vol. 3. Tokyo: Shin jinbutsu orai sha.
Tatsuki, Mariko. 1990. "Mitsui Bussan no setsuritsu to hatten [The Establishment and Development of Mitsui Bussan]." In Nakagawa, Morikawa, & Yui (1990: 36–7).
Telser, Lester G. 1980. "A Theory of Self-Enforcing Agreements." 22 *Journal of Business* 27 (1980).
Temin, Peter. 1988. "Product Quality and Vertical Integration in the Early Cotton Textile Industry." 48 *Journal of Economic History* 891.
Thompson, E. P. 1991. *Customs in Common*. New York: New Press.
Thompson, F. M. L. 1988. *The Rise of Respectable Society: A Social History of Victorian Britain, 1830–1900*. Cambridge, Mass.: Harvard University Press.
Tiebout, Charles. 1956. "A Pure Theory of Local Expenditures." 64 *Journal of Political Economy* 416.
Tokoro, Rikio. 1973. "Edo no dekasegi nin [Workers Away from Home during the Edo Period]." In Nishiyama (1973: 263).
Tokyo kabushiki torihiki sho (ed.). 1916. *Tokyo kabushiki torihiki sho shi [The Tokyo Stock Exchange]*. Tokyo: Keizai shimbun sha.
*Tokyo teikoku daigaku shiryo hensan jo (ed.). Various dates. *Dai Nippon shiryo [Historical Materials for the Great Japan]*. Vol. 12, No. 10 (1907); Vol. 12, No. 13 (1909); Vol. 12, No. 23 (1922); Vol. 12, No. 36 (1954). Tokyo: Tokyo teikoku daigaku.
Tomosugi, Takashi. 1984. "Shizen to shite no tochi kara shohin to shite no tochi e [From Land as Nature to Land as Commodity]." In Tamaki, Hatate, & Imamura (1984: 253).
Tsuchiya, Susumu. 1966. *Kangai suiri ken ron I [The Theory of Irrigation Rights, 1]*. Tokyo: Chuo daigaku shuppan bu.
*Tsuchiya, Takao. 1937. *Nippon shihon shugi shi ronshu [Essays in the History of Japanese Capitalism]*. Tokyo: Ikusei sha.
Tsurumi, E. Patricia. 1990. *Factory Girls: Women in the Thread Mills of Meiji Japan*. Princeton: Princeton University Press.
Uemura, Yukitada. 1918. *Urare yuku onna [Sold Women]*. Tokyo: Daito kaku. Reprinted in *Kindai fujin mondai meichosaku shu zokuhen [A Collection of Famous Authors on Women's Issues – Continued Series]*, vol. 5. Tokyo: Nihon tosho sentaa, 1982.
*———. 1929a. *Nippon yuri shi [The History of Red-Light Districts in Japan]*. [Tokyo:] Shunyodo. Reprinted, Tokyo: Fujimori shoten, 1982.

———. 1929b. *Nihon yuri shi [A History of the Japanese Pleasure Quarters]*. Tokyo: Shunyodo.

Ukai, Nobushige, Masao Fukushima, Takeyoshi Kawashima, & Kiyoaki Tsuji (eds.). 1973. *Koza: Nihon kindai ho hattatsu shi [Lectures: History of Development of Law in Early Modern Japan]*. Tokyo: Keiso shobo.

Umemura, Matsuji, Saburo Yamada, Yujiro Hayami, Nobuyuki Takamatsu, & Minoru Kumazaki. 1966. *Choki keizai tokei: Norin gyo [Long-Term Economic Statistics: Agriculture and Forestry]*. Tokyo: Toyo keizai shimpo sha.

Uno, Riyuemon. 1913. *Shokko chingin shiharai no shin hoho [A New Means of Paying Factory Workers]*. Osaka: Kogyo kyoiku kai.

———. 1915a. *Shokko kinzoku nen su cho (jo) [A Survey of Work Tenure among Factory Workers (1)]*. Osaka: Kogyo kyoiku kai (Shokko mondai shiryo, No. A163).

———. 1915b. *Shokko kinzoku nen su cho (ge) [A Survey of Work Tenure Among Factory Workers (2)]*. Osaka: Kogyo kyoiku kai (Shokko mondai shiryo, No. A164).

———. 1917. *Shoku hi teigaku no chosa [A Survey of Food Charges]*. Osaka: Kogyo kyoiku kai (Shokko mondai shiryo, No. B79).

*Usami, Misako. 1986. "Tokaido yado eki ni okeru meshimori onna no sonzai keitai [The Situation of Prostitutes at Inns along the Tokaido]." In Hayashi (1986: 345).

*———. 1993. "Meshimori onna [Prostitutes]." In Hayashi (1993: 39).

Viscusi, W. Kip. 1992. *Fatal Tradeoffs: Public and Private Responsibilities for Risk*. New York: Oxford University Press.

von Mehren, Arthur Taylor (ed.). 1963. *Law in Japan: The Legal Order in a Changing Society*. Cambridge, Mass.: Harvard University Press.

Wagatsuma, Sakae. 1923. "Hanrei yori miru 'ko no chitsujo zenryo no fuzoku' ['Public Order and Good Customs,' as Seen in the Case Law]." 41 *Hogaku kyokai zasshi* 904.

———. 1955. "Zenshakkin muko no hanketsu [Case Holding Indenture Contracts Void]." 93 *Jurisuto* 23.

*Wakita, Osamu. 1978. *Kinsei hoken shakai no keizai kozo [The Economic Structure of Early Modern Feudal Society]*. Rev. ed. Tokyo: Ochanomizu shobo.

Walkowitz, Judith R. 1980. *Prostitution and Victorian Society: Women, Class, and the State*. Cambridge: Cambridge University Press.

*Watanabe, Nobuo. 1961. "Shogyo teki nogyo ni okeru koyo rodo [Employed Labor in Commercial Agriculture]." In Ichikawa, Watanabe, & Furushima (1961: 43).

Watanabe, Ryokichi. 1931. *Nihon mengyo ron [The Theory of the Japanese Cotton Industry]*. Tokyo: Nippon hyoron sha.

Watanabe, Yozo. 1951. "Nogyo suiri ken ni kansuru horitsu [Laws Relating to the Agricultural Water Rights]." 68 *Hogaku kyokai zasshi* 713, 824.

———. 1962. "Chika suiri yoken no ranyo [Abuse of Right to Subterranean Water]." In 2 *Kenri no ranyo [Abuse of Right]* 80.

———. 1963. "The Family and the Law: The Individualistic Premise and Modern Japanese Family Law." In von Mehren (1963: 364).

———. 1973. "Kasen ho [Rivers Act]." In Ukai et al. (1973: VI-129).

Waza, Kazukiyo. 1960. "Onsen riyo no ruikei to onsen sogi ni okeru shomondai [Issues in Hot Spring Use and Disputes over Hot Springs]." 6 *Kanazawa hogaku* 98.

# References

Weingast, Barry R. 1995. "The Economic Role of Political Institutions: Market-Preserving Federalism and Economic Development." 11 *Journal of Law, Economics & Organization* 1.

Williamson, Oliver E. 1979. "Transaction Cost Economics: The Governance of Contractual Relations." 22 *Journal of Law & Economics* 233.

———. 1983. "Credible Commitments: Using Hostages to Support Exchange." 73 *American Economic Review* 519.

———. 1985. *The Economic Institutions of Capitalism.* New York: Free Press.

Wray, William D. 1984. *Mitsubishi and the N.Y.K., 1870–1914: Busines Strategy in the Japanese Shipping Industry.* Cambridge, Mass.: Harvard Council on East Asian Studies Publications.

———. 1989a. "Kagami Kenkichi and the N.Y.K., 1929–1935: Vertical Control, Horizontal Strategy, and Company Autonomy." In Wray (1989b: 182).

——— (ed.). 1989b. *Managing Industrial Enterprise: Cases from the Prewar Experience.* Cambridge, Mass.: Harvard Council on East Asian Studies Publications.

Yamaguchi ken (ed.). 1885. *Yamaguchi ken tokei sho [Yamaguchi Prefectural Statistics].* Yamaguchi: Yamaguchi ken.

Yamamoto, Shigemi. 1977. *Aa nomugi toge: aru seishi kojo aishi [Ah, the Nomugi Pass: A Tragic History of the Factory Women in the Silk Thread Industry].* Tokyo: Kadogawa shoten.

Yamamoto, Shun'ichi. 1983. *Nihon kosho shi [A History of Licensed Prostitution in Japan].* Tokyo: Chuo hoki shuppan.

Yamamura, Kozo. 1981. "Returns on Unification: Economic Growth in Japan, 1550–1650." In Hall, Nagahara, & Yamamura (1981: 327).

*Yamazaki, Ryuzo. 1961. "Settsu ni okeru nogyo koyo rodo keitai no hatten [The Development of Agricultural Labor in Settsu]." In Ichikawa, Watanabe, & Furushima (1961: 193).

Yasuba, Yasukichi. 1986. "Standard of Living in Japan before Industrialization: From What Level Did Japan Begin? A Comment." 46 *Journal of Economic History* 217.

———. 1987. "The Tokugawa Legacy: A Survey." 38 *Economic Studies Quarterly* 289.

Yasuda, Masataka. 1933. *Suiri ken [Water Rights].* Tokyo: Matsuyama bo.

Yokoyama, Gennosuke. 1899. *Nihon no kaso shakai [Japanese Lower-Class Society].* Tokyo: Kyobunkan.

Yonekura, Akira. 1985. "Horitsu koi [Legal Acts]." 59 *Hogaku kyoshitsu* 30, 60: 28, 61: 118, 62: 30.

Yoshida, Masashi. 1977. "Kinsei koyo ho no kozo to sono shiteki tenkai katei josetsu [An Introduction to the Historical Developmental Process and to the Structure of Early Modern Employment Law]." 41 *[Tohoku Daigaku] Hogaku* 53, 41 *Hogaku* 165.

———. 1978. "Kinsei koyo ho shi kenkyu no shinka no tame ni [To Deepen the Study of Early Modern Employment Law]." 11 *Shakai kagaku no hoho* 1.

Yoshimi, Shoko. 1984. *Baisho no shakai shi [A Social History of Prostitution].* Tokyo: Yusankaku.

Zaisei keizai jiho sha (ed.). 1936. *Nippon sen'i kogyo soran okutsuki [An Overview of the Japanese Textile Industry, with Appendix].* Tokyo: Zaisei keizia jiho sha.

# Index

187